Johnny Black Hawk

The Outcast Series
Book Three

SUSAN ILEEN LEPPERT

Paperback ISBN: 978-1-956467-06-2
Hardback ISBN: 978-1-956467-07-9
E-book ISBN: 978-1-956467-08-6

Printed in the United States of America
1 3 5 7 9 10 8 6 4 2

DEDICATED TO:

The GRANDFATHERS With humble gratitude
And
To all those who believe

WITH SPECIAL THANKS TO:

The Grandfathers—without your input there would be no books.

Bryan Locey—my so wise and so patient proofreader.

Jerry and Jane Ahrens—who believed enough to make the journey to Minnesota.

JoAnn Yager Brown—whose faith, strength, and encouragement never falters.

Laughing Water—whose friendship has always meant the world to me— then and now.

Margaret and Jim Curtis—for the wonderful hospitality they showed me while in Texas.

Duane Arnold—for giving freely of his time and talent as an artist.

And to:

The Rocky "S" Ranch—There aren't enough words to describe its beauty.

God Bless You all,
Susan Ileen Leppert

AUTHOR'S NOTE

For some life is a circle within a circle.

PROLOGUE

John Black Hawk Gentry grew to manhood in much the same way other boys in Hastings did in the 1800's. He was a handsome boy with straight black hair and smooth skin, noticeably darker than his class-mates. His dark, liquid-brown eyes set above high cheekbones, showing unmistakably his Indian ancestry. His eyes held one's attention when he looked at them and revealed a wisdom and understanding far beyond his years. They also seemed to look not *at*, but *through* a person, and to delve the very depths of their souls, making some folks highly uncomfortable.

He was a quiet child with an innate curiosity that drove him to study everything around him, however important or unimportant. He asked a million questions, always wanting to know more. Family and friends shook their heads, smiling, when again and again his interest in things took precedence over his mother's voice calling him to eat, or asking him to fetch a pail of water, or even to go to sleep. His appetite for knowledge was voracious!

Even before he was five, he poked and prodded in cracks and crev-ices, on the trail of insects. His mother, often the recipient of a beetle or other such bug, or a snail or snake. She would answer his many questions as best she could, or in the case of snakes, send him to find his father and ask him. Later, his parents would laugh quietly in their bed at night, discussing his insatiable thirst for answers.

At six, he couldn't eat an apple from the old tree in their yard, with-out wanting to know why it was a certain color or shape, why some were smooth in texture, and some were covered in raised, brown spots. Even the arrangement of the seeds within fascinated the boy. Nothing seemed to escape his scrutiny!

Sarah knew, even before he was three, that he was wise beyond his years. Other children, she noted, played with the wooden toys their fathers or grandfathers had carved for them, or wrestled playfully with each other, laughing, or crying when their games ended with a bloody nose or black eye. Johnny took little part in their revelry. He seemed only to answer an inner call, as though he were on a mission to soak up all the knowledge he could, forgoing the games of children. At five and six, his curiosity often led to questions his parents and other piers had no answers for, such as: Who was God? How did He make the world? As Johnny grew, his questions grew in magnitude and depth. A frequently asked one, some years later, was 'Why couldn't the white men understand the ways of the Indians, and try to live in peace with them?'

Sarah noticed, as years went by, that he was more and more drawn to his Indian heritage, to their ways, and more importantly, to their beliefs, as she was. She worried how this would affect his life, and if it would stand him in good stead in the white man's world. She saw too, that her own longing for adventure was part and parcel of her son as he grew to manhood. A longing that had taken precedence over the teachings of her father, years before, and led her to leave her home and loved ones to marry Gray Eagle, a Lakota Indian, and live among his people. She saw that same longing for adventure grow stronger, day by day, within her son, and wondered what affect it would have on his life.

CHAPTER 1

The first tragedy of my life occurred in 1861, when my pa, Moses Gentry, left to fight in the War Between the States. I was six, going on seven. The worst tragedy of my life occurred in 1865, when the war ended...and he didn't return.

Of course, we didn't expect him home right away. But often I caught my mother, Sarah Elizabeth Gentry, scanning the road as each hour passed, hope and strain etched upon her face. With each passing day, I couldn't help notice as her hope faded—little by little—as she busied herself around our place, trying to keep her mounting fears for my father at bay by continuously scrubbing, cleaning, and cooking.

A month later, word came that one of the O'Leary boys had come home; a shadow of his former self, his spirit broken, his body ravaged by illness and disease. My mother baked all through the night, loading a large basket the next morning with bread and cake, and a roast to take to his mother, Miz O'Leary, who could no longer do for her family; her hands long since bent and twisted.

Another O'Leary son, William, arrived home soon after, we heard, carried by buckboard to waiting casket, a scrap of paper pinned to his tattered shirt with his name printed upon it, and the name of our town. His lifeless body already stiff. They said Miz O'Leary fell down upon seeing him and had to be carried into her house, all the while screaming, over and over again, "Billy! Not my Billy! Oh, God, not my Billy!" Later, she sat in the dark beside his casket in silence, her head leaning against it, one claw-like hand reaching inside to tenderly pat the arm of her departed son. She sat there all through the night and the next day, no longer crying, aware only of the horrible pain visited upon her. No amount of comforting could begin to console her. As with so many other mothers of sons on both sides of the war; part of her had died, along with her son.

We went to town the following week, my mother and I, to visit my grandparents, Rosie and Angus MacGregor. Everywhere we looked, everyone we saw had that same look that now seemed permanently etched upon my mother's face; a look of anguish and pain. Little hope. It was a day I'll never forget.

After eating some of Grandma Rosie's good vegetable soup and thick slices of bread, slathered in fresh butter, Grandpa Angus and I left the ladies and walked to the Mercantile to see if there was any news posted on the bulletin board outside it. Old men with solemn faces read every word posted there, shaking their heads and staring out across the street, seeing in their mind's eyes a fading memory of their loved one as he waved goodbye and walked away to do his part in the war. Some coughed aloud to choke back tears, as they wiped the dampness from their eyes. Some sought understanding, some sought relief from sorrow and worry, and all sought news—any news—of those dear ones whose whereabouts had long been unknown. Dear ones, precious ones, who had still not returned.

A heated argument broke out between two of the old men, but ended as quickly as it had begun, when a wagon pulled by an exhausted horse—its ribs clearly too visible—passed by. The occupants of the wagon, all soldiers: Some sitting, some laying, some looking more dead than alive. All nearly unrecognizable in their present condition. Their garments, what was left of them that is, a poor substitute for coverings. The stench coming from those in the wagon assaulted our nostrils even from the distance that separated us. Bandages, black with filth, reeked with the putrid slime of seeping sores and wounds long festered. Bodies wounded and decaying, on men once strong and fit, once able to work from sunup to sunset to build a place in the wilderness for their families, now too beaten and broken to crawl or walk. Men incapacitated and enfeebled, and as maimed emotionally, as physically. Some, with bandages soaked with fresh blood, crying out. Some no longer capable of crying out, their suffering at long last over. Anxious eyes scanned those in the wagon, hoping beyond hope to recognize one of their own, to gather him up, and take him home.

"Mother, Mother," a young man that I guessed at not yet twenty, cried, reaching out, searching with his hands toward no one in particular, his eyes covered with bandages coated with dried blood.

Grandpa Angus gave me a penny and sent me into the Mercantile to buy a candy. But, I, too, had scanned those in the wagon, looking for my father. He was not amongst them, and I felt a wave of sadness flow over me, and then relief, that he was not. It was then, as I turned to go inside, I heard one of the old men on the porch ask, "Where you from? Where do you call home?"

A faint answer came, "We're the 1st Minnesota. 'Bout all that's left."

I ran inside, not wanting to hear anymore.

Grandpa Angus didn't tell my mother what we'd seen, and worse yet, what we'd heard. It would surely have broken her heart, and we both knew it. He put a finger to his lips to caution me to silence as we arrived back at the house, then motioned with his head for me to follow him out to the barn. That was the first time he spoke to me "man to man," and I knew by his words and the solemn tone of his voice, that my childhood was now a thing of the past. I was no longer Sarah and Moses' boy, though now ten, going on eleven. From now on, I had to become the man in our family, accepting it as my due till my father came home. *If* he came home. But the possibility of it faded, more and more, with each passing day, and left a chill around my young heart that would stay with me from that day on.

"Ye've got t' be a man now, Johnny," Grandpa Angus said. "I know yer only ten, lad, but, 'tis a load only a man can carry, tha' the good Lord's seen fit t' place upon yer shoulders. Ye've got t' be brave, lad, and strong. Got t' do wha' ye can to see yer mither through wha's t' come," his voice choked with emotion, his hand rested gently upon my shoulder. He cleared his throat, sniffling and shaking his head, and then looked away a long time, before continuing. "'Tis sad times upon us, Johnny. Sorrowful times, indeed." I gave my word I would do my best, thinking back to a similar talk I had shared in another place and time...a talk with my pa.

As the prospect of war loomed on the horizon, my pa had shown me how to do more and more of the chores, explaining that he was counting on me to do my best. That it was his duty to join up, though he hated the idea of leaving my mother and me. He said only the oldest men and those unable, like his friend, Cal Dunnevey, who had been blinded in a gunfight some years before, would be exempt from leaving to answer the call. He looked proud when he spoke of joining. Like it was a most solemn duty to do so, and yet I saw the sadness in his eyes when he spoke again of my mother. Of how I would have to do not only the chores, but would have to see that I helped her with all the heavier tasks. He laughed when he told me not to worry about milking, saying that was one chore my mother enjoyed doing. He spoke to me in a way that made me feel old beyond my years, and I did my best to assure him I would not let him down. He patted my shoulder then, and told me to run and get his gun from over the mantel. I looked at him, surprised at his words, but ran to do as he said. Every day for the next three weeks, he taught me to shoot that old gun. Taught me how to keep my eyes on the target and not flinch as I pulled the trigger. Soon, I could hit the target I was aiming at with a fine degree of accuracy, and knew the lessons he taught me would hold me in good standing, all the rest of my life. Oh, how I relished every lesson! Not only for what I was learning, but because my teacher was my father, whom I had always looked up to with great admiration.

In the evening, sitting before the oil lamp in our kitchen, I studied the lessons learned each day in school. Before most children were able to read, my mother had taught me many words. She had also taught me how to count. I was slow with numbers, however, because—for some unknown reason—I always inserted the number twenty-seven in my recitation. I would begin saying my numbers in their proper sequence, then insert twenty-seven between every fourth or fifth number. Mother thought it quite funny, at first, and laughed gaily the first few times I did it. But, it soon became cause for concern, when I continued to do so. She tried to no avail to teach me the right way to count, her frustration mounting, moment by moment. She picked flowers, counting the petals as she pulled them loose, letting them fall to the ground, making me repeat each number after her. When she was certain I had finally understood, she would then ask me to count by myself. I would bite my lip and begin: "one, two, three, four, twenty-seven, five, six, and so forth." Hard as I tried to please her, the number twenty-seven would slip from my lips and disgrace me.

In time, my mother gave up. She'd simply roll her eyes and shake her head, sighing, as the unwelcome number slipped from my lips, unbidden.

By the age of six, I knew twenty-seven could only follow twenty-six, but the habit had grown so strong that I had to be very watchful that—quite by accident—it didn't slip in elsewhere. On the occasions that it did, much to my chagrin and the delight of those classmates who found it great sport to tease me, anyway, because of my very noticeable Indian features, I would often arrive home from school with bloodied lip or black eye. I was *not* the only one! More than one of my schoolmates, on those occasions, showed the signs of my retaliation.

One boy, in particular, seemed to instigate most of our battles. Eli. Eli Hart. We were the same size and height, and equally as strong, and often fought until we were both too tired to continue, though egged on by other boys who yelled slurs at both of us, calling us names that we weren't always sure the meaning of.

Eli had red hair, the color of flames, and freckles that spread across his nose and cheeks. They called him "Red," and laughed at him as his face grew nearly as red as his hair as we fought, rolling and punching each other.

They called me "Injun," and sneered and gestured, holding three fingers up behind their heads, dancing around like I'd seen Indians do when I went with my folks to our Indian friends' village.

When Eli lost one of our fights, one day, they jeered and called him, "cry baby," and one of the older boys yelled, "Better run home to your maw, little bastard." Eli stomped over to the boy and hit him squarely on the jaw, surprising all of us, even me! The bigger boy stood there; holding his face, as all around him the others chanted, "Fight! Fight!" I don't know what made me do it, but I guess it was the look of pure hatred in that bigger boy's eyes. I hurried over to stand beside Eli, taking a deep breath, my fists clenched and ready, my heart pounding in my chest like a drum!

"You'll have to fight both of us," I said, my eyes narrowing and focusing unblinkingly on the eyes of the bigger boy. Eli looked at me, a questioning look, then a slight smile spread across his face. The bigger boy knew he had a poor chance of taking on both of us, and swore at us, threatening to get even, later. Then he stomped off, followed by the others. We watched them till they were out of sight, and then each took a relieved deep breath.

"Why'd you do that?" Eli asked, wiping the blood from under his nose that I had caused to be there.

"Why not?" I replied, my chin rising slightly.

"Don't make sense," he said, reaching down to retrieve his hat that had fallen off when I landed my first punch.

"Didn't want to see him get the best of you," I stated, smiling.

He hesitated a moment, looked at me out of the corner of his eye, then turned, reaching out slowly toward me. "Thanks."

I took his hand, shaking it, a good feeling inside me. "No need t' thank me."

We became friends that day, Eli and me. Never fought each other again, though we did stomp the stuffin's out of some of the others. More than once, we stood together, covering each other's back. A duo to be reckoned with as the years came to pass. We never spoke of the names we were called by those who—for one reason or another—didn't like us. It seemed only to lessen our respect for them, not damaging our own self-images. I knew where I had come from, knew the kind of parents I had, and grandparents. Knew the strong blood of both the whites and the Indians ran in my veins, and I was proud of it. I walked tall, my head held high, in spite of lesser men's remarks. Like my mother, I held the Indians in high esteem, having learned many of their ways on the many visits my folks and I had made to Standing Elk's village. Standing Elk had been a great warrior when younger. A man who judged no one by his color or race. He was a very wise man who spoke both the language of the whites and the Lakota. How could I not be proud of such a man? Why, I wondered, couldn't it be easily understood, the tremendous reverence the Indians had when it came to the earth and animals? Yes, I was proud to be a part of that heritage.

My father, Moses Gentry, through his mother, Singing Raven, was of the Blackfoot tribe to the west. My mother had been married to Standing Elk's son, long before her marriage to my father. Her husband then, Gray Eagle, had been a highly respected man amongst his people. 'Gentle of heart,' she told me, 'and very skilled in the ways of the People.' He had been killed while on a buffalo hunt, his body never having been recovered. My mother had grieved his loss many years, staying with his people for five years after his death. When smallpox struck the village, she returned to Hastings to get medicine to help the Indians survive. Sadly, she was told there was no medicine available to help them, only some that might bring a modicum of relief to their suffering. My father, Moses Gentry, returned to Standing Elk's village with my mother when she went back, and they were eventually married. I was proud of my mother, proud of her strength and courage. Of all the white women I ever met, I knew none who would have been as courageous. In years to come, her example would fashion my life.

Eli, on the other hand, was told early on that he was taken in by his aunt Lilly, and her husband, Jonas Hart, and adopted as their own. He told me, in one of our long chats, that his real mother, Lilly's younger sister, Lydia, had gotten in the family way by someone other than her husband, a preacher. Seems the preacher left town, shortly after finding out there was a baby due from that union. Lilly and Jonas were wonderful parents, he said. They showed him all the love that any parent could give a child, even one not their own, and he always felt secure in their love. Like Jonas, he also had a fondness for farming, and worked side by side with Jonas, learning many things from him that would be instrumental in his own farming venture, if that's what he chose to do with his life when he was grown. Being the kind of parents they were—showering him with a generous outflowing of love and understanding—and always compassionate in their discipline, if it was needed, Eli grew to be generous of heart, kind and considerate. Only the taunts and name-calling of the other boys, on rare occasions, provoked his ire. On those occasions, I stood by his side, ready to defend him to the death, if need be. He was my friend, from the day of our last fight when first I stood with him, and it was not a one-sided friendship. In years to come, when I was looked down upon by so many, Eli's friendship never wavered, and was never lacking. Never...for even one moment!

CHAPTER 2

The dark-haired man stood straight and tall before a group of head-stones in the cemetery just outside of Hastings. His long black hair hung well below his shoulders, a worn black hat covering his head and shading his eyes. Noticing him—for it was hard not to—a person had to wonder if the hat was for his benefit—shading his face from the sun—or to shield him from the curious stares of onlookers. He wore a black frock coat that came to his knees, as worn looking as his pants and boots. He drew attention both by his attire, and the way he traversed the distance from his horse to the graves he sought. Those watching could not help but notice his ease of movement, his head soon bending as if in prayer. Some thought they recognized him, though his back was to them, and waited for a chance to wave if he turned and looked in their direction. Others cast hurried glances, then rushed on, immersed in their own thoughts. Only for a moment did they wonder who the tall, dark-haired man was, and whose grave he sought in the cemetery. It was obvious he was a stranger in town, and even more obvious that he was an Indian.

Indians weren't welcome in town since the vicious uprising of '62. It had lasted an unimaginable five and a half weeks, ending in the death of many settlers, and an Indian was looked upon as a renegade and savage, no matter how peaceful-like he rode into town. No matter that he seemed unarmed and only interested in visiting some graves in the cemetery. The folks of Hastings knew an Indian didn't need a gun to wreak a whole lot of hell upon the good folks in a town, and for one to journey into town seemed an affront to all those who had died in the uprising. Few whites had any sympathy for the losses suffered by the Indians, or their reason for the uprising.

John Black Hawk Gentry felt the eyes upon him, sensing the bitter thoughts and outright hatred behind some of those that watched him. He knew it would make no difference to most people that he was both white and Indian. He looked Indian, and that would be more than enough to set off those who hated the Indians. Men that were set on hating—for whatever reason—usually let their feelings rule, never taking the time to make sensible judgments. Their resulting actions often leading to deadly conclusions! How many times had he seen how one angry boy at school could stir others to a frenzy, no thought given by any to the possible conclusion of such action. He shifted his weight from one foot to the other, his attention turning back to the graves that lay before him. He couldn't help wondering if he'd been wrong to return to Hastings. But, no, he knew in his heart it was the right thing to do. He had come to pay his respects to his grandparents: John Bruce, Angus MacGregor, and Rosie MacGregor. As thoughts of these dear ones came to mind, he felt a lump form in his throat. Not the first time he had felt it, and not the last, he was certain.

He'd been away from Hastings a long time. Three...no...four years now. Had left when he was sixteen, was twenty now. Twenty, he thought. He felt old, old and plumb tuckered out. Tired in his bones, and all through his body. Tired even in his soul. To his surprise, his eyes welled up with tears at these troubling thoughts. He wondered if his mother was well. He shook his head sadly, trying to dispel any further such thoughts. Sniffling, he looked at the graves that lay at his feet, his thoughts now turning to the dear ones who lay there beneath the cold, hard ground. He had heard of Grandma Rosie's death while on the road back to Hastings. That's why he'd made it a point to head for town, instead of cutting cross-country. He never expected to find Grandpa Angus here, too, beside his beloved "angel," as Angus liked to call Rosie. His eyes filled with tears again, and he wiped them away, sniffling as he did so. Then, kneeling on one knee, he placed his hand flat upon the mound of dirt covering the only woman he had ever called grandmother, knowing how very deeply he would miss her; miss her hugs and her joyful laughter, her welcoming warmth and the sweet scent of lavender that hung in the air when she was near.

Four years earlier, when he'd left to go in search of his father, she had filled a sack with his favorite slices of bread, strawberry jam oozing out from between. She had cried then, hugging him to her, telling him she loved him and to be careful. Telling him to come back safe. He smiled at the memories, bittersweet as they were. Four years ago, he had been a boy. Four years ago, he thought. It seemed more like four lifetimes ago!

He rose, brushing off the knee of his pants, and straightened his coat. As he did, he couldn't help notice the roses carved into the cross above her grave. "Rosie MacGregor, me angel" was carved below, the date of her birth unclear, the date of her death, June 27, 1875, clearly marked. She had told him she'd be awaiting his return: his, and his pa's. But instead, she lay beneath the dirt at his feet, and he knew just how deeply he would miss her.

"Best I get on my way," he said, shaking his head, sadly. He thought then of his mother, knowing how worried she'd be. He made no move to go, however, his thoughts once more turning back to when he was young. Thoughts of Grandma Rosie filled his mind: her happy laughter as she bustled around her kitchen, cooking the best food and telling him story after story of her own childhood in her beloved Ireland. It was only later that she told him of her trip to America, and how she had lost her sister, Margaret Mary, and so many dear friends during the voyage. Her lovely green eyes would fill with tears and she'd dab at them with a lace-edged handkerchief from her apron pocket, and push a plate of cookies toward him, or a thick slice of her sourdough bread, while she tried to compose herself. He thought she was the bravest woman he knew, back then.

She never spanked him,or punished him when he did something wrong. Even when he soiled her finest linen tablecloth by touching it with filthy hands, so intent on telling her something, that he wasn't thinking what he was doing. The only time he could ever remember her scolding him was when he had climbed the apple tree beside her house to see if there were any bird's eggs in a nest there, and fell with a resounding thud onto the ground far below! Even yet, he knew the scolding he received that day was because she had been frightened for him, not really angry. He had to smile, remembering how she had clasped him to her, burying his face between her ample breasts, nearly suffocating him as she held him there, saying, "Oh, my dear! Oh, Johnny! It's the death of me, you'll be, child!" She helped him up then, checking him over for broken bones, then ushered him into the house for a big bowl of stew, followed by an extra large piece of her Irish grandmother's special cake.

He stood there at her grave, his eyes closed and head bowed, remembering how tenderly she had run her hand over his head then, brushing his hair back out of his eyes, muttering to herself about how handsome a boy he was. Taking in a deep breath, he opened his eyes, pulling his coat closer around him, noticing that the wind had picked up somewhat and it had gotten quite a bit colder. It wouldn't be long now before the snows came.

"I've come back, Grandma," he said, quietly, "all safe and sound." He paused a moment before adding, "but alone." He tried in vain to shut out the thoughts that now formed, thoughts that had tormented him every minute of his journey. He was coming home alone, a crushing feeling of grief within him. He had failed. Failed his mother. Worse still, failed his father. But more than anything, failed himself. There would be no joyous homecoming, only the look of sorrow on his mother's face to greet him. Seeing the same look upon his face, she would not ask, would continue to grieve as she had ever since the war had ended, and his father had not returned.

Grandpa Angus would have known he'd done his best. Would have patted him on the shoulder. Would have accepted that he had done all he could. Or, would he? Doubts assailed him. He glanced at the wooden cross above the grave next to Rosie's, reading: "Angus Charles MacGregor—July 20, 1875." He had died soon after Rosie. That didn't surprise Johnny. Not a bit. He knew that older folks, who loved each other as deeply as they had, often didn't last long when they lost their spouse. Look at that old gunfighter-friend of my pa's, Johnny thought, Amos Culpepper. How many times had both Angus and Rosie told him the story? How he'd been gone, living outside the law, some...what...20 or 25 years? Then he'd gotten shot-up down near Mexico, and some old padre had told him of Jesus, of how He loved *all* men, and Amos had turned his life over to Him that day. He'd changed his ways, got pardoned, and come home to his wife, Amanda. Seemed she'd waited all those years, too, for his return. 'Loving him more than ever,' Grandma Rosie had said. A few years later, he had stood with Cal Dunnevey and Pa—who was the sheriff then—against three gunfighters, and had been killed. Johnny shook his head at these thoughts. For when Rosie and Angus went to tell Amanda the terrible news of Amos' death, they found that she had died, too, at the same time. 'Her heart suddenly giving out', the doctor had said. But they were certain she had simply gone to be with her beloved husband for the rest of eternity. He smiled; knowing deep within his heart there was no way Grandpa Angus would have kept the will to live, once he'd lost his "angel."

"You carved both your markers," he said. "Guess you knew, too, Grandpa, that it wouldn't be long before you went to join her." He glanced at the plain cross that marked John Bruce's grave. John Bruce, the grandfather he had never met, but was named after. His father's *real* father. Strange, he thought, how things sometimes work out. John Bruce had never known Moses Gentry was his son. He'd died in a shoot-out, saving my mother's life and giving his own in the process. John Bruce... Oh, the stories Grandpa Angus had told him about his real grandfather. How he'd loved two women with all his heart, in his lifetime, giving up a professorship at a college in the East when he discovered the first gal had married someone else. Truth was, John had been so busy earning enough money to assure them the life he wanted for them, that he forgot to write the young woman. After waiting for 3 or 4 years for some word from John, she figured he had taken ill at sea, or drowned, and went on with her life. When John heard she had married another, he walked out of that grand position, bought a horse and gear, and headed west. Smart as he was—and they said he was brilliant—he took off for the wilds, and darned near froze to death in the process. It was some kind of amazing luck, or amazing coincidence, that Angus—who had met John, previously, on the ship to America—was living with some Indians in those wilds, rescued John, nursed him back to health, and saved his life. Once well, he soon met and fell in love with his second love, Singing Raven, a pretty Indian woman who disappeared soon after she found she was carrying John's baby. Surprisingly, that baby was my father, Moses Gentry, Johnny thought. It was awhile before anyone figured that out, however. At the wedding of Moses Gentry and Sarah Justus, Angus had been near struck dumb when my mother pulled the round bone medallion from under the neck of her dress and placed it around my father's neck. Seems he had given it to her months earlier, as proof of his love for her. Strangely enough, Angus had seen John Bruce carve that very same medallion for Singing Raven and the babe she was carrying, and knew right then that Moses Gentry was the son of John Bruce, and not Frank Gentry. Moses had always thought Frank was his father: a mean son of a gun who had won Singing Raven in a card game. Seems some trappers had kidnapped her, as she left her camp to go to a secret destination known only to the Indians, to get a special gift for John. What that gift was, was never discovered. But in searching for Singing Raven, John and Angus had come upon a cave. A cave containing a vein of gold as wide as a small stream! That cave soon became the pot at the end of the rainbow for John and Angus, though John continued on with his search for Singing Raven, by himself, and finally ended up in Hastings. Angus named the mine "The Golden Lassie Mine," and registered the claim to it in both their names, making both himself and John Bruce extremely rich. John, however, never lived to learn of their strike, though Angus saw to it Moses received John's half of the riches. Johnny smiled at all the memories that flooded his consciousness, pulling his coat more tightly closed. It was nearly dark now. He had stayed a lot longer than he intended. The wind whistled around him, blowing leaves hither and yon, as he gazed out across the cemetery to the one lone birch. Only a decaying trunk reached for the sky now. The rest of its branches lay on the ground, sad reminders of the beautiful tree it had once been. He shook his head, sadly. He was tired of death. It's shroud of grief and sorrow weighed heavily upon him, burrowing into his soul.

As he stood there, the noise of the town assaulted his ears: the raucous sounds from the numerous bars that now lined the street, the many discordant voices and loud laughter heard from inside them, all mixed together with the sound of ship's bells, wagons passing, dogs barking, and the loud retort of guns, somewhere down near the docks. He shook his head once again, looking back toward the town. This was what most of the folks nowadays called progress. White man's progress, he thought. Progress that cut through the silence like the blade of a knife, blocking out the whisper of the wind, the music of the birds, the sweet melody of brook and stream as they hurried on to their destination.

Here in this white man's town there could be no communion with the spirits, no vision quest, no quiet soul-searching. It was not the way of the white man to do these things. They did not listen as the Grandfathers spoke, nor even as their own God spoke. It seemed greed was their god, and it saddened Johnny to see it even here in Hastings. Land deals flourished, the prices always going higher and higher. Nearly every day someone was killed over a claim. Lumber was a commodity to be sold to the highest bidder. Or stolen, when money was short. The river had brought the first settlers to town, Johnny knew, and the railroad now brought still more. Families looking for a new start headed west, as did gamblers and gunfighters, followed by saloon ladies, and those who worked in the houses down by the docks. Johnny had seen it all too often, in his travels to find his father. Towns springing up, the land clearcut, the waters dammed or polluted beyond use. Rubbish and rubble an all too common sight. Lawlessness prevailed, as laws were made and soon broken. No, there was no peace in the white man's town, or in his soul. He made promises he had no intention of keeping, uttering useless words to get what he wanted, caring not for the destruction and devastation that lay in his wake.

Johnny looked down at the ground, saddened by his thoughts. He had studied many long years so he could someday help these people, could lead and guide them. But could he? Would they let him? Would they listen to a man whose blood was a combination of theirs *and* the Indians? A man whose heart, more and more every day, chose the path of his Indian brothers? He shifted his weight from one foot to the other, a yawn escaping his lips, and felt suddenly very anxious to be on his way. Anxious to distance himself from all the things he found so disturbing. From death and deviousness, from failure and grief, from loss...and longing.

CHAPTER 3

Walking to his horse—an almost fluid grace to his movements— he patted its neck, took up his reins, and mounted. But he couldn't stop the thoughts that plagued him, and turned in his saddle, looking back at the cemetery and all the graves within it. He remembered coming here as a child with his mother. Remembered how few graves there had been then. He was well aware that time always brought such changes. He'd seen a lot of deaths as he traveled, more than most young men his age. And he'd read a lot about dying, when younger. Wasn't all that sure *he'd* welcome it. Not yet, anyway. But like his Indian friends, he believed death was not an ending, but merely a beginning. How often had he sat in Chief Standing Elk's tepee discussing such things? A man who lived honorably, who acquired respect by his deeds and was brave and trustworthy, one who grew in the wisdom of his father, and his father's father before him, had no reason to fear death. No, he thought, death was not to be feared or dreaded, though it often was. Thoughts such as these, made him think of his mother, Sarah Gentry. Once again, he saw in his mind's eye how she had looked as she waved goodbye to him, standing at the outer fringe of Standing Elk's village, the day he left. She stood there, her head held high, her back straight, her lovely auburn hair hanging to her waist in two long braids, neatly tied with buffalo sinew, her buckskin dress outlining her slim figure. The knee-high moccasins she wore, a pair her first husband, Gray Eagle, had given her many years before. She stood proudly, not weeping or wailing, or looking anxious of heart, and in her smile he could see the tremendous love she felt for him. He was so proud of her. No other white woman he knew would have had the courage to return to live among the Indians. Especially not now, when there was so much dissension and downright hatred between the whites and the Indians. Of course, he knew that Chief Standing Elk was a leader who favored peace, and wished only to live in the manner the Indians had long been accustomed to. He was brave, and had often shown his courage in battles in years past, either by fighting or counting coup. With age, however, he realized there were just too many whites to fight. They came in numbers as great as the buffalo had once been. Like the stars in the sky, too many to count. Having grown in wisdom, Standing Elk realized it was better to live peaceably, if at all possible. If only the steady flow of wagons would lessen, so the buffalo would return to sustain his people.

Johnny turned in his saddle, urging his horse into a slow walk. The stores were closed for the night now, only the noise from the many saloons shattered the silence. He pulled his collar up around his neck, and headed out of town. He wondered what his mother was doing. The winter was always especially hard on the Indians. He knew they would settle in, staying warm by their fires, the men going out if it was necessary to hunt, the women to fetch water from the nearby creek. Otherwise, they would busy themselves, making clothing from the various hides: deer, elk, fox, and wolf, to mention a few, that they had acquired for just such purpose. Occupying themselves, also, with the making of baskets, or moccasins, or the carving of necessary tools and utensils from bones. His mother was always happiest when busy, and he smiled as he envisioned her, bustling around, humming happily as she worked, her voice soft and sweet as a meadowlark's. She had learned well the ways of the Indian, and could not abide the cruel and insensitive remarks, or angry outbursts—one-sided as they were—when the townsfolk had blamed the Indians for all the trouble and strife that grew more and more rampant, day by day. Wagon trains full of settlers and those seeking gold pushed on through the land, heedless of the fact that this was a land of plenty, a land of unparalleled beauty and sustenance for the many different tribes living there. Even more important to the Indians, it was the land of their fathers, and their fathers' fathers before them. A sacred land, a sacred trust!

That was why, she had told him, she had to return to Standing Elk's village. She could not abide the terrible, unfair, and foolish remarks of her own people. She had tried to explain that it was the way of the Indian to worship Mother Earth and Father Sky, and to give thanks even to the animal that gave its life as meat, or the tree that gave its life to protect, in the form of a strong ash-wood bow. All of her words had fallen on deaf ears, and she had been told to go back to the Indians, if she liked them so. Angry words had been shouted at her then, not only by the men she had spoken to, but by their women. Women she had once gone to school with, had attended socials with, and helped care for when some sickness had forced them to take to their beds for a spell. Women she had called friends, believing them to be such.

She had come home from town that day, four years earlier, angrier than he had ever seen her. Had stormed through their house, her eyes flashing, and the track of dried tears upon her cheeks. When he'd asked her what was wrong, she had turned on him, furious not with him, but with the 'fools' in town! She had stood there, her hands on her hips, shaking her head; her eyes squeezed shut, frustration showing in her features.

"Mother, what is it?" he had asked, having never seen her so upset before.

"You're a man now, Johnny, old enough to choose your own way in life, son. And old enough to stand for the principles that speak to your heart. I, too, must do so! I cannot abide these ignorant fools that call themselves 'learned men,' and walk around town so pompous and pious! They spout off about things they have no knowledge of, things that flame a fire in the hearts of men even more stupid than they. I can't abide it any longer, Johnny." She turned from him, but not before he saw the tears start to spill from her eyes.

"What can we do, Mother? How can I help? You know that I feel as you do. I'll abide by whatever you think is best."

"Oh, son. You've always had to put up with this, haven't you? Always been the brunt of jokes and insults at school, because of your Indian features," Sarah said, feeling sadness in her heart for her tall, handsome son. "How you've suffered, simply because you resemble your grandmother, Singing Raven."

"I'm proud to be like her, Mother. I've learned many things from both cultures. You know that. I'm not ashamed to be either," he replied, his voice firm, but soft, and soothing to the ear.

Sarah walked to his side, reaching out to lay her hand upon his arm. His skin was warm and smooth to the touch, the tone darker than hers. "Do you have regrets, Johnny?"

"Of course not," he replied, laying his strong hand over hers, and smiling down at her.

She smiled at him, and then walked over to the table, sitting down, motioning him to do likewise. "John, I've made a decision. I've made it only for myself, trusting you to decide for yourself, also." She paused, looking up into his handsome, young face, trying to memorize every inch of it, even the slightest feature, be it hollow of cheek or strong jaw line. "I'm going back to Standing Elk's village, Johnny. I must go. I've waited till you were old enough to stand on your own feet. I've thought about it, ever since the war was over," she paused, a look of sadness in her eyes, then continued, "ever since your father didn't return." She smiled a sadly wistful smile; looking down at the table, then back up at him. "I've tried to raise you with a depth of compassion and understanding, so when this day came, you would be strong enough to stand proudly, as a man of *both* peoples, a man who is gentle, wise, and caring. I hope you will accept my decision to leave, John, and understand why it's necessary."

He saw the look of concern upon her face, the questioning in her eyes, and stood, pulling her up and hugging her to him. "I do understand, Mother. I've known for a long time that you would go back when the time was right." He felt her rest her head against him, heard her sigh of relief, and continued to stand there holding her. In his mind, he remembered back to another time, when he had come rushing into the house to find his father holding her in the same kind of comforting embrace. He remembered how his father had looked over at him that day, and winked, his smile telling him without words that whatever was wrong, he had handled it, and all was well. He smiled at the memory, as his mother stepped away from him. "When will you go?" he asked, looking down at her, noticing the many white hairs that stood out now amongst her auburn.

"Soon. Soon," she replied, and he could see the thoughts race across her mind of what she must do, of what she would need, of what she would take, when she did go.

"I'll see you safely there, Mother, and stay awhile. I've missed Chief Standing Elk, and Brave Foot, and the friends of my father. It'll be good to be with them again. We'll hunt, as we did in days past. I'd like to know there's enough meat to get all of you through the winter, before I leave." Sarah smiled up at her son, feeling great pride. Moses would have been so proud of you, she thought. Would have, indeed!

"And then, where will you go," she asked, already knowing.

"To find my father," he answered, his voice resolute.

Johnny gazed out at the tall trees on each side of the road, his thoughts, once again, going back in time. He had stayed a month with his mother, in Standing Elk's camp. Stayed, enjoying the company of the friend he had made, long before, called Brave Foot, and hearing again the stories told by Chief Standing Elk and the others. Stories passed down by word of mouth from generation to generation of the feats and daring of warriors like Crazy Horse, an Oglala Lakota, and Sitting Bull and Gall, both Hunkpapa Lakota. All were great warriors, and honorable and courageous leaders of the People. He had also joined in the hunt, taking both deer and a large elk. He knew that there would now be enough meat to see them through the worst winter weather, when fierce snows would blanket the earth and harsh freezing winds would whip the trees and reach with icy fingers into every crack and crevice, making it extremely difficult for the Indians. He felt content with his mother's decision, and did not try to talk her out of it. These were her people now, though she was white of skin. It wasn't a matter of skin. He understood that. It was a matter of heart. Ever since she had lived amongst the Indians as Gray Eagle's wife, she'd shared a connection with them that bound her, heart and soul, to them. She'd told him that, long ago, when he was a small boy. She had also told him how very dearly she had loved his father, Moses Gentry. Like Gray Eagle, Moses had one parent who was white, and one who was Indian. And as he learned the ways of the Indians, Moses, too, had developed a deep familial bond with them. Accompanying Sarah back to Standing Elk's village, years earlier, after she'd returned to Hastings in the hopes of getting some medicine to cure the smallpox killing so many of the Indians, Moses soon discovered a side of him that had long lain dormant: his Indian side. For the very first time in his life, he was proud of his Indian heritage…a feeling new to him. Since childhood, he had

believed himself to be the son of Frank Gentry, a man with a vile temper and predilection to drink, who often beat his soft-spoken, gentle,
Indian mother, cursing both of them, when he was drunk. Moses had
told Johnny these things, impressing upon him the fact that *no man* had
a right to cast shame on a child because he was different in any way.
Nor had he the right, *ever*, to hit a woman. That any man who did so
was the worst kind of man. And Johnny had listened, taking his father's
words to heart.

Moses also told him how much he wished he had gotten to know
John Bruce, his real father. How he had only seen or spoken to him
in passing, and would always regret that they had not spent any time
together. Because of her close friendship with John, from the time she
met him at the age of ten, to the time of his death, years later, Sarah was
really Moses' only link to John. She knew John better than any other
person in Hastings, and told Moses many stories—usually just as funny
as could be—of how he taught her the things he knew: mainly, how to
track and hunt, how to shoot and throw a knife with some degree of
accuracy, how to find her way by the stars or the sun, and many other
things. She also told him how John looked at life, and what his deepest
beliefs were. Moses told Johnny that many of those same beliefs were
now Sarah's. As time went by, especially after the war ended, and Moses didn't return—Johnny wished, too, that John Bruce was still alive.
He wished that he had gotten the chance to meet his grandfather—the
grandfather he was named after. But, John had died many years before,
and Angus had assumed that position when Johnny was born, and had
done a right credible job of it!

Night was closing in around the young man on horseback, and as
it did, he found a secluded spot far enough off the trail, where he was
certain he would not be disturbed by anyone. He wasn't afraid, just
cautious. It paid to be, with things the way they were now. You never
could tell just what was going on in a man's mind when there were
such hostile feelings between people. He dismounted, tied his horse to
a nearby tree, and removed his bedroll and saddlebags. Then he undid
the girth strap and carried his saddle over to where he planned to sleep.
His horse, a buckskin, nickered softly, then began to graze. Johnny was
fond of the horse. It had been a gift from Grandpa Angus for his fif-
teenth birthday. He'd named him "Buck," for lack of a better idea at the

time, and it stuck. Buck wasn't the fastest horse; he'd seen some a lot faster. But he was sturdy, and rode easy, never shying at loud sounds, or wanting his own head.

Johnny spread out his bedroll, getting the blanket out of his saddlebag, then, using his saddle as a pillow, he laid down, yanking his blanket this way and that, until it covered him sufficiently. The night air was cool, but not as cool as the wind had been, back at the cemetery. He had picked a good spot to camp, one that gave some protection from not only a person out to do no good, but also from the wind. He rolled onto his back, closed his eyes, then spoke, his words barely discernable, "Our Father..."

When he'd finished his prayers, he opened his eyes, scanning the stars above, his thoughts now of his mother. He wondered if he'd been right to leave her at Standing Elk's camp. Maybe I should have stayed, he thought, instead of leaving like I did. But he could justify—as he had many times before—his decision to leave, telling himself he had no choice, that he had to try to find his father. That Angus was too old to go, so it was his duty as Moses' son, to try and find him. Or, at least, to find out what had happened to him. But, he knew deep in his heart that wasn't the only reason he'd left. That was only part of it. He'd left because of a gal. A gal as pretty as ever he'd seen. A beauty with doe-like eyes and the prettiest lips, with skin as smooth as silk, and the promise of delights a man would die for. He groaned aloud at the thought. She was why he had left, and why he'd stayed away so long. He ran a hand across his stomach, an ache building within him at the mere thought of her. He rolled onto his side and closed his eyes, praying for sleep to come and ease his desire for his best friend's wife.

CHAPTER 4

The sounds of Hastings drifted on the air, carried upon the wind to where Cal Dunnevey slept, or rather, tried to sleep. A bevy of voices disturbed the night, mixed with the sounds of many pianos echoing in the background. Hastings had become quite a bustling town, what with all the boats that docked daily along the river front, depositing their cargo and tired passengers in one uncertain grouping with little care and few "fare thee wells." There were fifty-six saloons scattered here and there along the river front, catering to all sorts of clientele, from "fancy dans" in pants too tight to sit a horse, and ruffled shirts and polished shoes. To cowboys in buckskin, the toes of their boots, scuffed. Family men, looking worried and cautious, herded their wives and children away from the hustle and bustle, their Sunday best clothes showing wear and tear from the journey. You could hear the whimpering of the little ones, the whispered questioning of the anxious mothers. Soon they would spot the boardinghouse across the street, and as one, head for it, trying to avoid the horses and wagons that hurried past, seemingly unaware of them in their rush. The cowboys and drifters, cattlemen, and con men scanned the street, checking out the names on the signs in front of the saloons, and the attractiveness of the "ladies" who stood on the balconies, inviting their attentions and sizing up their ability to pay for a few drinks and an evening of "entertainment." Cal lay on the bunk in the back of the Mercantile, listening to the night sounds, as he did every night. Seeing in his mind the endless mass of humanity, rushing here and there, along the street. Rushing to their homes, to games of chance at one of the saloons, or to soft, waiting arms that promised a release from the drudgery and demands of a hard life. He shook his head, willing himself to think only of those others. Never of Lea. Lea. A muffled cry tore from him, as once again she entered his thoughts. He stifled the next cry and whipped the covers back, sitting up on the edge of the small cot, noticing the soft ticking of the clock that lay on the table before him. His world: a world of thoughts and sounds, devoid of comfort and beauty, devoid of love and hope. He stood, his arms outstretched toward the table, a sense of hopelessness coursing all through him.

This was all he had now. Might as well be dead, he thought. Or was he already? Wasn't this unending blackness the same as that of the grave? But, no, how well he knew it wasn't. In the grave, you lacked the one thing he still had—feelings. Oh, God, the feelings! They tore at him every minute of every day, ripping him apart. Tearing at him till he felt the terror start. Would he be like this forever? Was there no chance he'd ever see again? He shuddered as he felt the cold edge of fear fill him, and as it did, he heard the sound of breaking glass, and realized he had knocked his cup off the table. He steadied himself, gripping the edge of the table with one hand, as he reached forward, his arm flailing as he tried to find the chair at the end of the table. He was lost! Lost in the small room that he had lived in for the past twenty years. Twenty years! He clenched his hands into fists, knowing it would be impossible to pound them against the wall like he wanted to do. Why hell, he was no longer sure where the wall was! Had he walked away from the bed, trying to locate the chair? He stood still, his heart pounding like a drum within his chest. He had to get himself under control. He'd been lost before, had been lost in this very room, in fact. He coughed, forcibly unclenching his fists. "Steady," he told himself, aloud, the sound of his voice calming him, somewhat. "How far can you go, Cal, in one small room?" He laughed, an unsure laugh, and reached out in front of him, slowly, carefully. Nothing. Lower. Nothing. A niggling sensation began to build within him: the sensation of out and out panic. Would he ever get used to it? At that moment, his hand touched the edge of the chair, and he gave a sigh of relief. As he did, he remembered that he had moved the chair from its accustomed place at the end of the table, over nearer to the small stove that heated his room. "Fool," he cursed himself, used to talking aloud to himself. "Darned fool."

As his heart settled back into its regular rhythm, he felt for the edge of the table, finding it right where it was supposed to be. Then he felt, with his foot, for the broken cup. When he found it, he bent and picked up the pieces, hoping he had not missed any. Standing back up, he ran a hand through his hair, wondering if his shirt was still on the back of the chair. It was, and he gathered it to him, turning it this way and that, till he was sure it was not inside out. Then he put it on, finding and buttoning each button; a chore in the dark hell that he now resided in. He tucked the shirt into his pants, no longer sure if they were his nicer work pants, or the old pair that he wore on days when the store was closed. What did it matter, anyway, he thought, as long as he had pants on? He chuckled, half-heartedly at his own wry humor, not feeling any mirth. Again, a similar thought entered his mind…at least I don't have to check my hair in the mirror to make sure I'm presentable. He sighed, then, shaking his head sadly, all too aware that he had smashed it, the last time he had gotten lost in his room. He had reached out to get his bearings and felt the smooth edge of the mirror that hung beside his bed. Had grabbed it off its hook, and dashed it to the floor in one impulsive, anger-filled move, regretting it even before it hit the floor. He was not a man to show anger. Had never been that kind of man. Had been a gentle man, a man always in control of his feelings. He turned, and as he did, caught his foot in the corner of the blanket that had fallen onto the floor as he'd gotten out of bed. He stumbled forward, nearly falling, before he could catch himself and get his foot loose. "Damn!" It took him a moment to get his hands to stop shaking, a moment to gain his composure. He stood in the silence of his room, the beating of his heart drowning out the sounds of night in Hastings. A tear slowly coursed a path down one cheek. He knew he was feeling sorry for himself, but he couldn't help it. He had good reason! And once again, for just a moment, he wished *he* had been the one to die that day, twenty years earlier, when he, Moses and Amos Culpepper had stood against the Santiagos. It would have been better if I had, he thought, better for everyone concerned. But he hadn't, and no amount of trips to doctors had given him the slightest inkling of hope. He was blind, and blind he was going to stay. It was something about the nerve being damaged by the blast from the gun because it was fired at such close range. He shook his head, his grief at the tragic outcome still so easily able to reduce him to tears.

A soft knock at the front door of the Mercantile surprised him, and he wondered who it could possibly be, this late at night. Then he laughed, wondering if it really was late at night. When you live in a world of blackness, day and night, how can you be sure of the time? How can you be sure of anything, he thought, and heard again the knocking at the door. "Yes. Who is it?" he asked, trying to find his way to the door of his room and out into the store.

"It's me, Cal, Ophelia," the soft voice replied, and he moved slowly toward it, feeling his way among the counters and along the wall. "It's late. Were you sleeping?" she asked, and he was relieved to know it was still night, as he thought, and he had not been confused about that, too.

"No, Ophelia, I was up," he replied, as his hand hit the edge of a shelf, sending a shock of pain through the whole hand. He touched the area that hurt, checking to feel for blood or a cut, but found none. "I'm coming," he said, and he felt his way safely, this time, to the door, unlocking the lock and opening it to her.

"I'm sorry to disturb you, Cal," she said, her voice sounding sympathetic.

"You're *not* disturbing me," he replied, realizing his tone was a lot sharper than he had intended. "Sorry."

She placed a hand upon his arm, knowing he was upset. It was apparent he had not been sleeping. Even in the semi-darkness of the store, she could see the tiredness etched upon his face.

"Did you need something from the store, Ophelia, or just come to see me?" He laughed harshly at his words, standing still, noticing that she kept her hand upon his arm. There was a sense of comfort in her touch, and he took a deep breath, relaxing somewhat. It had been a long time since he'd felt a woman's touch. A long time since...

"I couldn't sleep, thought I'd come sit awhile, if you don't mind," she replied, the tone of her voice reminding him of Lea. He moved away, not wanting to think of her. He thought of her enough, as it was. Immediately, he bumped into a counter, a feeling of shame and embarrassment filling him.

Ophelia reached out, her touch gentle. "It's dark in here, Cal. I hope we can find our way to the back." He smiled at her attempt to put him at ease, and placed his hand over hers.

"I'm afraid you'll have to lead the way. I seem to be having a hard time of it tonight," he said, his words no longer sounding angry.

Slowly they made their way to the back, and as they did, he felt glad that she had come. He had always been alone, ever since his mother, Maggie, had been beaten to death when he was nine. He'd never told Lea about it. But after Lea had left, he had told Ophelia. Told her the whole story. Not just that his mother had worked for Victor Jalaco in a saloon far from Hastings, but that he had killed Jalaco. Shot him dead with one shot, and ran for his life, a mere child of nine. Ophelia had not been shocked, as he'd expected, or run screaming from him, but had continued to visit as though he'd said nothing. How many women would have done so, he wondered. Surely not Lea. His Lea was too sensitive and innocent, too childlike. He shook his head, and sighed.

"Can I make us some coffee, Cal?"

"Sounds good," he answered, having forgotten for a moment that she was even there. "Light the lamp, so you can see," he ordered, smiling in her direction.

"Guess I'd better, not sure I could make it in the dark," she hesitated, and he knew what she was thinking.

"Mine tastes terrible," he replied, hoping to put her at ease, "that must be why." They laughed together, then, the tension quickly dissipating. "I'm glad you came, Ophelia. Thanks."

"You're welcome. I hesitated to do so, it being so late, but sometimes I just feel so...restless. Do you know what I mean?"

"I've had those nights," he replied. "What time is it, by the way?"

"About nine."

He could hear her movements as she made them a pot of coffee, and asked if she could reach two cups down from up in the cupboard. "I had a little accident, broke one, earlier," he explained.

"Sure, I can get them," she said, but he noticed a hesitancy in her voice, and wondered why. She had never been one to be hesitant. In fact, in the many years that they'd been friends, often sitting and visiting late into the night, he'd never known her to hesitate at telling him anything that was on her mind. He had enjoyed their many talks, missing a woman's companionship dearly, ever since Lea had left. Ever since Lea had left... He wondered then, if everything in his life would always be measured by Lea. First, by her coming to Hastings, then by her leaving. He guessed that's the way it was with first loves; a fellow had a hard time getting over them.

"Cal? I asked if you want a piece of pie. I brought a couple pieces for us."

He jumped when she spoke, having been lost in his thoughts. He cleared his throat. "Sure. I thought I smelled pie. What kind?"

"Apple. I know that's your favorite," she said. "There are so many apple trees on the far side of the pond. I can't stand to see them go to waste."

He smiled, seeing in his mind the work she had gone to so they could enjoy the pieces of apple pie. He fumbled for the chair at the end of the table, and finding it, pulled it out and sat down. The coffee had begun to boil, and the smell of it pleased his senses. Carefully he felt in front of him for his cup, relieved when his hand touched it.

"Coffee's done. Here, let me fill your cup," she said, gently touching his hand, making sure he wouldn't move it and get burned. As she poured, he got the feeling she had something on her mind.

"Is something wrong, Ophelia?"

Again she hesitated. It was only a moment's hesitation, but he could tell, and hoped she'd speak to him about whatever it was that was obviously bothering her.

"Ophelia?"

"I need to talk to you," she began, her voice becoming a mere whisper in the room. "I need your advice, if you don't mind, Cal."

"I don't mind at all. What's wrong?"

He heard her slide her chair over closer to the table, then the unmistakable sound of her pouring a cup of coffee for herself. He sat still, waiting for her to go on, hoping she felt secure enough in their friendship to confide in him. She cleared her throat, and then spoke. "I've got two things to tell you," she said, and again he heard the hesitation in her voice. "First of all, I...um...I received a letter today from my Aunt Hilda." Cal felt his heart leap within his chest and then begin to race. A letter from her aunt could mean news of Lea. He sat still, the blood pounding in his temples, realizing he was holding his breath. "Aunt Hilda is coming to Hastings to live," Ophelia said, nervously. "She's coming to help me."

"To help you? What do you need help with?" he asked, more curious than ever to know what was wrong.

"I'm thinking of opening a...a hospital. Please don't laugh. I know it sounds like a silly notion, but you know how very large Johnathon's house is, Cal. I'd have plenty of room. There's...why there's at least seven rooms upstairs, alone! I can't use all of them. I haven't even opened all of them, in fact. I'm barely using half of the downstairs." She paused, and he heard her take up her cup of coffee and sip it, and took a sip of his own, waiting for her to go on. In a moment, she did. "I've talked to Doc Valentine and Judith. They said they'd be only too glad to teach me what I need to know. Judith has learned so much, being the wife of a doctor. I'm most impressed. And Doc said there's a tremendous need for a hospital, with the town growing as it is. Why everyday there's more folks that arrive, either on the boats, or by wagon train. Have you seen how many decide to stay here, and not go on west?" She stopped suddenly, realizing what she had said, and offered, "Oh, I'm sorry, Cal. I didn't mean..."

"I know. It's okay," he said, and he wished so much that he *could* see, so he could help her plans come to fruition. He could hear the enthusiasm in her voice as she continued, and realized she had given a lot of thought to the things she spoke of. It cheered him to hear how excited she was, and he hoped she'd tell him more.

"Would you continue to teach? Could you manage to do both? Teach and run the hospital?" he asked, feeling his own interest build.

"Oh, I think they could find another teacher. I'm sure of it, in fact. I've always wanted to take care of folks, Cal. I think, with a lot of training, I could get to be a big help to Doc and Judith."

"Are there enough people in our area, do you think, to warrant a hospital?" he asked, feeling foolish for asking. As she had said, any town that was growing like Hastings, had need of a hospital. It was a foolish question, and as soon as he asked it, he wished he hadn't.

But Ophelia seemed not to notice; so intent was she on telling him more. "Think about it, Cal! Most towns have to *build* a hospital when they need one. We already have a building big enough. Do you know how thrilled Johnathon would have been?"

She was beside herself with happiness, and her mood was so infectious that he, too, began to get over his previous gloom. "I think Johnathon would be as happy as you are," he said. "Have you thought of a name for your hospital? Why not name it after him. Call it "Clark Hospital." What do you think? That has a nice ring to it."

"Oh, Cal! I never thought of naming it. I *love* the idea!" she exclaimed, clapping her hands, delightedly. She leaned forward and much to his surprise, kissed him on the cheek. He was startled by it, not seeing it coming, and felt his face flush. Just as quickly, she rose and picked up the coffeepot, asking if he wanted more. He did, and as she filled his cup a second time, he suddenly remembered that she had said she had two things to tell him. He took a sip of coffee, and then asked her what else she had on her mind.

"I hope you won't think I'm terribly bold, Cal, with what I say next. I know it's probably going to shock you..." He waited, wishing she would get to the point. Finally, she did, and his shock was more than a little apparent! In fact, he was so shocked that he could not answer, but sat there feeling a plethora of emotions, while trying to get his thoughts in order.

"Ophelia, I..." he shook his head, not continuing.

She was silent, now, afraid that not only had she shocked him, but that—in her impulsiveness—she had done irreparable damage to their longtime friendship. She shifted in her chair, clearing her throat.

"I'm sorry. I was out of line. I didn't mean to offend you, Cal. It was foolish of me to...to...suggest such a thing. It's just that I enjoy our talks so much, and we could talk anytime we wished, if you lived with me. You shouldn't stay cooped up in this tiny room, living here like you do, all alone. It's not good for a person to be alone. I've been alone all my life, Cal, and I can't imagine being alone, *and* blind! I'm sorry, but it just isn't a good thing."

It was his turn to be silent now. Everything she said was true. No one should be alone, cooped up in small surroundings, and blind, too. But, what would people say, if he took her up on her offer? What would it look like, a grown man living with an unmarried woman? Her reputation would be shot. It could only cause her a lot of shame and embarrassment. As he thought that, he suddenly thought of Lea. What would Lea think of him living with her sister? If she had any feelings left, at all, for him—though he doubted it—what would this do to those feelings? True, he had told her to go away. Told her he no longer wanted to marry. Told her she should find a husband who could be a *real* husband to her. Could go places with her, do things with her, could *see* her! When she had insisted she wanted no one else, that she loved him, he had told her to get out. Had screamed at her, without thinking, "Get out of my sight!" There had been a horrible moment of silence that seemed to go on forever, and then Lea had flung herself into his arms, her tears wetting his cheeks as she tried to kiss him. He hung his head as he remembered. "Get out of here! I want you to *go!* I wouldn't be *blind*, if it wasn't for you!" He remembered how her slender body had trembled as she backed away from him. Heard her sobs, as she turned and raced from the room. Two days later, when the train pulled out of town, she was on it, and his heart went with her. He sighed, and looked up toward where Ophelia sat, watching him. It wasn't necessary for him to explain.

"I know what you're thinking, Cal. It's alright. I was wrong to ask." She reached out and patted his arm, a sad expression upon her face. Then she stood, picking up both their empty cups.

"Leave the dishes, Ophelia. I'll wash them," he said, knowing he had hurt her, and had changed the mood of her visit from joy to sadness. "I think your idea for the hospital is grand."

She took his arm. "Walk me out," she said, and he thought again of Lea, and how she had run from the store, and from his life.

When she reached the door, Ophelia rose up on her toes and kissed him quickly on his cheek, telling him to be sure and lock the door behind her. "Yes, Ma'am," he replied, and listened to her walk across the boardwalk, and hurry across the street. As he turned to go back inside, he heard her call, "goodnight," and he closed the door, his world once again so very small. He felt his way to his room, and sat at the table, wondering if he'd been wrong to drive Lea away. He'd only said what he did, to make her go. He didn't blame her. Not at all. He knew he'd go through it all again, gladly, to keep her safe. If only he could have made her understand that. But what was done was done. There was no turning back. He'd done it for her own good, knowing she deserved better than to be tied to a blind man. Even to a blind man who still loved her with all his heart!

CHAPTER 5

The next morning, Johnny woke before the sun came up. He hadn't slept a very restful sleep, and felt stiff and sore and out of sorts. Buck nickered a greeting, and Johnny smiled a half-hearted smile, then rose and walked off into the bushes to relieve himself. When he returned, he started a small fire, and put a pot of coffee on to brew. His stomach rumbled, as he rubbed the sleep from his eyes. And a deep yawn escaped his lips, as he sat down on a log to wait for the coffee to boil. There was a slight mist, he noticed, and he knew it wouldn't be long before the snows came. At the thought of snow, his mother came to mind, followed immediately by thoughts of their first day in Chief Standing Elk's camp, and his first encounter with Laughing Water. He shook his head, reaching out to pour himself a cup of coffee, and settled down— his back against the log—to enjoy it. No matter how hard he tried, he couldn't get that day out of his mind.

A boy can be sorely impressionable at the age of sixteen, and I had not been any different, he thought. It was late fall when my mother decided to go back to Standing Elk's village. We hadn't been there in a long time, and I readily agreed. The weather was perfect: not too hot, not too cold, a fine time to travel. I always looked forward to going, having many friends among the braves my age. I also liked to spend time with my father's old friend, Howling Wolf. We would talk long into the night, sharing stories of our lives, and especially the time we had spent with my father. Those talks helped, somehow, to ease the pain of his loss for both of us. Mother, too, seemed more at peace with the Indian women: Wind Runner and Little Moon, in particular.

Indians had a different idea of death than the white man: an acceptance of it, and no fear. To say they didn't grieve would be a lie. They did. And when they did, their keening could be heard throughout the camp. But to them death was a natural part of life, instead of just a loss, and it comforted us to be there. One of the worst things about my father failing to return was the "not knowing." Like so many folks on both sides of the war, we had no idea if he actually was dead, and if so, where had he died, and how? That caused many a sleepless night, our minds imagining the pain and suffering he might have endured. Of course, we also held out hope, though it diminished more and more as time passed, that he might still be alive. Could it be possible that he'd suffered a wound to the head, and might be out there, somewhere, wandering and confused, ravaged by pain, cold, afraid, and alone? The images these thoughts conjured up were the worst to deal with. They ate at both my mother and me, sickening us. Oh, yes, sickening us.

Howling Wolf spoke to me about my fears, encouraging me to be strong and not give up hope. I listened to him speak, his voice firm, and felt comforted by his words. He told me many stories of the times he and my father had gone hunting together, of my father's courage and strength, and above all, of his wisdom. I felt empowered by his words, and grew to believe that if he was alive, someday, somehow, my father would find his way back to us. If he was not alive, God, or Wakantanka, would watch over him, and eventually grant my mother and I surcease from our pain and worry. In the meantime, I prayed daily for his safe return, or some word of him, our lives not complete without him. Believing that God heard all my prayers, though doubt slipped in now and then, I trusted that the day would come when I would see him again.

We were welcomed warmly upon our arrival in the village, smiles appearing on the faces of all those who saw us ride in. We felt happy to see our old friends, and knew we had been wise to come.

My mother dismounted at the dwelling of Chief Standing Elk, embracing his wife, Wind Runner, and speaking to her in her own language, which seemed to greatly please her.

I slid from my horse, calling out a greeting to friends of my own, glad to see them after so long a time. They hurried to meet me, warm smiles upon their faces. I felt great joy at seeing them again, and looked around, trying to see all that was going on in the camp. Women sat outside some of the tepees, hanging meat strips to dry, or stretching hides on frames to cure in the sun. Dogs ran here and there amongst the younger children as they played, barking or scratching, or chasing each other, or their tails. Young boys practiced shooting at the far end of the camp, their triumphs acknowledged by their companions, as young girls helped their mothers or the older women of the tribe. Or if too young to do so, sat quietly playing with small dolls made of sticks and dressed with tiny pieces of cloth or leaves. An old, gray-haired woman, her skin wrinkled with age, walked through the camp, a large basket in her arms. I wondered what was in it, but was too far away to tell. Two braves, with eagle feathers hanging from their long, black hair, stirred up dust as they rode through the camp, one on a horse of shimmering black that reminded me of my father's horse, Midnight. They turned to look at a young woman who stepped from her tepee as they passed, and raised their bows in greeting. It felt good to see the quiet peacefulness of the village, and I was glad we had come.

I wondered why my childhood friend, Brave Foot—once called Crying Badger—had not come to greet me, and went to look for him. He had earned his name when very young, by counting coup on a cavalry officer who had attempted to shoot him off his horse when he was out hunting one day. The supply of meat having dwindled, and having heard—some days earlier—of a large buck at a watering hole a distance from the camp, he decided to journey there. He would have preferred to hunt buffalo, but they were all gone. Killed by the white men for their hides or bones, but mostly for sport. Slaughtered by the hundreds, their great bodies skinned, and left to rot in the sun! Chief Standing Elk had gasped in disbelief at the sight, Howling Wolf told me later, unable to understand men who would do such a thing. 'They have no heart,' he had finally said, and then turned away, walking slowly back to his horse.

As Brave Foot neared the place where the large buck usually drank, he saw a figure lying on the ground, the blue of his cavalry jacket, unmistakable. A horse stood nearby, its head hung down, one leg bent, the knee badly swollen. Brave Foot approached slowly, not certain of the condition of the man upon the ground. The man's horse raised its head, limping, as it began to move away. Brave Foot felt sad as he watched, certain that the horse would not be able to be ridden for a very long time, if ever again.

Suddenly, a shot rang out! Brave Foot yanked on his reins, the bullet zipping past his head, missing him by a mere breath! Before the man could shoot again—without even thinking—Brave Foot urged his horse straight at the man, surprising him so badly that he yelled out, dropping his gun as he cowered in fear. In the next instant, Brave Foot had leaned out and reached down, touching the man on his head with one hand, his shout of triumph resounding across the countryside!

That night, as dancing commenced, Brave Foot—then called Crying Badger—told of how he had encountered the man in the soldier jacket, and had counted coup, describing even the paleness of the man's face. His look of fear, and then surprise, as he touched his head, then rode away. Later that night, his father came to his tepee and—in a naming ceremony—gave his son his name, in honor of such bravery. From that day on, he was no longer Crying Badger, but Brave Foot.

Johnny walked through the camp, enjoying the sounds of the children at play. The little girls staying close to their mothers, the boys practicing their skill with small bow and arrows. Some of the women stole shy glances at him, smiling, and then went about their work. He felt good being there, good about himself. There was a sense of belonging every time he was among the Indians. Perhaps, it's because I look like them, he thought. But it was more than that, and he knew it. It was because he thought and believed as they did.

He walked on; his legs long like his father's, his arms strong and muscular, his skin taut and smooth. He stood 5'10" and weighed one hundred and sixty pounds. And his raven-black hair, thick and straight, hung midway down his back. From the chores he had done, when young, muscles rippled across his mid-section, and he prided himself on his strength. But his best attribute was his ability to run. He could outrun all the boys he knew, without getting the least out of breath. It was an ability he'd inherited from his mother, who had also been able to outrun all her friends, when she was young.

As he strolled through the village looking for Brave Foot, he happened to notice a young woman about his own age, as she knelt at the edge of a stream. He couldn't help noticing. Her long, dark hair glistened in the sun, cascading around her shoulders like a cloak. And her dress hugged her shapely bottom, as she reached forward, cupping some water into her hands to drink. He stopped in his tracks, unable to look away, hoping she'd turn toward him so he could see her face. As though she sensed his eyes upon her, she slowly turned. He knew he should look away, but the gentle curve of her cheek, the questioning look in her beautiful eyes, the delicate outline of her lips, captivated him, and he could not. He stood staring, spellbound by her loveliness, certain there weren't enough words written to describe such beauty.

It was then that he happened to notice the cradleboard on the ground beside where she had been kneeling. Tiny hands waved from within it, and he glanced from the baby to the young woman, realizing it must be her child. Realizing that she was a mother, and was, in all probability, married. He felt embarrassed and awkward.

She saw how uncomfortable he suddenly looked, as he noticed the baby, and quickly bent to pick up the child. Johnny smiled then, not knowing what else to do to end the uncomfortable situation he found himself in. Here he was, sixteen years old, staring at a woman who was obviously married, and a mother, to boot! He cleared his throat, smiling a nervous smile, and was more than a little pleased when she smiled timidly back. He turned away then, forcing himself to continue on his way to find Brave Foot, and put as much distance as possible between the lovely woman and himself. Wishing at the same time that he'd spoken to her, said something, anything, or at least asked her name.

He groaned aloud as he walked, aware of the new feelings that coursed through him, feelings he had never experienced before. No one, not even Katie Yeager, had ever stirred such feelings within him. He cut through some tall brush, taking a path that he could tell was seldom used, and sat beside the stream there, his thoughts jumbled. He thought back to the summer he had carried some packages home for Katie, laughing at something she had said. He remembered how her blonde curls bounced as she walked, her pale skin looking even paler, as her cheeks reddened. She was a pretty girl, fun to talk to, and he was certain he was the envy of any of the boys in town who saw them that day. But though she was pretty, she had stirred no feelings in him like those he had experienced at the sight of the Indian woman. He shook his head, an ache building in him at the mere thought of her. "Well, I'll have to keep my distance," he said aloud, "but find out who she is. Maybe her husband's dead, and she..."

"Johnny!" Brave Foot exclaimed, coming up behind him. Johnny jumped, startled, not having heard his friend approach. "I saw your mother in camp, and hoped you had come with her. How are you, my friend?" Brave Foot asked, hunkering down beside him.

"I'm fine," Johnny replied. "Yourself?"

"I, too, am fine." Brave Foot was a slight bit shorter than Johnny, of heavier build, lacking the muscle tone of his friend. But, he was as strong as Johnny, and could run as fast, when they raced. He was two years older, and though his eyes held a look of kindness, he could not be called handsome. From the outer corner of his right eye to the corner of his mouth, a raised, red scar ran, the result of a childhood encounter he had with a saber wielding white man. Apparently the man had been in a wagon train that the Pawnees had attacked, killing everyone except him, and his mind had snapped from the horrors of what he'd seen. Weeks later, crazed and delirious, he'd charged into the village, brandishing the saber, while screaming at the top of his lungs! Brave Foot had no chance to run, as the man bore down on him, slashing wildly, his eyes proclaiming his madness. Before the startled Indians could stop him, he had slashed the young child: a number of arrows soon ending his rampage. Brave Foot, then known as Crying Badger, endured the pain, his first encounter with the white men who were soon to cross the land by the thousands.

"And who is it, Black Hawk, that you must find the name of?" Brave Foot asked, smiling at his friend.

"I've seen a young woman, unknown to me," Johnny replied, pleased to have been called by his father's Indian name, and his own middle name. "She's even more beautiful than the setting sun."

"Ah-h," Brave Foot said, grinning. "And she has stolen your heart, Black Hawk, has she not?"

A wide smile spread across Johnny's face as he rose, throwing a playful punch at his friend, in response.

Brave Foot ducked and whirled around, countering, his fist landing with a thud against Johnny's shoulder. They sparred a few minutes, then straightened, laughing, and then walked side-by-side back to the camp.

"Come eat," Brave Foot offered, gesturing toward a tepee off to their right. "My wife is a good cook."

Johnny nodded in acceptance, brushing his hair back from his face, as they approached the dwelling. Brave Foot stepped inside, Johnny following close behind. The tepee was warm and inviting. Many buffalo hides lay within it, an assortment of baskets to one side, and a lance over near where Brave Foot now sat. There was also a quiver filled with arrows, and a fine bow. Johnny folded his long legs beneath him and sat down across from his friend, glad to be there.

Just then, the flap was pulled aside, and to his utter surprise, the beautiful young woman he'd seen at the water's edge stepped in, her baby secured in its cradleboard on her back.

"Black Hawk, this is my wife, Laughing Water. Bring food, wife," he ordered, smiling tenderly at her. "My friend, Black Hawk, is hungry."

Johnny had all he could do not to stare at her, her slender body shapely beneath her deerskin dress, her skin as smooth as satin, and of the nicest honeyed shade. She was even more beautiful up close. Her doe-like, dark eyes held his, for only a moment, and then looked toward her husband. She smiled at him, and then set about filling bowls with food. It was when she handed a bowl to Johnny, that he knew she shared the same intense feelings as he. The look in her eyes had told him so.

A whinny from his horse brought Johnny back to the present. "What is it, Buck?" he asked, looking around. His stomach rumbled, and he knew he should eat something. But he decided to saddle up and get on his way. He had done the honorable thing. Had ridden away as soon as it was possible to do so. Ridden away, from his mother, his friend, and his friend's beautiful wife. Knowing in his heart, that everywhere he journeyed, she was with him.

CHAPTER 6

Katie Yeager woke early, stretching and yawning, as she rolled out of bed. It was chilly in the house, and she dressed quickly, pulling on one of her older, more worn dresses. She knew today would be a day of work: a day of baking and cleaning. She hummed as she pulled on her shoes, hearing the sound of a rooster crowing. So I'm not the only one who's up early, she thought, smiling. She brushed her hair, turning her head this way and that, to see how it looked in the large mirror that hung on the wall. It had been her grandmother's mirror, from Germany, and though some of the glass was mottled with age, she was pleased to have it. It just took the slightest ingenuity to figure out where to look, when looking into it, to avoid those spotted areas.

She heard someone moving around downstairs, and knew it was either her father or her mother. Her father, Heinrich Yeager, had a habit of opening the store at exactly six o'clock each morning, except of course, on the Sabbath. He had made it a practice to open at that time, ever since the first day of ownership of the old Dawson store. Her mother, Ursula, also worked in the store, but made certain that most household chores were done before she headed there. Katie smiled at these thoughts, and quickly pulled the quilt in place upon her bed, smoothing it with a few quick motions. Nearly twenty-five, she helped with the household chores, enjoying the conversations she shared then, with her grandmother. Her grandmother had not wanted to come to America, but could not bare the idea of her only son, Katie's father, leaving her behind. Once he'd made up his mind to take his family and go, she very reluctantly packed her belongings, bade her friends a sad farewell, and joined her family in the "grand adventure," as Katie's father liked to call their journey. Heinrich liked everything he saw upon landing in America, and his enthusiasm soon seemed to have a positive effect upon his mother. Until, that is, he told her he had no intention of staying in one of the more civilized towns along the seaboard, but intended on journeying out into the Wild West. Oh, the upset that had caused! But, dabbing at her eyes, a beseeching look given to all, she soon adjusted, and here they were in Hastings.

Katie liked Hastings. She had made many friends, and enjoyed the many activities the town offered. Or, at least the ones her father let her enjoy. Her father was a kind and warm-hearted man, who would give the shirt off his back to a stranger, if he saw the need. But when it came to Katie, he was a bit overly protective. At least she thought so. He let her go to the ice cream socials, as long as the rest of her family also attended. And he let her go visit Miz Denton, the schoolmarm. But never had he let her go on lone rides a distance from town, and absolutely never to visit the O'Leary's. She had met Miz O'Leary at church one Sunday. Had helped carry her basket and her prayer book, the old woman's hands being all bent and twisted. As they walked to her wagon, Miz O'Leary had told her of the beautiful quilts she had made, before an illness made her hands curl into horrible claw-like appendages. Katie wished so much to see the quilts. Wished so much to learn to make quilts, such as Miz O'Leary had described. But her father had told her in no uncertain terms, that she was *not* to go there. Not because they were terribly poor, as everyone knew. But because there were rumors about one of the sons, and her father wanted her nowhere near him. Colin, that was his name. Colin O'Leary. Katie wasn't sure what the rumors were, not having heard them, herself, but her father was adamant. And, since she was not of a nature to disobey, she set aside her longing and did what was asked of her. She had to admit, however, that she was quite curious about this Colin O'Leary, and could not imagine what he had done to set her father so against him. It was not like her father to be this way. He was usually the first to extend a helping hand, and to give a man the benefit of the doubt. The more he enforced this rule, the more curious she became. She had asked her friend, Eli Hart, if he knew Colin. Asked him if he had ever heard any rumors. But living so far from the O'Leary's, and always busy at his family farm, he told her he didn't have time to listen to stupid gossip. Told her she shouldn't judge a man, till she'd met him herself. Told her one of his friends had been an outsider, all the years they had attended school together. Not so much because he was both white and Indian, but because he *looked* Indian! He told her that once he got to know him, they had become the best of friends, and he now looked upon him as almost a brother. She learned later that he was talking about Johnny Gentry, a young man with the most beautiful dark eyes and hair, whom she had met at her father's store. She liked Johnny. Was fascinated by the fact that he was an honest-to-goodness Indian. Her father seemed to have no problem with that. Said his father had once been sheriff, and that his mother was a beautiful lady, who'd been taught at a young age to hunt and shoot, better than most men, by his grandfather, John Bruce. There was a whole story that everyone in town seemed to know, about how Sarah Gentry, Johnny's mother, had run off with an Indian, married him, and after he died, came back to Hastings. Seems she'd come for medicine, there being an outbreak of smallpox in the Indian village. The sheriff had been her friend, long before she left with the Indian, and well, she wasn't sure of the whole story, but it seems he was part Indian, too, and in time they had married and had a baby. That baby was Johnny. He also had an Indian name, he told her one-day, as he walked her home, having asked to help carry her packages. It was Black Hawk, he said, and she thought it highly romantic and very fitting. He looked Indian, with his long, black hair, and dark eyes. She had never seen any other Indians. Certainly not living, breathing ones! Only a picture of one that had been hanging on the bulletin board in front of the Dawson store, when they bought the store. That Indian was real old, however, his face pockmarked, his eyes wild looking. Johnny didn't look anything like him. Why, half the girls in town had thought John Black Hawk Gentry quite handsome. Though they wouldn't have considered being courted by him, of course, him being Indian, and all. I might have considered it, though, she thought, smiling pensively.

"I'm going to help your father at the store now, Kate. Are you awake, darling?" her mother called from downstairs.

"Yes, Mother. I'll be right down," Katie replied, hurrying to tie a ribbon of the softest blue around her head, to hold her golden curls back from her face. She tied a small bow, and with a quick look at her room, made sure she had left everything in order. She had heard that Mr. Dawson's father had died in this very room. Died in the same bed she slept in now, in fact. At first, it had frightened her. When they first moved into the house, she would lay awake all hours of the night, the quilts pulled up to her chin, watching as ghostly shapes floated here and there across the walls of the room. She'd lay there, only her eyes moving, and listen to the night sounds, wondering if his ghost would visit the room before morning. It seemed ages till the silly fears abated, and she actually grew to like having this room as her own. It was a much larger room than the one she had previously shared with her grandmother, back in Germany. Larger, and so much brighter, with the window right across from the foot of the bed. Some nights, the moon would shine right in the window, its radiance lighting up the whole room. She would lie there, on those nights, and envision what her life might be in years to come. She'd plan and dream. Would she marry and have a large family? Would she and her husband travel by wagon train to California? Or would they buy a little home right here in Hastings, and raise a lovely family: two boys and a girl, perhaps? Oh, how she dreamt, when the moon shone in her window, and spread its glorious golden light all across her bed.

"Morning, Mother," she said, as she came down the stairs. "Good morning, Grandmother. How are you feeling?" she asked, seeing that her grandmother already had a pan of water heating on the stove, and was ready to start cleaning.

"Good morning," her mother and grandmother both answered at the same time. "Your breakfast is on the table, dear. Eat, before it gets cold," her mother told her, smiling.

Katie washed her hands at the washstand near the door, and hurried to the table.

"Today, we clean," her grandmother said, walking over to the pan of boiling water upon the stove. "I've never seen so much dust! Every time someone goes by in one of those big wagons, all the furniture gets covered with dust. This wouldn't happen, you know, if we lived by the water."

Katie and her mother exchanged glances, smiling at the older woman's remarks. They both knew she would, in all probability, have found something to find fault with by the water, too. It seemed to be her nature to complain. And, too, they both realized how difficult it had to have been, at her age, to suddenly pack up and leave not only her lifetime friends, but also even the country she had called home for nigh on to sixty-some years. In truth, it had been hard for all to make the transition. Except, of course, for Katie's father. Once he'd made up his mind, the man could not be dissuaded! There were times when Katie's mother felt that he would have tried to swim to America, if that had been the only way to get there. Oh, how he had gone on about the new beginning they would have. The house he would find for them. The fine business they would own, in some grand town that was only just beginning to grow. A town with a railroad and stage line, and oh, just all kinds of wonderful possibilities for all who lived there. By day he talked to all his friends, and late into each evening he studied the books he had discovered. Books filled with pictures of wagon trains heading west, of towns springing up in a land of such immense beauty, and of all the opportunities for a man who was not afraid to work hard to make his dream come true. As one after another, his friends left for America, he became more determined to go. With every letter that arrived from those who had found the courage to venture out—often against great odds—Heinrich became more and more intrigued and empowered, and more intent on making his hopes and dreams for his family a reality.

At last, one blustery day in October, with the wind blowing fiercely and waves as tall as a man, he hurried his family aboard a waiting ship. With tears in their eyes, they bid farewell to friends and family, waving from the shore. Frightening, as it seemed, there was no going back. The "Lady Lydia" was heading for America, and Heinrich Yeager and his family were just beginning the adventure of their lives!

Katie finished her breakfast, washing the bowl and spoon, at once, so her grandmother wouldn't have to mention it. As she washed off the table where she had eaten, her thoughts turned again to Johnny Gentry. She wondered if his life was filled with danger, because of the way things were between the whites and Indians. She hoped he was safe, and doing well, wherever he was. She'd heard someone say he had taken his mother back to the Indian camp, then left to go in search of his father. But she wasn't certain if that was true or not. After all, many years had passed since the war, and it wasn't likely his father was still alive, if he hadn't returned by now. Knowing how kind and caring Johnny had always been, however, it wouldn't have surprised her, if it were true. He was always concerned for the welfare of others, she remembered. Yes, besides being handsome, she thought, he had always been exceedingly nice. I wouldn't have minded being courted by him, she mused. She wondered if he was married now, or had a gal he liked. Oh, well, she thought, he's been gone a long time. Was it four years, or five? She sighed, shaking her head, her blonde ringlets bouncing, as she did so. She wondered if he knew his grandparents had died. With that thought in mind, she walked into the other room to help her grandmother with the cleaning. These days, when Indians are looked upon with such hatred, there's probably little chance he'd ever come back to town, she thought. Little did she know, that only the day before, he had stood in the cemetery at the edge of town, at the graves of his grandparents.

CHAPTER 7

Colin O'Leary lay on his bed, his eyes wide open, staring at the ceiling of the room he once shared with his brother, Patrick. A week's growth of beard covered his chin, his expression sullen. He hated Hastings. Hated the way the folks in town had looked at him the day he returned from the war. He could see the same hatred mirrored in their faces, as he rode along, his gray uniform coat tattered and torn. His feet wrapped in strips of cloth, his boots having fallen apart, long before. He'd wondered if his maw was still alive. Had heard his pa was gone. He had a right to come back to Hastings. Didn't matter what anyone thought. He'd *earned* the right. His home was here. The home he'd left at the start of that hellish war. The only home he'd ever had. Let them look and point. He wasn't the only one who had chosen different. Why hell, he hadn't been anywhere near these Minnesota boys. Hadn't done them any damage. Hadn't killed a one of 'em. All he wanted now, now that the accursed war was over, was to be with his maw, and his family. All he had ever wanted was to be with them. To hold each one of them in his arms, as he had, in his heart, all through the wretched war. There had to be some way to heal the pain inside him. Some way to stop the nightmares from what he'd seen, and what he'd done.

Seeing his family would help, he thought. He hoped it would, any-way. Something had to! He knew he couldn't go on this way: unable to eat, unable to sleep. The nightmares tearing at him, night after night, till he thought about doing whatever it took to get away from the memories that haunted him.

He'd had trouble sleeping, long before he'd run into his brother, William, at Andersonville. Had seen to it he'd gotten away safely, with no one even realizing they were brothers. Felt like the wind had been knocked clear out of him, when he first saw William. Never expected to see one of his own family there. Never expected to have to watch, as days turned into months, and William slowly wasted away. Thought he'd go crazy, as he tried, frantically, to find a way to get him out of there. He'd finally devised a plan; a dangerous plan that he wasn't sure would work. If it didn't, he knew, not only would William be killed, but so would he. No easy death. Hung, as a traitor! If his men didn't get to him first, that is, and do what he'd seen them do to another, earlier on in the war. Every moment of every day, he worked on a plan, desperate to save his brother. Every time he thought he'd covered all the loopholes, there'd come another. And he'd have to shuck those plans, and try to devise some other way to get him out.

He'd never forget that last night, hiding William beneath a wagon-load of stiffening corpses, on their way to be buried. Told him not to move, not to cough, and not to breathe amid the terrible stench of those bodies: some covered in maggots and swollen to near bursting from the heat. He'd gotten him out, hadn't he? Gotten him past the guards, and past the gates! Had stood on the parapet, watching till the bodies were all dumped, a cold sweat breaking out, as one of the guards yelled that he'd seen one of the prisoners move, and grabbed his gun and shot into the mass of bodies! His knees felt like they might buckle, as he walked over to see if it was William who had been shot.

"What's all the commotion, Private?" he asked, his stomach churning from the sickening stench, and his over-wrought emotions.

"Nothing, Sir. Found a live one, that's all, Sir," the young man replied, smiling a gaping smile, four front teeth missing.

"Good work," Colin said, nearly choking on the words, trying his best to keep his hands from shaking, as he lit his pipe. He breathed in, sucking the smoke deep into his lungs, and as he did, his eyes searched the pile of dead, trying to locate his brother. His heart was pounding, as he scanned the mass of bodies. Five hundred had died that afternoon. Five hundred more would be dead by morning. Or maybe more. There had been days when fifteen hundred died. Fifteen hundred! He shuddered, and then he saw William. He lay among the decaying bodies, near the side of the long, narrow ditch, blood covering his shirt, his mouth open, his eyes staring straight at Colin. A gasp escaped his lips, as he saw him, thinking he was dead. And then, as if in answer to a prayer, he saw William wink. It was the only move his brother made. The only sign that he would get, that the plan still had a chance to work. Colin took a deep breath, and turned quickly, facing away from the ditch, yelling at the top of his lungs, "Halt! Who goes there?" A moment later, the men were running off in search of an elusive figure. Hell bent on catching some Yank escaping. And as they disappeared, Colin reached down and gave his brother his hand, pulling him up, and then squeezing it in a final embrace. William ran behind a nearby shed, hiding till night under a pile of filthy wet straw.

He hadn't heard any shots that night. Had lain awake all night, praying with all his might that William had gotten away. Praying the many patrols on the outer perimeter of the prison wouldn't catch him. That William would make it to the other side, safe and sound, and before long the war would end, and they'd both be on their way home.

There'd come no word to the contrary, and as days passed, he began to feel a slight sense of relief. He didn't learn till much later that William had gotten all the way to the Yankee line, surprising the sentry on guard, and was shot, point blank, the bullet hitting him in the chest. He'd lived long enough to tell one of his fellow soldiers his name and the town he was from, and to please see he got home. Then he closed his eyes and slowly bled to death.

Colin closed his eyes, feeling the dampness, as tears ran down his cheeks. He had done what he could, and it had all been in vain. One look at his mother's face, when he rode into the yard, and he knew there would never be peace in his soul again. She'd looked so frail, standing there on the porch, when he'd first arrived. Her face showing clearly, the pain and suffering the loss of his brother had caused her. He sat there, noticing how rundown the place looked, the fences barely standing, and the barn near falling down. And as he looked, his mother slowly stepped down from the porch. She stopped, looking at him questioningly, and then opened her arms to him. He was, after all, her son. Her son, come home from the war. A feeling of relief swept over him as he dismounted, watching her. Then he walked into the comfort of her waiting arms, his tears wetting the shoulder of her dress, as he held her close, and cried.

He'd slept that night, for the first time in months. Maybe because he was so tired, or maybe because he felt safe, at last. Whatever the reason, the nightmares were held at bay, starting up again on the following night. He'd collapsed on the bed, in the room that had been his, and his brother Patrick's. Collapsed, and slept like one dead. He didn't move, didn't snore, didn't dream. Didn't take off his tattered coat, or remove the strips of cloth from around his feet. He simply lay down on his bed, totally exhausted in body and in spirit. When sleep came, moments later, it was a deep, healing sleep. But he already knew there could never be enough healing. Though his body showed no wounds, they were there, hidden deep within his very soul. As long as they didn't surface, he'd be all right. He'd get through the hours and minutes of each day. But he already knew that there had to come a reckoning. There had to be a time of recall, when he would remember all he had seen, and remember...all he had done. When the wounds of his soul surfaced, he knew that only God would be able to heal him. If... he could heal.

He got out of bed, forcing himself to do so. He'd been home a long time now. Hadn't planned to stay, but couldn't leave. His mother was barely getting by, her hands paining her more and more each day, and hardly able to do any chores. How he wished his sister, Mary, hadn't married that Dawson fellow and moved to California. If she were here, it would have been a lot easier for their mother. She could have done the cleaning and baking, fed the chickens and done the milking. But she'd moved a long time ago, and their mother had done the best she could. He didn't see how she'd been able to do near as much as she'd done, also having to care for his brother, James, who'd come home from the war, broken in spirit and sickly. He'd had one illness after another, he told them, till finally dysentery had about killed him. All the soldiers in his troop had gotten it, some so bad that they wasted away in a matter of weeks. James had always been a stalwart fellow, powerful and indomitable. A man with unending courage, fearless and tireless. Now he sat in a rocker by the window, jumping at loud sounds, his eyes looking, but not seeing. Maw tended him, speaking softly to him about happy things, and happy times. She brushed his hair back out of his eyes, and spooned his food into his mouth, only her eyes betraying the grief she was feeling. I could not leave them, even if I had wanted to. Not now, not with things like this. What man could? I knew I'd stay, at least till Patrick came home, *if he* came home. He'd left soon after William, kissing Maw on her cheek, telling her not to worry, telling her he'd be back. Three years had passed till she heard from him. A letter came, the writing on the envelope faded, few words able to be read. Maw read what she could, never saying a word, then tucked the letter into her Bible. At night, by lamplight, she'd take it out and read it, again, straining her eyes to make out the faded words. Thankful to have some vestige of her younger boy to keep near her, safely tucked within her well-worn Bible. She never told us what the letter said. Just that he was getting by. Had found his rightful path through life, and would come home, when the time was right. I hoped it'd be before she died.

Patrick had always been her favorite, of the lot of us. Could make her laugh when things were bad, though he often made her cry by things he did. I had to laugh, as I remembered how he'd fallen off the barn roof, breaking his leg, while trying to fly. And how he'd set the barn on fire, claiming all he'd been doing was praying. Or the time he had almost drowned, trying to see how far out into the lake he could swim, when real little. Any time there'd been trouble, there'd been no doubt but that it was Patrick who'd started it, or finished it—usually by breaking some bones, and worrying Maw to death. Why I could count on my hands, at least ten accidents, resulting in breaks, Colin thought. First, he'd broken his leg trying to fly. Then he'd broken his wrist trying to ride our old milk cow. Then he'd broken his leg again, jumping into the swimming hole too close to the shore, where the big rocks were. Claimed he'd seen someone out on the rocks. Colin shook his head, smiling, his thoughts continuing. After he broke his arm—don't remember how he did that—the rest of his breaks were small, much to Maw's relief. Colin began to laugh as he thought back to those memories, surprised that he had temporarily forgotten—for a moment—the horrors of the war.

CHAPTER 8

It was nearly noon when Johnny rode across the pasture toward his family's old home. Even at that distance, it appeared to be in poor condition. One of the barn doors lay on the ground, a pail resting on its side beside it. The gate to the main pasture stood open, tall grass growing across the lane that led to it. The house looked dark and uninviting. Deserted. He was glad his mother could not see it like this. It'd break her heart. He rode on in, slowly, saddened at the sight.

When they'd left, four years earlier, to go to Standing Elk's village, his mother had sold the farm to Michael O'Leary. Michael knew the place better than anyone, even better than they did. Had taken care of it, tending the animals, fixing the fences, and doing most of the work required to keep it going, for years. Johnny was shocked at how it looked now, just four years later. No sign of the cattle, he noted. No chickens running about the yard. Deserted.

He dismounted, tying his reins to the fence post. Then patted Buck's neck, wondering what to do next. He had planned to spend the night. Planned to see how Michael was doing, and spend some time talking awhile with him. It looked like no one had been here in ages.

He brushed the dust from his coat, pulling his collar up around his neck, then took a deep breath. Well, if it's deserted, he thought, I might as well spend the night. Who is there, to say I can't?

Michael had offered right off, to buy the place, when they told him they meant to sell it. Told them he'd liked the place, since he was young. Ever since he'd gone to work for Johnny's pa. Had wished that it could someday be his. Johnny shook his head. Funny, he'd let it get like this, he thought. Just didn't make sense. But then, so much didn't make sense nowadays, ever since the war. He thought of his father, wishing he was here, and things could be like they used to be.

His mother had sold the place to Michael, giving him a very good deal, and was more than a little surprised when he'd come the very next morning with all the money. Said he'd been saving it up, for a long, long time. Both she and Johnny didn't say anything, but both of them thought, then, of Michael's mother, Miz O'Leary. If Michael had saved so much money, why hadn't he used some of it to ease the suffering of his own mother? Why, how many times had my pa sent food to them, Johnny thought, trying to help them get by, after Mr. O'Leary died? Sent a dozen or so chicks, too, and some fine laying hens. And later, even a cow that was soon to calve, so they'd have milk and butter. Johnny felt perplexed, thinking back to these things.

He walked to the house, seeing that the door stood ajar. Spider webs spread across the opening. He brushed them away, and went in. It was damp and dreary inside, the table lying on its side in the middle of the floor. One chair overturned. His mother's rocker lay in pieces, one arm—partially burned—protruding from the fireplace. It made Johnny's heart sick to see it. He shook his head, sadly, then took up the red twig broom that leaned against the wall by the door, and swept away the many cobwebs that hung suspended, here and there, throughout the room. Then he walked over to the bed, bunched up the old quilt that lay upon it, and walked outside. He shook the dust from it, shaking it again and again; to remove the worst of it, then carried it back inside. As he spread it out on the bed, he realized that it was the same quilt that his mother had made, long before. She had left it, offering it to Michael from the goodness of her heart, just before they left to go to Standing Elk's village. Johnny looked around. The whole place smelled dank and musty. He sneezed, and then sneezed again. Then he walked outside, sneezing once more, as he walked to his horse. He untied the reins from the fence post, and walked toward the pasture gate, leading Buck. A few minutes later, Johnny watched as the old horse ran, unencumbered, across the pasture, kicking up its heels as playfully as a colt! He watched, enjoying the sight, then picked up his gear and headed for the house. A few minutes later, he walked to the stream that ran beside the house, and filled his coffeepot with water. It wasn't long before a fresh pot of coffee was boiling on the stove, its aroma adding warmth to the room. His stomach rumbled, as he smelled the coffee. It'd been awhile since he'd eaten, and he wished there was a big pot of his Grandma Rosie's stew heating on the stove, and some of her delicious sourdough bread sitting beside it, hot and fresh from the oven. His stomach rumbled even louder as he thought these things, and he grabbed up a large, wooden bucket that sat beside the stove and walked back outside. The path to the stream next to the house was overgrown; making him certain no one had been here in a long time. He washed out the bucket, making sure there were no dead bugs in it, then filled it with the cold, clear water. It would be good to wash up. Had been awhile. His skin felt dirty from all the miles he had traveled, and he wished he wasn't so tired. If he hadn't been, he'd have carried in enough buckets of water to take a real bath. He'd seen his mother's old tub, over in the corner of the small adjoining room. But, suddenly he felt bone-tired. Wanted only to get the warmth of a good, hot cup of coffee inside him, and sleep.

He'd been on the road more days than he could count. Asked many questions, gotten fewer answers. Most of no consequence. Everyone, it seemed, had an opinion about the war. Most were extremely verbal about it, and not at all embarrassed to speak their minds. Everyone had a story to tell. And, sadly, everyone had lost someone dear to him or her, it seemed. In this, he was not alone. How many times had he asked them to keep their eye out for his father, showing them the old picture his mother usually kept with her? Telling them he came from a town called Hastings, in Minnesota. And how many times did they pull out a picture of their own, repeating his question, asking him if he had seen their loved one? It grieved him, more and more, as he journeyed across the land, always hoping and on the alert, always praying that somewhere, someone would say, "Oh, sure, I saw him. He's right down the street at the boardinghouse...or the barbershop..." After awhile, he didn't let his hopes get built up so high. Didn't let his heart begin to dance with the least anticipation. In time, he'd lost all hope he'd ever find any word of his father. Lost all hope...he'd ever... find his father.

He swilled down the cup of coffee, barely waiting for it to cool enough, the rumbling in his stomach easing. Then he pulled the partially burned arm of his mother's rocker from the fireplace, piled some wood that lay nearby in it, and in a few minutes had a sizable fire going. It wouldn't take long to get the chill and dampness out of the house, and would feel good to be warm again. He took off his coat and hat, hanging them on the one remaining nail by the door, then poured himself another cup of coffee. It was all the coffee he had left, and he hoped he'd find more when he searched the cupboards the next day. Right now he was dead on his feet, too tired to worry about coffee, or anything else, for that matter. He sat down in his father's rocker, in front of the fireplace, and removed his boots, then his shirt. He shivered slightly, walking over to bolt the door. Didn't want any surprises. Then he walked to the bed, curled up in his mother's quilt, and was soon fast asleep.

As he slept, he dreamt that he was a little boy, and he and his pa were walking in the woods, looking for something that was always just over the next hill. No matter how far or fast they walked, they could not get to whatever it was they sought. Johnny mumbled in his sleep, tossing and turning, a feeling of hopelessness and frustration tearing at him. Next, he dreamt of his mother. She stood, as she had the day he left her at Chief Standing Elk's village, smiling at him. As he smiled back, he saw her expression turn to one of surprise, then joy, and he turned to see what she was looking at. As he did, he saw his father standing there, in shadowed surroundings. He had on his old slouch hat, and the same clothes he'd worn when he left to fight in the war, and he waved at Sarah, smiling broadly at her. Johnny raised his arm to wave, so happy to see him, and as he did, Moses' expression changed to one of anguish. Followed by a look beseeching Johnny to come to his aid. Johnny began to run—running as fast as he could, yet not able to lessen the distance between them—as Moses smiled sadly and faded from sight. Only a mist remained where he'd been standing. Johnny woke with a start, fully awake now, his heart pounding in his chest, the quilt twisted around him, his thoughts jumbled from the too real dream. "Pa!" he shouted, feeling so sure that Moses was near. It took him some time to realize that it'd all been a horrible dream. The same dream he'd dreamt so often, as he traversed the country, looking for his father. And his heart felt heavy with despair, as it had for so long a time. He untangled himself from the quilt, noticing that the fire in the fireplace was burning nicely, and layback down. Sleep eluded him now, and he lay there, reliving his efforts to find his father.

When he left his mother at Standing Elk's village, he was a mere boy of sixteen. A smart lad, Grandpa Angus liked to say. But having never journeyed far from home, he'd had much to learn of the wiles and weaknesses of his fellow man, and of their treachery and cunning. He was a "babe in the woods" when it came to dealing with the unscrupulous characters he came upon, but deal with them, he had. He was on a mission. With every mile he rode he became more and more determined to succeed, and to prove himself. On and on he had traveled, far from the ones he loved, through all kinds of weather. The farther south he traveled, the hotter it got, and he often walked beside Buck, wanting to put no unnecessary strain on the old horse. Grandpa Angus had made a list of every place the 1st Minnesota had fought, that he knew of, and Johnny rode from town to town, no matter the weather, or the distance, searching...always searching. The story was always the same; no one had seen his father. Johnny lay there on the bed, a great sadness overcoming him. He'd been from one end of the war-torn land to the other. From the hills of Kentucky to the shores of Florida and Georgia, through Mississippi, South Carolina, Arkansas, North Carolina, through Tennessee, Louisiana, and Pennsylvania. Had traversed the land for longer than he cared to remember, crisscrossing his own path, while following first one lead, and then another. All to no avail. Any time there was even the slightest hope that his father had been spotted, that someone "might" have seen someone that fit his description, Johnny journeyed on, hoping and praying.

The war had ended years before, but he'd been too young then, to go in search of Moses. Sarah wouldn't hear of it. Four years after, she'd still held out hope that someday they'd look up from their chores and see Moses walking up the road, or across the field, coming home. Johnny had pleaded with her to let him go search. Then waited, accepting her reluctance, biding his time, till he was a man. He set himself to learning all he could, in the meantime. Studying every day, the lessons learned at school. Often discussing them with his mother, or Grandpa Angus. Having seen the world, and knowing the ways of it, and the many different people who abided there, Angus would often explain things in a different manner than his teacher had. Would often give

Johnny insights on issues Miss Denton had only skirted, either because of her own lack of knowledge about the subject, or because she always followed strictly the lessons in the books. Grandpa Angus, on the other hand, had a tendency to go into far more detail, often giving him more than one view of a subject to consider. Johnny was always impressed by his grandfather's logic and considerable wisdom, and often thought that he'd learned far more from his talks with his grandpa, than he had from Miss Denton at school. He was still a voracious reader, a man who soaked up knowledge with a passion. He wanted to know, not only the "how" of things, but the "why." Wanted to understand not just surface details, but the inner working of things, whether of man, or machine. His grandfather understood this, and had passed on as much information and knowledge as he could, amazed and pleased by the younger man's grasp of even difficult concepts and ideas, and his eagerness to learn.

Johnny rose, walking over to pour himself another cup of coffee, noticing it was still warm. So, I haven't been asleep for long, he thought, shaking his head. The dream had seemed to go on and on, but he realized now it had only taken a minimum of time, since the coffee was still warm. A minimum of time, he thought, and yet it had ripped at him, tearing at his heart, the expression upon his father's face, so vivid!

Year after long year, that same dream had driven him on. Was his father, he wondered, the elusive subject just over the next hill? Was it a sign that he had to keep looking? That somewhere, just ahead, Moses—or his grave—lay waiting to be discovered? Lay waiting for his son to come find him and take him home? He hung his head, sadness overwhelming him, once again. He had failed. Failed his father. Failed, too, his mother. But, most of all, failed himself. These were the thoughts that rode with him every day, no matter where he journeyed. Rode with him, filling his heart with unbearable sadness, the pain never-ending, and razor sharp!

CHAPTER 9

Miles away, far to the west, across the wind-swept prairie, Sarah Elizabeth Gentry—known now as Red Bird—walked from the tepee of her friend, Little Moon. A slight breeze was blowing, causing some strands of hair to blow across her face. She brushed them back, thinking she should have braided her hair that morning, upon rising. It had been just as windy then, but she'd had other things on her mind, and had not given it a thought. She'd been concentrating on the fine buckskin dress she had just finished making for herself. She smiled, at the thought of it. Her young friend, Laughing Water, walked by, her little girl at her side. Sarah greeted them, speaking to them in the Lakota dialect. The little girl giggled, her eyes filled with happiness.

Years before, when she was about the same age as her daughter, Laughing Water had stayed with Sarah, her mother having died of the smallpox that was so rampant in the village at that time. She'd been orphaned when her mother passed, her father having died, previously, in a buffalo stampede. As was the way of the Indians, Laughing Water was looked after by everyone in the village, and she had often stayed with Sarah. It was a comforting arrangement for both, as Sarah's husband, Gray Eagle, had been killed by a renegade Indian named Spotted Dog, who had on his person, at the time of his death, years later, a Bowie knife that had once belonged to John Bruce. That knife had been given to Sarah after John's death, because she had been his closest friend. Sarah, in turn, had given it to her husband, Gray Eagle. The only way Spotted Dog could've attained the knife, was if he had killed Gray Eagle, as he had boasted to Moses as they fought, years later. Funny, how things turn out, Sarah thought. Years before, John saved my life, throwing his knife at a bank-robber who was intent on shooting me, as I started to cross the street in Hastings. John's skill with the knife had killed the robber. But, as he fell he pulled the trigger, and bullets struck both Moses and John, killing John. Oh, how I remember that day! I was so shocked when I turned and saw John laying there on the walkway in front of Dawson's Store. It was then that Moses came across the street, blood soaking the side of his shirt, and dripping from his fingertips. I knew he was in serious trouble, by the amount of blood he was losing, and prayed, over and over again, that God would not let *him* die, too. The loss of one best friend was horrible enough. Sarah shook her head, thinking back to that day. Moses had pulled through, thank God, and was soon up and on the mend, though she still looked upon it as a double tragedy, and prayed there'd be no more. But that was not to be.

The second double tragedy came when Spotted Dog had raped her, causing her to lose Gray Eagle's baby. She'd been devastated by the loss, and wondered how she would ever tell Gray Eagle, when he returned from the buffalo hunt. But, he hadn't returned, and when Wind Runner came and told her that he'd been killed, Sarah's world became a dark void. She had lost both her baby, and her husband, and no longer cared to go on living. Overwhelmed by her grief, she lay in her tepee, not eating, or sleeping. Her life was over, as far as she was concerned. For days upon days, she wept, blaming herself for their deaths. Believing that it was her punishment for hurting her father so badly, by marrying Gray Eagle.

Her father, for as long as Sarah could remember, had hated the Indians. She didn't know why, but he'd made his feelings extremely clear. Samuel Justus had been a good father, had always seemed a fine judge of men, having been a captain in the cavalry at a fort far to the north, before her mother died. He had been in charge of many soldiers, and not one of them had ever questioned his authority. He was a good leader: levelheaded, honest, and decisive. His only flaw lay in his intense hatred toward the Indians.

Sarah smiled at some young children playing in front of one of the tepees. I'm certainly not like my father when it comes to these beautiful people. I couldn't love them more, she thought. She entered her dwelling; her buffalo hide bed and baskets she had made, giving her a sense of accomplishment. A bow was near at hand, a quiver nearby, filled with arrows. She had been practicing with the bow and arrows, nearly every day, and was getting fairly accurate. Johnny will be proud of me, she thought, when he returns. She had actually shot a large fish the other day, sharing it with her friend, Little Moon.

She dished up a bowl of food and sat down. As she ate, her thoughts were of her son. She wondered where Johnny was, and if he was safe. He'd left, nearly five years before. Nearly five years! Time had seemed to drag, when first he left. Seemed like everyday her thoughts were filled with him; wondering if he was well, wondering if he had eaten, and was warm. She'd prayed to both God and Wakantanka, asking them to watch over him and to protect him wherever he journeyed. Prayed that he would have no trouble of any kind. Prayed and prayed and prayed. The majority of prayers being that he'd find his father, and bring him home, though common sense told her it would not happen. She knew, beyond a doubt, that if Moses had still been alive at the end of the war, he'd have come home, somehow, soon after it had ended. Would have walked, or crawled, to get back to her and Johnny. Nothing would have kept him away...only his death, and she knew it. She took a deep breath, no longer interested in the bowl of food. Johnny had to learn about...things like this. Telling him had done no good. Had done no good, at all. Whenever she had tried to tell him it looked hopeless, hope would spring eternal on her handsome, young son's face, in spite of her words. Like her, he could not believe his father would never return. And seeing the hope in his eyes, she held her tongue, unable to speak to the contrary and break his heart.

She'd watched him go, that day, so long ago. Saying nothing to hold him back. Knowing that, young as he was, he was wise beyond his years, and determined. Oh, so determined! She had hoped maybe he'd stay at the camp, sharing a friendship with his father's friend, Howling Wolf, knowing Moses would have liked that. One day—not long after they had arrived—he came to her, however, telling her he had to leave. Telling her he had no choice, though he couldn't explain. Telling her she had to trust his decision. She had no clue as to why it was so imperative that he leave. No clue, that is, till Laughing Water came by to speak with her. One look at her son, and she knew! The love she saw in his eyes for the wife of his best friend, left no doubt that the decision he'd made was the right one. She felt a deep sadness for him, but at the same time, a wealth of pride that he would deny his own feelings, to not betray his friend, Brave Foot.

Sarah picked up her awl, and set to work on a buffalo hide, making a coat for Johnny, as she had for his father, years before. It would keep him warm, no matter how strong the winter winds would blow, or how deep the snow. She glanced at the corner, where a pair of fur-lined moccasins sat, waiting to protect his feet from the bitter cold that would soon be upon them. She wondered if he'd return this year, or if she would have to wait another long year. In mid-summer, Silas Haverty had come to tell her of Rosie's passing, and of Angus's, only a month later. She wished she could have returned to Hastings to pay her respects, but it was out of the question. The troubles between the Indians and whites were escalating, and besides, she wasn't sure she was up to making such a long trip. She'd noticed a slight decline in energy the past year, and some aches and pains she'd never had before, definite signs that she was getting old.

She set the buffalo hide aside, and stood, then walked outside.

She missed Johnny. Missed hearing his voice, and the sound of his laughter. Walking to the edge of the stream that ran along one side of the camp, she closed her eyes, and listened to the sounds of it as it rushed along. She wondered if someone else was standing beside this same stream, somewhere far from where she stood, thinking of their son, too. It wasn't easy, being a mother. Too easy to make mistakes. Too easy to say the wrong thing, or do the wrong thing, and hurt the ones who meant more to you than life itself. Sarah thought she and Moses had done a reasonably good job of raising Johnny. He was kind and caring, and genuinely concerned for the welfare of others. Best of all, he was honorable. His very leaving had proven that. She shook her head, looking down at the water, as it raced along to wherever its journey would take it. Moses would have been so proud of Johnny. How many times had he stressed to Johnny the need for honor? Even as he was leaving to go off to war, he'd sat on the porch, talking with Johnny, explaining that it was an honor to be asked to fight for your country. An honor to be amongst the first troop to go, and most of all, to stand tall, helping other less fortunate folks gain their freedom. He told Johnny that no man had the right to own another. And that the good Lord must be absolutely heartsick to find such a thing going on. 'Honor, Johnny, honor is what it's all about, son. Always remember that,' Moses had told him. Sarah shut her eyes, holding back the tears that threatened to flow, remembering how Moses had hugged their boy, then, holding him close, a look of love upon his face, as he did so. The look of a father who knew he might never see his son again.

As she stood there, thinking these thoughts, Sarah felt a drop of moisture touch her nose. She opened her eyes, surprised to see a smattering of delicate snowflakes in the air. She stuck out her tongue, trying to catch some, but they melted too quickly. Better get busy, she thought, and she turned and walked up the path to her tepee, intent on getting right to work on the warm buffalo coat that she soon hoped to give her son. He'd been gone four years, and that was far too long!

CHAPTER 10

It has been said that a good woman is worth her weight in gold. If that is true, Hastings received—one cold and blustery day—more than its fair share of gold in the person of not only Annathea Blossom, affectionately known as "Aunt Hilda" by her nieces, Ophelia and Lea Denton, but also Dorothea Blossom, called "Auntie Belle." The fact that they had chosen nicknames so far-fetched from their actual given names, gave one a forewarning as to the mischievous spirit of the two maiden aunts.

Both Dorothea, better known as Auntie Belle, and Annathea, called Aunt Hilda, had chosen at a much younger age these oddly different names. When asked why, they had spoken in chorus, giggling and covering their mouths with a hand, asking in reply, "Why not?" The names had prevailed from that day forward, as if cast in stone.

Aunt Hilda, at age fifty-five, the eldest by a year and being of a more dominant character, made most of the decisions for the twosome. Auntie Belle, on the other hand, was of a more humble nature, and happily deferred to her sister, going along with her decisions with a contented smile upon her face.

They were as unalike in character as they were in looks. Aunt Hilda was tall and slim, of solid build, with strong arms and stronger features. Her dark eyes looked at a person with deliberate focus, not blinking or questioning. Her cheekbones were set high, smooth flesh covering them with nary an ounce of fat to give a hint of softness to her features. She could not be called beautiful, or even attractive. A better word would have been "handsome."

She had worked hard all her life, taking in wash and sewing, till she could afford her small house near the Mexican border, having not found a husband among the few candidates that courted her. She had grown to like living alone, tending her garden, milking her old cow, and caring for her six hens—the rooster having long before ended up in the soup pot. The milk and eggs from her animals, and the vegetables from her garden kept her healthy. Her income, small as it was, covered her needs and gave her a sense of satisfaction. Many times, she had taken a basket of eggs or vegetables to one of her neighbors, glad to be able to help them. She had also taken such fare to her youngest sister, Ophelia and Lea's mother. She was hard put to understand why her sister would put up with their father's incessant drinking after his injury, but knew marriage was a sacred union, and far be it for her to get in the middle of such as that. For years, she had sat on the sidelines, holding her tongue, biting back tears on occasion, determined to be there if needed by her sister. Instead, she was there for Lea and Ophelia, taking them into her home when the unthinkable had occurred. When in his drunkenness, their father had attempted to accost Lea—his mind obviously sick from the effects of liquor.

To her dismay, however, soon after the death of their parents, Lea had agreed to marry Diego Santiago, a heartless Spanish don with vast acreage and beautiful hacienda. He possessed a violent temper, it was rumored, and was capable of tremendous cruelty. Those tales were soon proven true when it came to pass that Lea appeared at her door seeking shelter from his horrible and unjust acts of brutality: whip marks criss-crossing the flesh of her back!

Aunt Hilda had hidden Lea, facing Diego when he came searching for her, fearlessly standing up to him and threatening to call the sheriff if he gave her the least reason to do so. Then, under cover of night, she saw to it that Lea was spirited away in the carriage of her friend, the local doctor. She had dressed Lea in her own garments and best bonnet, its brim shielding her niece from the watchful eyes of an unsavory looking fellow who lingered across the street, obviously hired to watch the house and report back to Diego, Lea's whereabouts. Instead, her longtime suitor—the good doctor—had arrived as he usually did on a Saturday evening, escorted his lovely friend to his waiting carriage, and off they had driven. Unbeknownst to the lone scoundrel who stood watch, that the lady in question had not been Aunt Hilda, but Lea, disguised as her aunt.

To her great relief, Lea had gotten away, and after a long and arduous journey had arrived in Hastings, safe for the time being in the company of her sister, Ophelia. Safe, that is, until the day Diego Santiago and his sons had arrived, and been ultimately killed, in a gunfight with the Hastings sheriff and his deputies. Aunt Hilda had been relieved to learn of the Santiagos' deaths. Relieved the ruse had worked, and Lea would never have to live in the shadow of fear again.

Then, sometime later, a note had come from Ophelia, telling her of the plans she had to make a hospital of the large and stately home that had been bequeathed to her upon the death of her suitor, Johnathon Clark, who had also been killed in the same gunfight, by a stray bullet.

Annathea had pondered Ophelia's request, sizing up the possibilities it offered, and before the month was up had sold her small but comfortable home and her cow and hens. She packed her meager belongings in trunk and garment bag, and with sister Dorothea in tow, set off for Hastings.

Dorothea Blossom, or Auntie Belle, as she liked being called, was delighted with the opportunity to move to Hastings and live with her sister and niece, Ophelia, in her big house. She loved being around people, had always been happiest amongst a lot of folks, whether at church, sewing bees, or socials. She was much more outgoing than her older sister, Annathea, and far more gregarious in nature. She reminded one of a butterfly, flitting happily from flower-to-flower—or person-to-person—her cheerful countenance welcomed readily by all. Decisions had always been made for her, first by her parents, and later—more often than not—by her sister. So much so, that it had become second nature to her over the years, and accepted as rote, But unlike Annathea, her bubbly spirit and effervescent personality enabled her to make friends easily, and because of this, she found life a most joyful experience. She stood just over five feet in height and though younger than her sister by only a year, had a matronly build, being short and decidedly plump. Her face glowed prettily, her apple-like cheeks blushing soft pink when she smiled—which was often—her light green eyes seeming always to twinkle merrily.

She had lived far across town from her sister, respecting Annathea's desire for a place of her own, but would much rather have
shared a home with her. She kept busy to assuage the feelings of loneliness that this caused, and had acquired a habit of talking to herself
on a regular basis when not in the company of friends, of which she
had many. Annathea chided her for this, having herself the habit of
saying little—*even* in the company of others—and certainly *not* of
speaking to herself! It was a habit she thought prevalent only in the
dottiest old women.

The facts of Lea and Ophelia having stayed with Aunt Hilda, and
the reason for it, had been kept from Dorothea in an attempt to put
less stress or sadness upon her. She was thought to be too genteel
for such knowledge, having not that long after to deal with the death
of their youngest sister, which they could not conceal. Having many
friends who were concerned for her and constantly showered her with
their heartfelt sympathy, she soon knew more than was suspected. It
saddened her greatly, and she spent many hours seeking solace in her
worn and tattered Bible, many hours in deeply contemplative prayer.
Of the sisters, she was the one who turned more often to the Lord
for guidance. He was her constant support, her companion, and her
friend. If Annathea had spent much time with her, she would have
discovered that most of the talking Dorothea did when alone was
not to herself, but to her Lord whom she believed, wholeheartedly,
walked beside her every moment of every day, His great love always
strengthening her.

When she had heard of the hospital Ophelia intended to start in the
town of Hastings, she was more than delighted for the opportunity to
go there and to be part of such an adventure. She knew that God had
a way of leading her exactly to where she was most needed and could
be most helpful, and she could barely contain her joy at the prospect!
She had hurried to tell her many friends, hugging them to her in warm
embrace, telling them how dearly she had enjoyed their friendship.
Promising to always think of them and pray for them, she'd chatted
on and on, her own happiness so apparent that they could not help
but focus on it. Her leaving, and the loss of her companionship in
the days and years to come, was overshadowed by her tremendous
outpouring of joy.

And so, on a cold and blustery day, as the train pulled into the town of Hastings, little did the folks at the station who watched the two sisters step down onto the platform, one smiling happily, her cheeks rosy, one with frown upon her angular face, realize that the town of Hastings had just been blessed with a gift as precious as gold!

CHAPTER 11

"Oh, my, isn't it a nice looking, little town," Auntie Belle remarked, stepping down from the train. Her eyes twinkled merrily, as she looked this way and that, happily surveying all the activity that was taking place.

"We'll see," replied her sister, more concerned with where their trunks were, and if Ophelia would be on time to fetch them. She found the noise, hustle and bustle, the shouts and loud clatter of wagons and carts near the platform very distracting, and wanted only to find their belongings *and* their niece, and be on their way. It was obvious that, given half the chance, Dorothea would dilly-dally as long as possible, wanting to see everything that was going on and speak to as many strangers as possible. "Come along, Dorothea," she ordered, her voice rising above the noise of their surroundings.

"Yes, dear," Auntie Belle replied, nodding at the couple approaching them.

"How do," the man said, tipping his hat, a gesture Dorothea found so elegant. She smiled in return, tipping her head in response.

"Morning, Ma'am, watch your step. Can I help you with your bag?" a courtly gentleman asked, reaching out tentatively toward her.

"Dorothea!" Aunt Hilda exclaimed, glaring slightly at both her sister and the fellow. He bowed slightly and backed away, much to Auntie Belle's disappointment. "I do declare, Dorothea, you're going to get your bag stolen if you're not careful! You can't just go smiling at every stranger you meet. Why who knows what kind of unsavory character might be lurking in this town, ready to rob you? Please stop grinning at everyone and follow me. Isn't that Ophelia heading our way? Why I wonder where her carriage is?"

Auntie Belle was already waving happily in Ophelia's direction, a wide smile upon her face, her eyes dancing with delight.

"Aunt Hilda, Auntie Belle," Ophelia called, hurrying to them. "I'm so happy to see you. How was your trip? Have they unloaded your trunks yet? Oh, I'm so happy you're here," she said, hugging first one, and then the other, noticing Dorothea's flushed cheeks, and the worried frown on Annathea's face. Aunt Hilda always was the one to fret, how well she remembered. And also the one in charge, it seemed, where the maiden sisters were concerned.

"Where's your carriage? Certainly you don't expect us to carry our trunks on our back, Ophelia? Didn't you expect us to arrive today? I sent you a telegram stating our arrival time," Aunt Hilda said, her questions, one after the other, showing Ophelia the degree of upset she was feeling.

"A friend of mine will be arriving any moment to fetch us and will see to your trunks. Please don't worry yourself," Ophelia replied, thinking how different her two aunts were. Auntie Belle was giggling softly, one plump hand held to her mouth, a mischievous twinkle in her eyes. Her other hand clasped both the handle of her garment bag and Ophelia's hand. There was no doubt that she was happy to be in Hastings. No doubt but that she had a far more adventurous nature than her sister.

"Where's Lea? Isn't she coming to meet us? Why I certainly thought you'd both take time to be here," Aunt Hilda stated, looking past Ophelia's shoulder to see if she could see Lea anywhere.

"Lea isn't here," Ophelia answered, wondering how to explain. She hesitated momentarily, well aware of her aunt's questioning gaze fixed firmly upon her. "I'll explain when we get you settled," was all she could think of to reply.

Aunt Hilda shook her head, and was about to say something, but at that moment she spotted the trunks being unloaded further down the platform, and without further ado, hurried off to see that they were not mishandled.

"Oh, I'm so glad you're here," Ophelia whispered, squeezing the hand, gently, of her other aunt, Auntie Belle. "Let me carry your bag,

Auntie. Are you tired? Do you need to sit a moment, until my friend arrives?" she asked.

"Oh, no, I feel fine," Auntie Belle replied, turning her head this way and that to take in all the activity. "I like your town, Ophelia. I'm so glad to be here. Don't mind Annathea. You know how she is. She means well, but gets a little out of sorts when she feels overwhelmed." They both laughed then, knowing just how true her words were.

"Oh, here comes my friend," Ophelia stated, letting go of her aunt's hand and walking quickly away. Auntie Belle craned her neck to see her niece's friend, and saw a tall, very nice looking, dark-haired man approaching, a man who walked carefully, with cane in hand. A man who was obviously blind. At that moment, Ophelia reached his side and took his arm, smiling happily and speaking to him, though Dorothea could not hear her words through the din going on around her. She watched her niece's face light up at something the man said, and was suddenly certain that there was more to Ophelia's friendship than, perhaps, *she* even realized. She smiled again, happily imagining what the future might hold for her niece.

At that moment, Aunt Hilda approached, her voice strained, her movements brisk. "Where's Ophelia gone off to? Oh, there she is. Who's that she's talking to? Isn't her friend here yet? I do declare, Dorothea, no one but I seems eager to take control of this situation, or to be responsible for seeing us safely settled! That's certainly not the friend who is supposed to see to our trunks, is it? Why, he's blind. Whatever can Ophelia be thinking?"

"Hush, Annathea," Auntie Belle ordered, softly. "Yes, that's obviously Ophelia's friend, sister. Mind your manners, please," she stated, totally surprising, not only herself, but also her older sister to the point of actual speechlessness!

"Well...I never..." Aunt Hilda began.

"Hush," Auntie Belle whispered, putting a finger to her lips.

It was then that Ophelia and her friend approached. "Aunts, I want you to meet my dear friend, Cal Dunnevey. Cal, this is my Aunt Hilda," and she guided his hand toward Aunt Hilda's, "and my Auntie Belle. The Blossom sisters." Cal noticed the firm grip as he shook first Aunt Hilda's hand, and the softer grip of Auntie Belle's, not to mention the soft giggle of the second sister.

"Ladies. I'm happy to make your acquaintance. Welcome to Hastings. I hope you find our town to your liking," Cal said, wondering if the second sister, Auntie Belle, was ever going to let go of his hand.

"Oh, we like your town already," she quickly replied, once again giggling softly, and he felt the other sister nudge her. Pulling his hand away, he could not help but smile. Obviously, Ophelia's aunts were very different in character, the one with the softer grip having a much sweeter disposition. He liked her, already.

"Well, Ophelia, and now that we've met your friend, how do we get our trunks secured?" There was a moment's silence and then Cal spoke, realizing this aunt had to be dealt with firmly to assuage her feelings of concern.

"Your trunks will be delivered to Ophelia's house in a matter of minutes. I give you my word. They are quite safe where they are, I assure you, for the time being, dear ladies. The station master is a friend of mine, and has been keeping his eye on them every moment, since they were unloaded."

Auntie Belle looked at Ophelia, winking, and then turned to look at her sister, a triumphant look stealing across her face.

Just then a young woman they had not seen approach spoke from behind Ophelia. "I'm sorry I'm late, Ophelia. I hope your aunts will forgive me."

"Aunt Hilda, I'd like you to meet another of my friends, Miss Kate Yeager. Katie, this is my Aunt Hilda and my Auntie Belle," Ophelia said, hugging the young woman in quick embrace, "and you know Mr. Dunnevey, don't you?"

"Yes, of course. Hello, Mr. Dunnevey. It's nice to see you," the young lady replied. Greetings were exchanged, and then they all made their way to Miss Yeager's waiting carriage.

Annathea Blossom looked about as the carriage moved along the street, her thoughts troubling her. She wondered if their trunks were indeed safe, sitting on the platform in full sight of any scoundrel that might come along. Well, she thought, I've done all I can to see them safely here. If Ophelia trusts this blind man so greatly, I will just have to hope her judgment is sound. She straightened her bonnet, feeling it was slightly askew, though it was not. After all, it was very important to give the right impression, if anyone happened to notice their arrival. Far be it for her to have someone think she was not a proper lady!

Dorothea Blossom sat behind her sister in the carriage, smiling happily, and occasionally waving or nodding to those the carriage passed. Some smiled and returned her gesture, some moved along, lost in their own thoughts and attending to their own business. She was delighted to see the large bank, and not one, but two general stores, not to mention, a livery stable, sizable cemetery, and many fine houses along the way. This certainly was a town she would enjoy living in, that she already knew, just from what she could see of it. There was a sturdy looking sheriff's office, one she was sure would be adequate, if needed, and a doctor's office. She smiled contentedly, anticipating all the opportunities a fine town like Hastings might offer. The sounds from the many saloons further on down the street did not bother her, or cause her any concern. Nor did the many cowboys, seamen, and obvious ruffians and gamblers that she noticed, walking along, here and there. She was not one to be put off by folks such as these. After all, they were as much God's children, as she. He loved them as dearly as He did her. And she knew in her heart that there was good in *all* God's flock, even if they had chosen a different path than her own. She brushed an insect away from her face, taking in a deep breath. This was where God wanted her to be, of that she had no doubt. This was where she could be of the most use to Him. She closed her eyes for just a moment, a word of thanks upon her lips, her heart filled with abounding joy.

CHAPTER 12

Cal Dunnevey caught himself humming as he made his way back to the Mercantile that night. It wasn't anything specific that caused this, that he could put his finger on. He just felt...good. Happy. It had been so long since he'd felt anything even remotely like this, that he was more than a little surprised by it. It was as if there was some kind of... magic...yes, magic in the air. Some kind of...he tried to think of words that would explain just what it was he felt. Some kind of...hope, that was what he felt, though there was no reason for it, as far as he could tell. Must be getting silly in my old age, he thought, stepping carefully, feeling his way across the street, trying to judge just where he was and where the Mercantile was.

He had to laugh as he remembered the day he had pushed open the door to what he thought was the Mercantile, shouting "I'm home," only to discover he had walked into the sheriff's office by mistake. The sheriff, a surly fellow by the name of "Gator" MacKay, had been slumped in his chair, half asleep, and had sprung up, not at all happy with being startled out of a sound sleep. He'd let out a yell and grabbed for his gun, before he realized it was just Cal who'd come bursting into his office. Cal had to smile, as he remembered how mad the sheriff had gotten. Had swore at him, asking him just what in tarnation he thought he was trying to pull. Cal laughed aloud, wishing he could have seen the expression on the poor fellow's face. Served him right, he thought, for sleeping on the job. You wouldn't have caught Moses sleeping, when he was sheriff.

The thought of his old friend, Moses Gentry, saddened him. Of all the men who went off to war, he had been sorriest to see Moses go. They'd been friends ever since the first day Cal had moved to Hastings. Good friends, special friends. Moses knew all about him, knew he'd killed Victor Jalaco when he was a mere boy of nine, after Jalaco had beaten his mother, Maggie, to death. Some lesser man might have arrested him, might have thought Maggie deserved it, being a saloon gal, but not Moses. He had a decency and understanding that surpassed the "book laws." Sometimes, justice wasn't as "just," as it was supposed to be. Sometimes the punishment didn't fit the crime.

Moses had listened to him, that night so long ago, as they sat in his office drinking coffee and reminiscing. It was quiet that night in Hastings, and on quiet nights he often walked on down to the sheriff's office to chat with Moses. How the subject came up, he no longer remembered. But it no longer mattered. He'd told Moses all about his childhood, all about Maggie, and all about Jalaco. Moses had sat there, tilted back in his chair, sipping his coffee and listening. Cal hadn't intended to talk about the past, certainly hadn't intended to confess to killing Jalaco, but was glad he had, when he was through. It felt like a heavy burden had been lifted off his shoulders when he had finished. He'd picked up his own cup then, and drank down the last of his coffee, wondering what Moses was thinking. At last Moses spoke.

"I'd say you did what you had to do, Cal. You were young, and you'd just seen this swine beat your mother to death. I'm glad you've told me about it. Never can tell when some relative of Jalaco might ride into town and want to settle the score. Far as I'm concerned, it never happened, my friend. No cause for us to speak of it again."

Cal was surprised to feel a wellspring of emotion as he walked along, remembering that night. Yes, sir, Moses had never broached the subject again, and they had remained the best of friends. I would have been by his side, he thought, when he left to fight, if I hadn't been blind. He'd felt so helpless, standing there along the sidelines the day the group of men he'd long known, and been friends with, had marched out of town to go and fight. Moses had come over to him, shaking his hand, understanding all the emotions he was feeling. He'd told Moses to be careful, good luck, that he'd see him when the war was over. Never dreamed that Moses, like so many others, would not return. Nearly all of the 1st Minnesota had been killed, he'd been told, when the fighting was done.

"Cal, I have a favor to ask of you, my friend."

"Anything," he had replied, still clutching his friend's hand.

"If Sarah needs anything, or my boy..." he'd always remember how Moses' voice had choked up then, how he hadn't finished what he had started to say, couldn't finish.

"You can count on it, Moses. You can count on me," he'd replied, and Moses' grip on his hand had tightened for only a moment, and then he was gone, marching away with the others. So many who were never to return.

Cal's knee hit the edge of the bench that sat out in front of the Mercantile, and he winced, never quite used to bumping into it, though he did it often. He fished his keys out of his pocket, his mood somber from the memories that besieged him. He felt his way to the door, found the keyhole, got the key into it, and let himself inside the store. Slowly, carefully, he made his way to the back room where he lived; his thoughts rushing back to the days that followed Moses' leaving...

Sarah had come to the store about a week after Moses had left, gathering supplies for the farm. He'd felt clumsy and like a dumb ox, as he tried to help her get a jar down from the top shelf, and had instead, knocked it to the floor, breaking it. The contents had spattered everything close by, including himself, and Sarah. He'd felt so small and stupid, and wanted to curse not only himself, but also the blindness that caused so much misery in his life. Life? What kind of life was it, he remembered thinking, to blunder around, unable to do any of the normal things he was used to doing? A sense of shame had filled him that day, the same sense of shame he felt now, in remembering the incident. He had stammered an apology, trying to move without knocking anything else down, feeling his face grow hot with embarrassment.

It was then he felt Sarah's hand upon his arm. "It's okay, Cal. No harm done. Please, dear friend, it's alright."

He'd felt almost like crying at the sound of gentle caring he heard in her voice. Or was it because of her touch, as her hand rested softly upon his arm? He hung his head, as he remembered.

"Let me help you clean it up," She had said, asking where some old rags were.

"No," he'd said. "I'll manage, somehow. I'm sorry, Sarah. Did any of whatever it was get on your dress?"

"Not a drop," she replied, and he was sure she was saying that only to ease his mind. "Now tell me where the rags are, Cal. I'm going to give you a hand cleaning it up, and I'll not hear another word about it. It's some kind of horse medicine, I believe. Don't worry about it, you have about ten other bottles of the same and won't run out anytime soon, by the looks of it." She laughed softly, and he had to laugh with her, her mood was so infectious.

He smiled at the memory, and felt his way over to his bed. Once he'd ascertained its whereabouts, he took off his shirt and tie, pulled off his boots, undid his pants and let them drop. He hung his clothes on the back of his chair, standing his boots side-by-side. Then he reached for the blanket at the foot of his bed, got himself situated comfortably in the bed, and yanked the blanket up around his shoulders. Then he lay there, a long time, deep in thought.

Sarah had not spoken of Moses that day, and he had only asked if there was anything that needed doing around the farm. Anything he could give her a hand with. "I'm not as clumsy out of the store," he'd said. She had shushed him, telling him the bottle had been too near the edge of the shelf, and anyone could have knocked it down. He doubted that was true, but had thanked her for saying it, knowing once again, just how very lucky Moses was to have found her first.

He rolled onto his side, his thoughts going back to the arrival, in Hastings, of Ophelia's two maiden aunts. It was safer to think of them. Safer to *not* remember how his feelings had grown for his best friend's wife, in the years after Moses had left.

CHAPTER 13

There comes a time in every man's life, when he has to do some mighty deep soul-searching. A time when he realizes the decision he makes will affect the outcome of, not only his own life, but also the lives of others. That time had come for Cal about two years after Moses had left for the war.

It was a warm, sunshine-filled day, and though he couldn't see the beauty of his surroundings, he could feel the warmth of the sun upon his back as he went to fetch a bucket of water from the stream that ran beside Sarah's cabin. He was well aware that she or the boy could have carried in the water, but it made him feel good to be of some help, this being something he thought he could do. He made his way to the water's edge, trying to judge by his cane tapping the ground in front of him, just exactly where the area was where the water bucket was usually filled. He had done this before on one of his visits to their place, and though cautious, was not concerned that there might be the possibility of danger in doing so.

On that particular day, however, he misjudged the distance and found himself in an area of small rocks and brush. He backed up, turning slowly, trying to get his bearings with the cane. He could hear the water to his right, but was no longer certain just where he was. It would have been easy to call out for Johnny or Sarah, but his pride kept him from doing so. He stood still a moment, and then began to move slowly toward the water. The ground was uneven in spots, and made it difficult for him to proceed, but proceed he did. He continued on, his heart beginning to pound at an exhilarated speed in his chest, until he could hear it even in his ears. "Silly," he told himself. "I can't get lost this close to the house. Can hear the water to my left..." and then he stopped where he was, panic starting to fill him. The water should be on my *right*, he thought, not my left! He realized he was clenching the handle of the water bucket. Steady, he thought, steady. He stood still, listening, trying to get his bearings. The water's to my left, I must have turned around, he thought. I'll just turn and head the other way. He began to do so, his foot catching on a fallen limb, and to his dismay, he began to fall! He dropped the bucket, reaching out to block his fall, his arm and side striking against some rocks as he landed. He groaned, feeling his side and his arm, fairly sure he'd broken no bones, or done no serious damage. Then he sat up, and reached out for the bucket. It was not within arm's reach, but that didn't surprise him. He shook his head, feeling not only disgusted, but also terribly unsure of himself. He breathed in and out, slowly, trying to calm his nerves, then got to his feet. His arm was skinned where it had hit the rocks, but otherwise, he was fine. Relieved, he took a deep breath, determined to conquer the immense fear that threatened to overwhelm him. He wasn't lost. He could still hear the water. He knew he couldn't be far from Sarah's house. Why, he was bound to run smack into either the water, or the house, if he struck out in a direction. But *what* direction? No. No. He wouldn't let himself panic. And he wouldn't yell for help. After all, he was a man. Blind, yes, but still a capable man...or was he? Again his heart began to beat loudly in his chest, till he could hear it in his ears. He rubbed his hands together, and then held his face within them. All right, he thought, I can do this. Take it easy, Dunnevey. Don't make a bigger fool of yourself. Just start out slowly...It was then he realized that he had dropped his cane when he fell, and any confidence that had remained, evaporated with the realization. He started to stride, not slowly and carefully, but at an almost running gait. The brush that tore at the legs of his pants did not concern him, nor did the unevenness of the ground, nor the fact that the rocks seemed to be getting larger, the farther he went. He could hear the sound of rushing water ahead of him, and it drove him on. Throwing caution to the wind, he hurried toward it, oblivious to all else. Suddenly, he caught his foot on a large rock! Propelled forward, the motion of his body made him unable to stop. He put his hands out in front of him as he felt himself fall, and called out just before he hit the water and went under, his head hitting a large rock beneath the surface. Then all was black.

The next thing he knew, he was laying on his side on the ground, coughing and sputtering. Sarah was saying his name over and over, her hand upon his cheek, her concern for him evident. "Cal, can you hear me? Oh, Cal, I'm so sorry. You're safe now. It's okay. I'm right here."

He continued to cough, reaching up to take her hand, trying to assure her he was all right. "It's okay, Sarah. Not your fault. I got lost, couldn't tell where I was. Didn't mean to frighten you," he said, feeling both stupid and relieved at the same time. He sat up, slowly, thoroughly shaken by all that had happened. "I hit my head," he said, reaching up to touch where it hurt.

"I know," she said. "You're bleeding. It doesn't look like too deep a cut. I'll bandage it when we get to the house." She patted his arm, so glad that she had heard him call out, and had been in time to get to him before he drowned. "Can you stand? Here, let me help."

Cal stood up, realizing he was shaking. At the same time, he felt Sarah's arm go around his waist to steady him. Felt her body close to his, her hair against his chin as she moved in closer, so he could lean on her. The dress she wore was soaked, and clung to her. "Can you walk, Cal?" she asked, turning to look up at him.

Without the slightest intention of doing so, he turned toward her, bent his head, and kissed her. He had wanted to; ever since the first day she had entered his store. Even before he knew her name, or that she was betrothed to his best friend, Moses Gentry, Hastings' sheriff. He had lived alone too long without a woman, to not be aware of her beauty, and the desire he felt at the mere sight of her.

The kiss consumed him, wiping out all rational thought. It took every last ounce of his strength to pull away, and end it. "Sarah," he said, his voice sounding raw with desire. "I'm sorry. I didn't mean to..." he began, taking his arms from around her, wondering if he had destroyed their friendship, by letting his feelings get out of control.

Sarah stepped back from him, breathing rapidly. "We'll talk no more of it, Cal. You're not the only one to blame," she said, her voice a mere whisper.

"It won't happen again," he said, feeling both shame and guilt.

"I know," she replied. "Now let's go to the house, and get that cut bandaged." He felt he should say more, but every time he tried, she stopped him, changing the subject.

Later, when he'd had time to think, he realized he would have to be on his guard so it wouldn't happen again, if he hoped to honor his friendship with Moses. For though he'd tried to deny it, he knew, beyond a doubt, that Sarah had returned his kiss!

CHAPTER 14

"Let me tell you, the news spread rapidly around Hastin's, delightin' the Irish folks in particular, when word came a Catholic Church was goin' to be built at the far end of town, on the other side of the old cemetery," Old Man Pearly said to the fellow who shared his cell. "Fer years, the church-going folks o' Hastings had attended the little church on Old Mill Road, quite a distance from town. Of course, circuit ridin' preachers had come through town, preaching against the unholy doin's at the other end of it, where all the saloons, houses of ill repute, and disreputable boarding houses stand. They occasionally got the opportunity to marry a couple, or baptize a baby, and sometimes even preached a sermon or two down by the stream where the folks liked to gather for socials and picnics, and that sort o' thing. Other than that, they went on their way, traveling here and there, tending their flock where they found 'em. There was always need fer a preacher. More often than not, there was a buryin' to say a few words at. Hastings had seen its share o' them circuit-riding preachers, and even had one of its own in years past, though there's few still alive who remember the Reverend Emory Mitchell. There'd been that young preacher fellow named Cole, of course, Reverend David Cole. He was the one...well...most folks have forgotten about that poor fella and that wife of his. Some things are best forgot, I always say, like bein' drunk, and gettin' the tar beat outta you. I ought to know that, fer a fact. Can't tell ya how long I been drinkin' up the town. Had my share o' fightin', that I did."

The other fellow nodded, and then closed his eyes, hoping the old man would take a hint, and finally shut up. He'd never met anyone who talked so much. How he'd even ended up in here with the old fool was beyond him. He'd ordered a drink, his first, and then all hell had broken loose! Next thing he knew, he'd landed in jail. He rolled onto his side, hoping he could fall asleep before the old man started in talking again. He'd had enough of this fellow, and this town!

Old Man Pearly, as folks called him, had awakened sober as a judge, the third morning of his stay in the Hastings jail. He lay on a cot in the small cell, his thoughts running rampant, but clear, for the first time in years. And because of it, for the first time in as long as he could remember, he felt ashamed to be there. His thoughts went back to some nights earlier, when he and some Irish lads were drinking at Gilhaney's Saloon, celebrating the new Catholic Church that was being built in town.

The memory of his old friend, Emery Mitchell, came to mind. He was the *only one* of them preacher fellows who had ever taken the time to sit down and talk with me, he thought, and he shook his head, remembering how sad he'd felt, the day he learned the good reverend had caught the pox and died. Truth was, he was my only real friend, he thought, and there'd never been another, since. He was like a father to me, the old man mused, as he eased up off of the cot to go relieve himself. The other fellow who'd been in the cell with him was no longer there. But, used to having only himself to keep him company, his thoughts continued as he walked along. He shuffled his feet, noticing he was a little off balance. Sheriff MacKay never locks my cell. Says he has no reason to, since I'm the only one I'm a danger to, he thought, and he laughed aloud. His thoughts turned then to his daughter, Nancy. She'd been a good daughter, and pretty, too, but always hounded him to give up his drinking, before she went and married up with that trapper fella. Been a long time since I seen her. Hope she's doing all right. He finished his business and walked back into the jail cell that had become a second home to him over the years. But this time he noticed the filthy floor and walls of the cell, the cobwebs across the corners, and the dried vomit. He wondered if it was from him, or the fellow who'd been lodged there with him. He knew he'd been in there awhile, and was pretty sure he was the one who'd been sick. His shirt showed traces of the same mess, and looking down at it made him gag. He staggered to the cot, eased down upon it, and ran a hand through his long, tangled gray hair. He could feel dirt and sticky grime on his fingers as he did so, and shook his head, sadly. I've got t' straighten up my life, he thought, and with that thought came an immense desire to head over to Gilhaney's for just one whiskey. Just one. No more. One would get him through the day. One would get him in shape to head home and get a fresh start at cleaning up his place. He'd intended to do just that, he remembered, but had to come into town to get some soap and a broom. He'd only planned to have one drink. Then he'd planned to head back home. But it hadn't turned out that way. It never did. A couple of them Irish lads had been celebrating the building of their church, and... well... one thing led to another, and he didn't know what started it, but there were words, and a fight, he remembered that. He could still feel where some of those lad's fists had pounded on him. He smiled, rubbing his arm where it was tender. "Well, I got in a few licks of my own," he said aloud. "Or at least I think I did." It bothered him that he couldn't remember. That was happening more often, of late. He lay down on the cot, noticing it smelled of stale beer and vomit. Wiping a hand across his nose and mouth, he saw the nicks and cuts and dirty fingernails of his hand. He laid still, his thoughts turning to other things.

When word had come that the Catholic Church was gonna put up the big, old church, right there on the main street, the Irish folks were all praying that one of their priests from over in the Old Country would be called to head it up. They had two priests, in particular, they were praying would lead them, he recalled, and pretty soon some of them Irish boys got into a brawl over it. Some wanted a Father Mike Finnegan, and some, a priest named O'Malley. When the fightin' was done, twelve of them lads were bleeding like stuck hogs, and I ended up in here, he thought. And not one thing's been settled, I'm sure of that. But that's how it is with them Irish. You get a little drink into them lads and there's bound to be a fine fight, sure as can be. His arm felt awfully sore, he noticed, and he saw that he sported a large bruise on it, and his shirtsleeve was torn completely off. He'd worn his coat into town, he faintly remembered that, but it was nowhere to be seen.

More thoughts besieged him. He remembered watching as a fine load of lumber had been unloaded, and folks' utter dismay, when word came that during the night every last piece of that lumber had vanished. Sheriff MacKay, being Irish himself, didn't send his deputy, Roy Dupree—who was looked on as just about the dumbest man who ever lived—out to look for the scoundrels who had stolen it. Instead, MacKay, himself, had hurried over to the church site, and searched and searched for some clue as to whom might have done the dastardly deed. The old man snickered as he remembered how the sheriff had walked this way, and then that way, crossing back and forth, checking out the wagon tracks that pressed into the ground beside where the pile of lumber had last stood. He'd rubbed his chin, a few times, looking deep in thought, and folks stopped to watch. A couple times he bent down and ran his hand over the slight indentations, as if by touching them he'd get some clue as to who the thieves had been. Then he stood, shaking his head slowly, and took a pipe from his back pocket. He tapped it a couple times on an old stump that stood nearby, and then surveyed the crowd that had gathered. Sniffed the air, then, like some hound might do, and everyone had all they could do not to laugh aloud at such goings-on. Knowin', as we all did, that he weren't that friendly a fellow, most held silent, just watching, like I was doin' myself. You couldn't help wonderin', though, if he had some kind of special sense, or somethin'. You know, like them there people has that seem t' know stuff there ain't no way to know. But then, t' our surprise, he turned and walked on down the street toward the jail, and t' my recollection, that was all that come o' the stolen pile of lumber. Old Man Pearly laughed so hard at these thoughts that he had a coughing fit, and had to sit up on the cot in order to catch his breath. He remembered that the next week when another load of lumber was delivered, two men were hired to guard it, till the fellows came the next day to turn it into a strong west wall. He got to laughing again at the memory, and had tears in his eyes, before he could stop and once again, catch his breath. "I've got to get a hold of m'self," he said, getting to his feet, weaving a bit. "The good Reverend Mitchell would be mighty unhappy if he could see what's become o' me. I best try t' straighten up, that's fer sure. Who knows, maybe I'll join that new Catholic Church," he said, and he left the jail, shuffling off down the street, knowing he had a long, cold, walk ahead of him before he'd reach home. A dozen times he stopped outside the many saloons, along the main street, a look of tremendous longing upon his face. But he didn't go inside. Lord, how he craved a drink! Just one. But he'd made a promise to his friend, the good Reverend Emory Mitchell, a long, long time before. A promise to give up the devil's brew. *And this* time he planned to do just that, no matter how hard it was for him to do so!

As the days and then the weeks went by, the good folks of Hastings continued to watch the comings and goings of the men who were hired to build the church. And it wasn't long before the building was done. The only problem seemed to lie in the fact that the priest who arrived was not one any of the townsfolk had hoped for. In fact, he was terribly ill fitted to lead any church. He was old, and drooled when he talked, and oft' times let a little wind pass, at the most inopportune times. As if that weren't bad enough, he had a habit of forgetting, and would suddenly stop in the middle of the Mass, look around—totally confused—and then proceed to talk about whatever odd subject came into his mind. Clearly, he was too old to lead a parish, and it soon became evident—when he mistakenly set the altar cloth *and* part of the altar, itself, on fire—that something had to be done.

Then one fine Sunday morning, soon after, as folks knelt and said their prayers—surprisingly, a sober Old Man Pearly amongst them—a young priest stood before them. He had hair the color of flames, and a smile that stretched from one side of his freckled face to the other. He looked small in the robes he wore, as though a slight wind might blow him over. And he wasn't very tall. But in his eyes there shown a love for God and all His creatures. And in the words he spoke, the people knew they had found the priest they all wanted. His name was Father Patrick O'Leary, and he was one of their own!

CHAPTER 15

No one could have been more pleased, or more excited, than Mrs. O'Leary had been, a week before Father Patrick arrived at the church to say his first Mass. It was the day the telegram had arrived from her son, Patrick. She had let out a squeal upon reading it, which was highly unusual for her, and began to cry and laugh at the same time. Colin was in his room when he heard her, and came rushing into the main room, a worried expression upon his face. He saw the paper clutched within her bent and twisted hands, and his heart leapt in his chest, a feeling of dread filling him. At the same time, he saw the smile upon her face, and thought perhaps, the news was so bad that it had caused his maw to suffer some kind of spell. Patrick, he thought. To affect her so seriously, it had to be news of Patrick. He hurried to her side, trying to get his own feelings under control. "Maw? What is it, Maw? What's happened? Is it Patrick?" He just knew it had to be about Patrick. Something inside him told him so.

His maw began to dance around, the telegram falling to the floor, as she raised both hands and tears streamed down her weathered face. Colin reached out, enfolding her within his arms, not at all sure what to do to help her. Even James, who usually sat without moving, in a rocking chair over by the window, turned his head, a look of concern upon his face.

Mrs. O'Leary bowed her head, laying it against Colin's chest, her body trembling within his arms. Then she raised her head, and Colin realized it was joy she felt, and that the news that had come was not bad, as he had suspected. "Maw? Maw, what is it?" he asked, not knowing whether to smile, or still be concerned. "Is it Mary, Maw? Tell me what's happened."

Mrs. O'Leary stepped back from his embrace, a wide smile upon her small, wrinkled face. She clasped her hands to her heart, grinning like he had never seen her do before. "'Tis news of your brother," she said, at last. "Patty's coming home. He's coming home," she repeated, as if by saying it, she'd believe it to be true.

"Is he alright, then?" Colin asked, a worried look still fresh upon his face."

"That he is," she said. "That he is. He'll be coming soon."

Colin felt himself relax a bit at her words, but still didn't understand what it was that made her so beside herself with joy. "Can I read the telegram, Maw?" he asked, bending to pick it up.

"'Tis best ye wait," she replied, her eyes dancing with joy.

"I don't understand. Wait for what?" he asked, wondering now if it was indeed bad news, and had affected his mother's mind. He knew how she was about Patrick. Knew that though she hadn't intended it, Patrick had always been her favorite of all the O'Leary children. Patrick, the troublemaker: the one who always worried her the most. Ah, yes indeed. It was as if he was the one most certain to break her heart, as quickly and as often, as he broke his bones. Ever since Patrick was born, Colin could remember how their maw had been forever saying, "Watch out for your brother. Take special care to keep watch on Patty, Colin. Don't let Patty out o' your sight, Colin. Don't let Patty get in with the bull, Colin. Take care o' Patty, when ye go t' the stream t' fetch the water, Colin." Colin scratched his head, smiling slightly at these memories. He hadn't been home when Patrick had left to fight in the war, but could just imagine how worried it must have made his maw, seeing her child so prone to accidents, walking away to fight. He could almost imagine the many fears that his maw must have felt that day, knowing that troubles always seemed able to find this child of hers. He was glad he hadn't been there then.

"Go make your bed," Mrs. O'Leary said, surprising him. "Then get the chores done. Hurry." He looked at her, wondering if she'd suddenly gone daft. But she turned away, rushing to the cupboard, getting down her old, tattered recipe book. "'Tis a fine day," she said, rushing about, a liveliness to her step that he had not seen in more years than he cared to remember. Her mood was infectious, and he began to smile, a feeling of hope and anticipation suddenly filling him.

"'Tis a fine day, indeed," he replied, starting to believe it, as he caught sight of James, struggling to stand. He stood still, not believing his eyes, as James got to his feet, steadying himself on the arms of the rocker. As he watched, James straightened, and then began to take one step, then two.

Mrs. O'Leary turned to say something to Colin, but caught the look of surprise upon his face, and quickly turned to see what he was staring at. "Oh, Saints be praised," she whispered, not believing her eyes. "James," she said, and hurried to his side.

"Maw, I'm back," James said, his voice a mere whisper. And Colin felt tears well up in his eyes and quickly turned and headed for his room, his heart bursting with the first real joy he had felt in a long, long time. He didn't understand why James had suddenly come back to them. Didn't understand why they had received not one, but two, such blessings. But he had no doubt that they had been blessed. Word that Patrick would return had been the first blessing. Little did he know, it would be the first of many!

CHAPTER 16

Johnny spent a week at his family homestead, a week that not only eased his sense of hurt from not finding his father, but rested his body after the many, many long and tiring miles he had traveled.

On the second day he walked the property, feeling as though he was seeing it for the first time. He climbed the hills, startling deer and wild turkeys, rabbits, and a fox or two. They scurried away at his approach, and he watched them go, feeling a sense of serenity, as they did so. Traversing the shallow river on the far side of the property, he enjoyed the fresh breeze that stirred the few remaining leaves on the trees along either side of the water, his mind coasting as peacefully as the eagles that flew above him, their wings outstretched, their call piercing the stillness. Johnny felt free. Free as the Eagles. Free from the heavy weight that had crushed down upon his young shoulders, ever since his father had not returned from the war. Free of the burden of responsibility he believed to be his, and his alone. He felt as though his soul floated free, up amongst the clouds and rays of golden sun. Its only companions, the two eagles that soared effortlessly, there.

He walked along, his thoughts going back to the day, many years before, when he'd come out of the woods near their cabin, a rabbit he'd shot in one hand, and his father's gun in the other. He'd stopped in his tracks, his mouth falling open, as he saw his mother in the arms of Cal Dunnevey. Saw the kiss they were sharing, beside the stream, near the small falls. He'd been so surprised, that he'd dropped the rabbit, anger filling him at the sight. He didn't remember moving, but suddenly found himself behind some bushes, his eyes never leaving his mother and Mr. Dunnevey. He remembered thinking, "Some friend you are! Wait till my father hears about this!" That was when he became more convinced than ever that he would go in search of Moses, as soon as he was old enough to do so. He'd bring him back, telling him what he'd seen, telling him that his "friend" wasn't the friend he thought him to be. Angered by the memories, he began to climb the hill before him, his steps quick and careful.

As he reached the top of the hill, he stood on the precipice of a huge, overhanging rock, and surveyed the scene before him. He looked about, and the anger flew from him, as the land in all its majesty seemed to enfold him, bringing him comfort. He thought of Chief Standing Elk, and Howling Wolf. Thought of his friend, Brave Foot. And just as quickly, his thoughts were filled with a shame of his own. The shame he'd felt, when he had done the same thing Cal had done. The shame he'd felt, after he had kissed Laughing Water, the wife of his best friend. He sat down upon the large, smooth rock, watching the two eagles as they soared across the sky a distance from him, their shadows gliding across the valley far below.

I am no more able to judge Cal Dunnevey, he thought, since I'd done the same thing as he, in a moment of weakness. My mother's a beautiful woman, after all. Perhaps Mr. Dunnevey had been aware of that, and could no more help himself, than I, the day I kissed Laughing Water. He sat there, noticing a herd of deer grazing far below, his thoughts stilled for a moment.

Laughing Water had just left his mother's tepee, having gone there to speak with her. As she walked along the path that led to the stream, Johnny had followed. She'd turned at the sound of his footfalls upon the path, looking surprised to see him. "I didn't mean to frighten you," he'd said, walking up to her.

"I am not afraid," she'd replied, lowering her eyes, a slight smile upon her lips.

"I'm leaving in the morning," he'd told her, noticing a slight frown cross her face. He'd hesitated then, for only a moment, before adding, "I have to."

"Because of me?" she'd asked, her soft voice caressing him.

He wanted to say "No. Not because of you. Because I must find my father, who didn't return from the white man's war," but he knew he could not lie to her. Knew she would read the truth in his eyes. "Yes," he had answered, and suddenly she was in his arms, her body pressed against his, the sweet scent of her blinding him to all reason. He held her tightly then, his heart racing within his chest, kissing her, long and hard. His lips pressed against hers, in tender embrace, and then harder, as his body responded to her closeness. Only the sense of decency that his father had instilled in him saved him from taking her as his own! He knew she would not have stopped him, knew she wanted him, as he did her. He had to garner every last ounce of strength, to pull back from her, the pain within his body showing in his eyes. "No, I cannot...I'm sorry. I must not dishonor Brave Foot," he managed to stammer, backing away.

Laughing Water stood before him, her heart beating rapidly, her eyes filled with pain. Then she closed her eyes and hung her head. "I love you, Black Hawk," she whispered, looking up at him with tears in her lovely, liquid brown eyes.

"As I do, you," he had replied, and he'd reached out to take her hand, raised it to his lips, and brushed it with a kiss. Then he'd turned away, walking without faltering, his steps determined. Soon after, he'd left to find his father, telling his mother he could not stay in the village of Chief Standing Elk any longer. He was certain she thought it was because of his longing to find his father, but could not tell her it was because of the desire he felt for his best friend's wife.

Johnny rose, stretching his legs, and felt the ache within his body and heart that the memory of that day caused. He took a deep breath, understanding at last, why Cal Dunnevey had kissed his mother. His feeling of anger toward Dunnevey dissolved, as did his own anger toward himself. It was different, looking at such things as a man. He understood now, why his father had spoken to him so often, of honor and the responsibility that came with it. A man had to be strong to deal with the feelings that arose, especially where a woman was concerned. Desire was not an easy thing to overcome, especially when you loved the woman who stirred that desire. He wondered then, as he walked on down to level ground, if Cal Dunnevey had loved his mother. But he knew enough about feelings to realize that a man's desire wasn't always because of love. No, sometimes it was about the needs a man had. He glanced around, noticing a flock of geese flying above, the eagles no longer in sight. Dunnevey hadn't come back to the farm for a long time after that day, he remembered. And when he did, Johnny had noticed how he stayed outside, sitting on the bench that was over near the barn, and didn't go into the house until *he* did. As he thought back to that day, he realized that Dunnevey had made it a point, in fact, to keep a distance from Sarah even when she shopped at the Mercantile. He had proof of that, because she always took him with her when she went there. Johnny shook his head, a relieved, yet questioning feeling filling him. If he hadn't seen them kiss, he would never have imagined his mother and Dunnevey to be anything but the most distant of acquaintances, he thought, or was he wrong? Like the distance he had put between himself and Laughing Water, had Cal purposely distanced himself from his mother? He wondered. Well, what did it matter now, he thought, for soon after she had decided to return to Chief Standing Elk's camp, and had not come back to Hastings, to his knowledge, in the four years that he'd been gone. He smiled, walking toward their old cabin, a feeling of contentment within him.

CHAPTER 17

The rest of the week Johnny busied himself, fixing things in the house and around the homestead. He couldn't understand why Michael had left it in such a shambles, and the possibilities worried him. For as long as he could remember, Michael had tended to all the chores around the place, seeing to it that fences were mended and everything was in good order. In fact, both his mother and father had commented, more than once, that they didn't have to even mention to Michael the things that needed fixing. He always took it upon himself to see that everything was kept up. The fact that it was in such sorry condition now worried Johnny. He decided that he'd fix what he could, spending a week doing so, and if Michael hadn't returned by then, would go to see the O'Learys. Perhaps, Michael, or his mother, Miz O'Leary, had taken ill. No other explanation came to mind.

Johnny felt good, fixing things around the old homestead. It gave him a sense of pride to see his efforts pay off, slowly but surely, as the place began to look like he remembered it. He felt an under-lying feeling, too, of wishing his mother had not sold it. Wished that it still belonged to his family. He wasn't used to such feelings, and was surprised by them. He'd always been certain that—like his mother—he, too, would go to live amongst the Indians when he was ready to settle down and raise a family of his own. He shook his head, sadly. That was out of the question now. He knew he could not live in Standing Elk's village. Could not bear to see Laughing Water, and know that she belonged to his best friend. That she slept beside his friend, night after night. He groaned aloud, taking in a deep breath. No, it was not something he could tolerate; being so near to the woman he loved, knowing he loved her, and she, him. It wouldn't take long, he knew, for his desire for her to grow, stamping out all reason. "I'll go to see my mother," he said, speaking aloud. "Will spend a month with her, at most." I should be able to be there a month, he thought. I'll just make sure I'm never alone with Laughing Water; make sure I never let temptation grow between us. He shivered, slightly, wondering if he was capable of doing so. He doubted it.

But it seemed an eternity since he had last seen his mother, and he knew he would have to go to the village. Had missed her gentle touch, her softly-spoken words of caring. Had missed, so greatly, the love she always showed for him. Knew also, that he must tell her that there had been no sign of his father, anywhere, no matter how far he'd traveled. I'll go in a week, he thought, before the heavy snows come. Will finish up a few things here, and then go speak with the O'Learys, if Michael still hasn't returned. After that, I'll leave for Standing Elk's village, and spend some time with my mother. For just a moment, the image of Laughing Water crossed his mind, and he took a deep breath, wondering if he'd have enough control of his feelings to be the honorable man his father had intended him to be. He would try, that he was sure of. But he knew deep within his heart that it would be the hardest thing he had ever succeeded at, *if* he succeeded.

The sound of approaching hoof beats caused him to look up, and he saw four men riding into the yard on fancy horses. He stopped what he was doing, and walked out of the barn to see who they were and what they wanted. They looked trail weary, and their horses were lathered, obvious signs of being ridden hard. He noticed the bulge of guns the men wore, concealed beneath their voluminous white linen dusters, and wondered if they meant any harm. He'd seen men such as these before, on his travels to find his father. Men who had the look of prosperous businessmen, but who were often not on the side of the law. He wished he had strapped on his gun, but knew it hung in his holster, inside the house. Cautiously, he approached them, having not been noticed, as they swung down from their saddles, laughing loudly and busily taking their saddle bags from the backs of their horses.

"Can I help you?" Johnny said, seeing the oldest looking fellow reach for his gun, as he whirled around to see who had spoken. "What do you want here?" Johnny asked. The other men turned, too, their guns pointed at him. Johnny stood his ground; hoping bravado alone would keep them from shooting him.

"Well, what have we got here?" the oldest fellow asked. "An Injun, by the looks of it," he continued, his gun still pointed at Johnny. His eyes were mere slits in his face, his deeply carved features tanned by long days in the sun. And unlike the clothes the others wore, his shirt and pants were stained with dirt and sweat.

Johnny stood still, not moving a muscle, watching intently the re-actions of the other men who still had their weapons pointed at him. "What do you want here?" he repeated, his chin raising, as he spoke.

The old fellow, whom Johnny guessed to be in his late fifty's, stopped walking, a frown crossing his face, as he tried to figure just how to deal with this Indian that spoke better English than he did, and had a tone of authority to his voice. "Better tell me who ya are," the old man said, his eyes, Johnny noticed, having a peculiar glint to them. "You best tell us who ya are, 'fore ya git yerself shot."

Johnny noticed that the old fellow often glanced back at a much younger looking man, and realized that the younger fellow seemed to be the one in charge, though he stayed in the background, silently watching what developed. One of the other fellows, whom Johnny judged to be well over six foot, ran a hand through his dark hair, then spoke, looking at the young fellow who Johnny was certain now was the leader of the bunch. "Let him go, Jessie. He looks harmless. I don't feel like standing here all day, want to rest a spell before we head for home."

"Shut up, Frank," the young one ordered, turning his attention back to Johnny.

"I'm John Gentry," Johnny stated, not knowing if this bunch knew his father had been the sheriff in Hastings, or not, and if so, wondering if it would make any difference.

"Gentry?" the old man questioned. "Moses Gentry's kid?"

"Yup," Johnny replied, still not sure if it was to his advantage or not.

"Why hell, son. I knowed yer pa. Way back 'fore he was sheriff. How in tarnation is he? We was told he sold this place. Didn't think anyone lived here anymore, that's a fact."

The young man who Johnny guessed to be in charge, cut in then, "Quit your jawing, Jubal. Is he okay, or do we have to shoot 'em?" he asked, glaring at the old man.

"He's fine, Jess. No need to worry. I knowed this fella's pa, way back. Way 'fore he set foot here. He's okay," the old man said, and Johnny saw the others holster their guns, as he spoke.

"I'm Jubal Cade," the old man said, reaching out to shake Johnny's hand, "and these are my...ah...my boys, Jess, Frank and...ah...Thomas. We been travelin' west o' here, o'er past Black Dog."

Johnny nodded, watching the others head for the house and go inside like they owned the place. He felt certain they had stayed here before, and most likely were the ones who had left it in the mess he had found it in when he first arrived. "How long you planning to stay here," Johnny asked, not sure just how to handle the situation.

"Oh, we'll be moving on soon enough, son," Jubal Cade said, and he cleared his throat and spit into the dirt, then walked back to his horse, gathering up his saddle bags. "How long you staying here," he asked, as he picked up his reins and started to lead his horse toward the barn.

"I'm waiting for Michael to get back. Michael O'Leary," Johnny replied, surprised to see the look that crossed the old man's face. It seemed to be a look of shame, or something close to it. The old man stopped walking, spit again, and then turned toward Johnny, his head cocked to one side.

"You a friend o' his, son?"

"I am," Johnny replied, curious as to why he asked.

"I see," came the reply, and Jubal turned and continued to walk toward the barn. Johnny followed; certain Jubal knew something about Michael. He waited as long as he could, his patience growing thin.

"He hasn't been around for a long time by the looks of the place," Johnny finally commented. "I've been waiting for him about a week. You don't happen to know where he's off to, do you?"

Jubal Cade took his time answering. Took his saddle off his horse, and his bridle, patting the horse on its neck before he spoke, "I don't think he'll be acomin' back, son. Not fer as I can tell, that is. Got hisself int' some mighty bad trouble, 'bout two weeks ago, o'er in the town o' Chaska. Kilt a man. Shot him down in cold blood. Might be dead, by now, fer all I know. They was gonna hang him, last I heard." He spit, wiping his mouth on his already filthy sleeve, then opened the gate and led his horse into the stall that used to be Glory's.

Johnny felt his heart skip a beat at the old man's words. Michael wasn't one to shoot somebody down in cold blood, and no one knew it better than he. Why, Michael had a hard time even shooting a deer, when the meat was badly needed. Johnny's thoughts were racing. "I need to go tell his family," he said. "You got any problem with me leaving?"

"Shucks, no, son. But I'm tellin' ya, yer probably too late," the old man said, his words laying harsh on Johnny's heart.

A few minutes later, Johnny was racing toward the O'Leary's place, his gun strapped to his side, his frock coat billowing out behind him as he urged Buck on, fast as he could run. He had no idea what, if anything, he could do to save his friend, but knew in his heart that he had to try. He also knew that he had to be careful not to alarm Miz O'Leary. Lord knows the woman had suffered enough, what with the pain in her crippled-up hands, and the loss of her son in the war. I have to find someone to help, Johnny thought. If I go riding into that town alone, looking Indian, it's bound to cause a panic. No telling how I could help Michael then. If there's no one at the O'Leary's who can help, I'll head for Eli's. He'll be more than glad to ride with me. He clung low along his horse's neck as it raced along, fearing that the fate of his friend, Michael O'Leary, had already been decided. Fearing he would be too late to change it!

CHAPTER 18

Pounding hooves shattered the stillness of the night, causing Colin O'Leary to jump out of bed and grab his gun from his holster that hung from a hook, nearby. He pulled on his pants, as he hurried through the house, peering out the kitchen window. Scanning the yard, he saw the silhouette of a man out by the corral. Carefully, he opened the door, sliding out into the semi-darkness. It wasn't late, but dark and menacing clouds covered the sky, the promise of a storm more than apparent. He edged toward the corner of the porch and stepped down onto the ground, keeping the intruder in sight. He hadn't had any trouble with the folks who lived in Hastings, though a few of the men had plenty to say, threatening him, as he rode through town on the day of his return from the war. He wasn't afraid, but sure didn't want any trouble to come to his maw and James because of a few liquored-up fools who might feel they had a grudge to settle, since he had fought for the South. He hunkered down behind the rain barrel, his heart pounding in his chest, his hand tightly clenching his gun, making certain he didn't step on anything that would make a sound and give him away. He listened intently, hearing only the beating of his heart.

Suddenly, a voice spoke from behind him, causing him to freeze where he hid! "You're the noisiest white man I've ever known, Colin O'Leary."

Colin whirled around, not certain if he'd heard right, and not quite certain he knew who it was who had snuck up on him. "Johnny? Johnny Gentry? Is that you?" he asked, lowering his gun, a feeling of relief running through him.

"Sure is," Johnny answered, reaching out to clasp Colin's hand, a grin crossing his face.

"Well, I'll be. You've sure grown. I see you're still more Indian than white," he said, smiling, embarrassed that the younger man had been able to sneak up on him.

Johnny laughed at his friend's remark, knowing it was said in kindness. But there wasn't time for talking, and as they walked back around the front of the house, Johnny told Colin the news he'd heard.

"Damn!" Colin exclaimed, and then lowered his voice so his mother wouldn't wake up. "I don't want my maw to know 'bout this. Have to think of some way of leaving that won't cause her any suspicions," he said, calming somewhat, so he could get his thoughts in order.

"Why not tell her a friend, over by Chaska, needs your help?" Johnny offered.

"Could do that," Colin replied.

Johnny walked quickly over to the corral fence where his horse stood, his coat draped over the post there, looking in the semi-darkness as if a man stood there. Colin saw now how he'd been snuck up on, and had to smile at the trick Johnny had played on him. "You're one smart Indian, kid," he stated, as he set out for the barn to get his horse. Wish James could ride with us, he thought, very aware that his brother was in no condition to do so. He wondered if there was any chance that he and Johnny would be able to help Michael, or worse, arrive in time to see him hung. His heart filled with sadness as he thought of the pain that would cause his mother, and he whispered a silent prayer that God would not only get them there in time, but would help them find a way to save Michael. They'd need a miracle, that was for certain. Soon, his horse ready, he handed the reins to Johnny and ran toward the house, slipping quietly inside.

Johnny pulled on his coat and flung himself up onto Buck's back, just as Colin came out of the house, coattails flying. His hat was pulled down against the rain that threatened, as he swung up onto his saddle, spurring his horse as he did so. Johnny followed, his thoughts racing ahead, fear for the safety of Michael, now his only concern.

They raced on as fast as they dared go, cutting through the woods and across the gullies, urging their horses back and forth through rough terrain, as night came on. A pouring rain drenched the men, and Johnny pulled his own hat down upon his head, glad that he'd put it on as he left his old homestead to go for help. The going was hard, but time was of the essence, both men knew.

When they came to Big Bear Pass, Johnny remembered the story he'd been told by his Grandpa Angus of how, many years before, a cougar had lain in wait as his pa rode by this very spot. How it had jumped his pa, causing him to fall, nearly killing him. And how Gray Eagle—at that time, his mother's friend—had seen it happen, and had killed the cougar, saving his pa. That was long before his mother had married Gray Eagle, he remembered, and he felt an outpouring of gratitude. If Gray Eagle hadn't been there, Johnny thought, Pa probably would have died: changing the course of all our lives.

Buck sidestepped, nearly causing Johnny to fall, as the horse came close to going down. Johnny tightened his grasp on the horse's mane, squeezing his legs tighter around its sides, till he felt Buck gain his footing. "Good boy," he whispered, leaning forward. Buck's ears turned back at the sound of his young master's voice, and he nickered softly in response.

"You alright?" Colin called, turning in his saddle, as he spoke.

"Was rough for a minute," Johnny replied, adding, "but we made it."

"Almost went down myself," Colin said, and then turned in his saddle, urging his horse on again. The rain made seeing difficult, and many times Johnny felt the branches of trees whip his cheeks and chest as he raced on. Occasionally, his leg would scrape along the side of a tree trunk, but still he hurried on. He knew that Colin was enduring the same, and both would have sore bodies at journey's end.

About midnight Colin pulled up, motioning Johnny to stop. The rain had finally let up, though it had drenched everything before doing so. "What say we stop a minute? I need to relieve myself," Colin said, and Johnny agreed, having the feeling his own bladder was about to burst. They dismounted, tied their horses' reins to nearby branches, walked off in opposite directions, then soon returned. "You ever heard tell of that old fellow, what'd you say his name was...Cade, wasn't it? You ever heard of him before?" Colin asked, as he stretched his arms above his head to relieve some of the stiffness he was feeling in his back from riding so long.

"Nope, never. Not till they rode in," Johnny replied. "Not much to tell. I had my suspicions about them, right from the start, though. That Cade fellow questioned me about my reason for being there, but I got the impression he was only the "front man," so to speak, for one of the younger men...a man called Jess."

Colin looked down at his boots, a frown crossing his face. "You don't happen to remember what the other fellow's names were, do you?" he asked.

"Ah, let me think," Johnny said, swinging back up onto his horse. "I think he said they were his sons. Let's see...he called the one Jess, and, if I'm remembering right, the others were...Frank, that's right, Frank and Thomas. Why? You heard of 'em before?"

"Guess not," Colin replied, adding, "*if that was* their real names. I suspect they weren't. Heard of an old fellow, once, last name of Cade, but that was a long time ago, before I left for the war. Not the neighborly type. He was old, then. Doubt he'd still be alive. Maybe this old fellow was kin of his."

"Don't know," Johnny answered. "Let's ride."

Colin mounted quickly and they traveled as fast as they could amongst the rocks and trees, up hill and down, slipping and sliding, as the trail coursed its way through thick woods, along narrow trails, and across a wide river, the current threatening to topple the men and their mounts before they could reach the safety of the other side. On they rode, their only concern, whether they'd be in time to somehow save Michael's life, or only in time to carry him home and bury him.

CHAPTER 19

Chaska was a small town a short distance from Black Dog. A town with few buildings: a church, a trading post, a livery stable, a saloon and a stage stop. If it weren't for the stage, there was a good chance it would have fast become a ghost town.

John Gentry and Colin O'Leary rode into Chaska in the early hours of morning when the sky was still a dark canvas. The only light to guide their way came from the moon high above, and the saloon in the middle of town. They rode in quietly, not knowing just what to expect, as neither had ever been there before. Half way down the street, they saw the jail and wondered if, indeed, they had come too late. It looked dark and empty. A rat ran from beneath some boards that lay beside the jail, as they rode by, and both men hated the thought of Michael ever having been a prisoner there. They rode on in silence, not wanting to draw any attention to themselves, though the street was empty. The only sounds came from the saloon.

As they neared the saloon, Johnny pulled up on his reins, motioning to Colin. He glanced in the direction Johnny had pointed, and to his dismay, saw the platform at the far edge of town, the hangman's noose dangling from it. A shudder ran through Colin as he saw it, and he bowed his head, his heart racing at the sight.

Johnny urged Buck on toward the saloon, knowing Colin would follow. He dismounted, tying Buck's reins to the hitching post. Pulling his hat farther down to better protect himself from the eyes of onlookers, he saw Colin do the same. Then together they walked into the saloon.

The bartender looked up as they came through the door, but continued washing off the bar, making no attempt toward friendliness. Two men, both looking half asleep, sat at a table near the front of the saloon. They were drunk—to all appearances—and seemed not to notice the newcomers. At the other side of the room, near an old piano, stood a tall, thin woman, her hand stroking the keys. Her red satin dress looked too big for her, and her smile was anything but pretty.

Johnny and Colin walked up to the bar, and Colin ordered two whiskeys. "Got the money to pay for 'em?" the bartender asked, wiping his hands on the front of his shirt.

Colin laid his money on the bar, never taking his eyes off the man. "That suit you?" he asked, in the tone of a man that didn't appreciate being asked.

"Yup. Can't never be too careful," the bartender replied, adding, "don't usually get any strangers in town. Where you boys from, if you don't mind me asking."

"I mind," Colin said, picking up the drink the bartender set before him, swallowing it down in one gulp. "Heard you had a hanging, that right?" he asked, and Johnny saw one of the fellows at the table sit up, reaching out to nudge the other one. Johnny turned so he could keep both men in better view.

"You fellas marshals?" the bartender asked, trying to get a better look at Johnny. "We been waiting for you, if you are. Ain't often the stage gets robbed this close to town."

The two men were now watching Johnny and Colin closely, and acting mighty jumpy. They looked like they were spooked aplenty, and Johnny wondered why. He shifted his weight from one foot to the other, still looking directly at them.

"What about the hanging?" Colin asked, sitting his empty glass in front of the bartender, who looked as if he wished he was anywhere else but there.

"The hanging was two weeks ago."

Colin's heart sunk at the words, a lump seeming to form in his throat. Beside him, Johnny felt the same. So they were too late. Michael was dead. Colin's hand shook as he picked up the newly refilled whiskey glass, drinking it down again, in one gulp. He felt the fire inside him as the whiskey ran down his throat, but it was nothing like the fire that burned inside his soul. He wanted to lash out, grab the bartender by the throat, and smash his face. Wanted to cause someone as much pain as he was feeling.

Johnny sensed his feelings, feeling much of the same. "Let's get out of here," he said. But Colin remained where he was, ordering another whiskey.

"Where's the body?" Johnny asked, turning toward the bartender.

"You boys ain't marshals, are you?" the man asked, answering Johnny's question with a question of his own.

"No, sir. We aren't. We're here to take him home," Johnny said at last, watching the men at the table through the large mirror behind the bar. They got up slowly, and edged toward the door, not realizing they were being watched. Johnny nudged Colin, making him aware of them. Then he sat his glass down and turned, just in time to see the men run out of the saloon as if they were on fire.

The bartender leaned forward, looking at the door, and then smiled, suddenly more than anxious to talk. "I'll tell you where he is. You'll have to work fast. The judge is due back in town tomorrow. Best you get him and get out of here as soon as you can. If you don't, well, I don't know what'll happen." He looked at the door again, then at the tall, thin woman. He nodded, and she hurried over, a smile on her face.

"Took you long enough to get here," she said, looking intently at Colin, then at Johnny. "Thought you was his kin, with that there red hair, and all," she stated. "You wouldn't care to take a quick walk upstairs, would you, Hon?" she asked, looking at Colin.

"No, thanks. I just want to take my brother home," Colin replied, the sadness he was feeling, showing in his eyes.

"Suit yourself," she said, and turned away, walking toward a door in the back of the saloon. "Well, you coming, or not?" she asked. "I don't like waiting, handsome."

"Go with her, gents, if the fellow they hanged was yer kin. She'll take ya' to 'em," the bartender said, then quickly turned away, as three men walked into the saloon, one wearing a sheriff's badge.

They paused, seeing Colin and Johnny, then spread out around the room. "You boys are new in these parts," the one wearing the sheriff's badge said. "Mind telling me your business here?"

"We don't want any trouble, sheriff. We heard talk of a hanging. Thought it might be a relative of mine," Colin stated, feeling the tension in the air.

"That right?" the sheriff replied. "Well, he could be a relative, I suppose. Had the same color hair."

"What'd he do?" Colin asked, his anger mounting at the obvious game of cat and mouse that was going on.

"You don't know?"

"If I knew, I wouldn't ask," Colin replied, his voice rising.

"Shot a fellow. A good fellow. A fellow who was minding his own business, not bothering a soul. Shot him down in cold blood," the sheriff said, a grimace crossing his face. "My friend," he added.

"My brother wouldn't do that," Colin stated, his anger more than apparent.

"Well, that's the way I seen it," the sheriff said. "And maybe you're the ones that robbed the stage. Since the judge ain't here yet, I want you boys to accompany me over to the jail. We don't need more of your kind causing trouble in our town. Hand over your guns." The men with the sheriff drew their guns, aiming them at Colin and Johnny. Colin slowly reached to unfasten his holster, anger burning in his eyes. Johnny did likewise, seeing it was futile to do anything else. It wouldn't do them any good to end up going home in a box. One brother going home that way was enough.

Then just as Johnny started to unfasten his holster, the back door to the saloon burst open, and one of the men who had been sitting at the table earlier—looking drunk—rushed in, his gun drawn! "Put down your gun, boys," he ordered, just as his partner, the other man who'd been sitting with him, stepped through the front door.

"Do as he says," the other one said, "or we'll fill you full o' holes!"

Johnny looked at Colin, who looked as surprised as he; neither of them understanding just what was going on.

"You're gonna regret this," the sheriff said, dropping his gun. The men with him did the same, the looks on their faces showing both surprise and anger.

"Maybe, maybe not," came the reply, as the two men quickly began to tie up the sheriff and the men who were with him. Colin and Johnny looked at each other, not knowing what to think, and quickly fastened their gun belts. Colin turned to the bartender, knowing most of them had at least one shotgun within easy reach behind the bar. He could tell by the look in the man's eyes that the same idea had crossed his mind. "Hand over your guns," Colin ordered, his own gun drawn. The bartender hesitated only a moment, and then reached slowly beneath the bar. Johnny drew his gun, his heart pounding in his chest like a drum. "Don't try anything," Colin warned, not sure whose side the man was on, and not wanting to take any chances.

The bartender's expression changed then, softening somewhat, and with no further hesitation he straightened, laying a shotgun on the bar. Colin picked it up, unloaded it, and carried it over to one of the far tables. Johnny kept watching the bartender, the hair on the back of his neck tingling. Used to trusting his senses, he walked over to the bar. "I'll take your *other* gun," he said, never taking his eyes off the man. "Now!" Johnny ordered, never blinking.

Colin had turned to watch the exchange between the two men, as did the other men in the saloon. The gal in the red dress smiled a wide smile—a gap showing where one of her teeth were missing—and laughed a loud, unfeminine, braying laugh. Colin glanced at her, and then turned his attention back to Johnny and the barkeep.

The bartender eased a small pistol from beneath his belt, laying it on the bar where the shotgun had been. "You'd both be dead, if I had my way," he said, and Johnny saw him wink. The woman walked back to the piano, no longer interested in the goings-on, now that the excitement was over. She wasn't going to help the two strangers now that the sheriff was around. They'd had their chance. Be no point in getting in trouble and ending up in jail, she thought. Especially when they weren't interested in buying her a drink or two, or spending a little time upstairs with her. She'd seen the money Colin had laid on the bar. He could've at least offered to spend a little on her, business being slow, and all.

Johnny turned, smiling a slight smile at Colin, and then they hurried to follow their two rescuers out the back door of the saloon. When they got to the livery stable, they rushed through it and out the back door to waiting horses. To their surprise, their horses were waiting there, too. They quickly mounted, racing after the two men, though still unsure as to why they'd rescued them from the sheriff's clutches. There was obviously something going on, but it was not the time to stop and talk.

About two hours later, with the sun just starting to peak over the horizon, they came to a narrow canyon surrounded by cliffs. The going was rough, and the men slowed their horses to a walk, going single file. Before long, one of their rescuers pulled up, jumped from his horse, and scurried up a path in the rocks to where he could survey the surrounding territory, and check for any pursuers. He returned, mounted, and followed behind Colin and Johnny as they, in turn, followed the other man. He was a swarthy fellow, about the same height as Colin, and had dark hair and a thick beard. The other fellow was much shorter, possibly younger, on the thin side, and bald. He deferred to the taller fellow, more times than not, Johnny noticed, and he couldn't help wondering just who they were, and what he and Colin had gotten themselves into.

As they turned this way and that, following the canyon trail, it suddenly opened into a wide valley, and beyond, dense woods. The man in front let out a yell, and spurred his horse into a gallop, racing along on a narrow trail that was all but hidden behind some massive boulders. Johnny and Colin raced along, too, certain they were now nearing their destination. The man to their rear followed close behind, the sun beating down upon his baldhead.

Soon they entered the woods. It was dark because of the many trees, and a good deal cooler. Johnny slowed his horse to a walk, as did the others. The bearded fellow was sweating, great stains showing on his shirt, beneath his arms. The younger man wore filthy buckskins that were big and loose, and both had bandanas tied loosely around their necks. He wondered if they were the men who had robbed the stage. Wouldn't do to let them get wise to such thoughts, he figured, taking off his hat and brushing back a strand of hair. He saw the lead man glance in his direction, a curious look upon his face before he turned back the way they were headed. He knows I'm Indian, Johnny thought. I could see it in his eyes. He glanced back at Colin, who followed close behind, the grief he felt, obvious, knowing they'd been too late to save his brother. Johnny wished he could say something to cheer his friend, but there were no words to ease such a hurt. He knew that, firsthand. How well he knew it.

Just then, far to their right, Johnny saw a thin trail of smoke in the sky, and soon after, a small cabin. It was well hidden. The perfect hideaway for a gang of robbers, he thought, and once again wondered just what he and Colin had gotten themselves into.

Colin saw the cabin, too, and was thinking the same. The yard stood empty, not a sign of man or beast. No corral, no chicken house, no barn. Only the cabin, hitching rail, and thin trail of smoke rising up into the air. Colin reached down, running his hand over the butt of his gun, wondering if he and Johnny had stumbled into more than they could handle. It was obvious they'd gotten themselves involved in something. No telling just what, he thought.

The two men pulled up to the hitching rail, dismounted quickly, and tied their horses' reins to it, then hurried toward the cabin with nary a glance back at Johnny or Colin. Colin dismounted, and then watched as the two men tapped at the door of the cabin, whispering something they were unable to hear. There was no answer. The men looked at each other, frowning, and then the bearded one tapped again, louder. He asked the other man something, glancing toward Johnny, as he dismounted, and went to stand beside Colin.

"How do I know?" the other replied, turning back to the door and whispering something, his mouth close to the door.

Colin and Johnny watched from beside their horses, not sure just what to do. It was obvious the men had expected someone to be waiting at the cabin for their return.

"Well, if that don't beat all," the bearded fellow said, wiping his arm across his face.

"Better not o' lit out," the bald one said. "Not after all the trouble we went to t' git these here fella's."

"I'm going t' look around," the bearded one said, spitting into the brush beside the cabin. "You fella's stay here," he ordered, looking at Colin. "Don't be runnin' off, if n ya' want t' take yer brother home, that is."

Colin looked at Johnny, and then started to ask the two men a question, but they rushed off, heading in the direction of the woods. Colin looked at the ground, shaking his head, then over at Johnny. "Well, what do you make of all this? Got any idea what's going on?"

"Sure don't," Johnny replied, and before he could say more he heard a gun cock behind them.

"Stay right where you are, gents, or I'll blast you full of holes," a woman said, her voice low.

"We mean no harm, Ma'am," Colin said, not moving. He wished he could turn and get a look at her.

"Take off your hats," she ordered, surprising the two men.

Colin reached up slowly and removed his hat, wondering just what in the world she'd want them to do that for. Johnny followed suit, wondering if the gal had others with her, and if he could turn fast enough to surprise her and get her gun.

"Tell me your names," she said, "and where you're from."

"John Gentry," Johnny replied. "From Hastings."

The woman said nothing, waiting for Colin to answer. She had seen his red hair, and felt a wave of relief, but had to be sure. "Well?" she said, an anxious tone to her voice.

"Colin O'Leary, from..." but before he could finish, the woman interrupted, a squeal coming from her that caused both men to turn and face her.

"Well, why didn't you say so!" she exclaimed, lowering her gun, and grinning from ear to ear. "What took you so long?"

"Beg pardon, Ma'am?" Colin replied, wondering what she was talking about.

She stared at him, the smile leaving her face. "Don't you recognize me, Colin O'Leary? Have I changed that much?"

It was Colin's turn to stare, as he tried to think of where and when, if ever, he'd seen her before. She was a pretty thing, or had been, he decided. Needed a bath, by the looks of it, and a good hair combing. Not to mention, a clean dress. He ran his eyes over her, trying to remember. Her body was pitifully thin. He looked at her face: the pretty smile that once might have promised a man many delights.

"Fine memory you've got," she said then, realizing he hadn't the slightest idea who she was. She turned away, pouting, and walked up the path toward the cabin.

Colin rubbed his head, sure now that somewhere in his past he had seen that pout. He remembered one gal...a gal from Hastings...but no, she had been a really pretty gal with soft ringlets, and a plump figure abounding with curves. A figure that could cause a flame to burn in any man...even a church-going one. He watched the woman go into the cabin, and suddenly he remembered. "Lydia Benedict," he said aloud, and he stared at the cabin door as it shut, wondering what on earth had happened to her in the years since she'd left Hastings. The years after he'd been one of her admirers, and had enjoyed more than a few of her many favors. "Come on," he said to Johnny, and hurried up the path to the cabin.

Lydia sat at a table, three cups of coffee poured and steamin' before her. "Well, about time you remembered," she said, her voice lowered, as she saw his look of recognition.

"Sorry, Lydia. I didn't expect to see you here," Colin replied, straddling one of the chairs across from her. Johnny sat down, wondering where the other two fellows had gone.

Lydia looked at him, sizing him up, then motioned toward the cups of coffee. "Help yourself," she said.

Both Colin and Johnny took up a cup and began to drink. Just then there was a knock on the door, and Lydia grabbed her gun from the table, standing and pointing it at the door. Both men drew their guns, wondering if it was the two men who stood outside, or the sheriff and his men.

"Miz Liddie," came the call from outside. "Are you there, Miz Liddie? We brung them fellows."

"Come on in," Lydia ordered, laying her gun back down on the table. She sighed, reaching into a deerskin bag that had been tied at her waist. The two men entered, nervously glancing from Colin to Johnny and back again, then toward Lydia.

"We brung 'em, Miz Liddie, just like you said," the bearded one said again, and he smiled a toothless smile at her, never taking his eyes from the deerskin bag she held in her hand.

"I knew I could count on you, boys," Lydia said, smiling at them as if she was still the prettiest girl in Hastings. Colin felt his cheeks flush with embarrassment, remembering a few of the delights he'd shared with her, years before. And then, to his surprise, Lydia emptied the deerskin bag onto the table. More money than he'd seen in a long time spilled onto the table. And as he stared in surprise, the bearded man and his partner scooped it up by the handfuls, jamming it into their pockets, smiles covering their faces from ear to ear.

When all the money—down to the smallest coin—was secured on their persons, the two men bowed to Lydia—still grinning from ear to ear—and turned and rushed from the cabin and to their horses. Lydia smiled as the sound of their horses' hoof beats grew fainter, and shook her head. "Well, I guess that takes care of that," she said, not noticing the perplexed looks upon Johnny and Colin's faces. She stood, patting the empty deerskin bag, then spoke. "We shouldn't be dilly-dallying around here, gents. The law can't be far behind you, you know. If you want to be taking your brother home, Colin, it's best we see to it."

Colin started at her words. "You know where Michael is?" he asked.

"Sure do," she replied. "Sad thing, what he went through," and as they watched, tears began to fill her eyes.

Colin sat still, hoping she'd tell him what had happened. He didn't have long to wait.

"A fella got...well, you know..." she paused, sniffling, that pout he remembered so well, once again upon her lips. "Tried t' impose himself on me," she said, her voice lowering. "I told Michael t' calm down, that I could handle him. Wasn't like I hadn't handled his kind before." She shook her head, sadly, before continuing. "I told the fella I wasn't interested. Told him I had me a fella, but he said no man worth his salt would let his gal work in a saloon. Said he wasn't taking no for an answer, and grabbed my arm..." She pulled aside the torn sleeve of her dress, and both Johnny and Colin were shocked to see the large black and yellow bruises that still covered her upper arm. "I saw Michael get up from the table where he'd been sitting. Saw the look on his face. Tried to get to him, to stop him. Knew the sheriff was standing there grinning and just awaiting." She started to cry then, wiping fresh tears on the sleeve of her dress. Colin cleared his throat, seeing in his mind the events as she had described them. He hung his head, looking down at the table, wishing he'd been there. Wishing now he'd shot the sheriff before they'd ridden out of town with the bearded fellow and his partner.

Lydia wiped her eyes on the sleeve of her dress, again, and then continued. "In a flash it was all over. I never even seen Michael draw his gun. I was trying to get my arm free, you see." She sniffled, before going on. "Then the sheriff's men knocked Michael out and drug him over to the jail. I tried to stop them, but they shoved me aside and laughed at me." She looked down at her hands resting in her lap, and both Johnny and Colin could see the look of shame upon her face. "Told me only a fool would shoot somebody over a...a whore like me." She turned away, and Colin felt an immense sadness flow through him at her words. Then she turned back, and stood, saying the words he'd been dreading, "A few days later, they hung him."

Colin felt a stab of pain, his eyes filling with tears. It was a few moments before he could get control of himself enough to speak. "Where's his body?" he stammered, his voice choking up.

"What?" Lydia asked, a strange expression upon her face.

"His body, where is it?" Colin repeated, aware of the look of total amazement that now shown on her face.

"Didn't they tell you? Oh, my heavens! You don't know, do you?" she asked, sitting down abruptly, and staring at him.

"Know what?" he asked, wishing she'd explain.

She stared at him a full minute, before she started to laugh. Colin wondered if she'd lost her mind. He looked at Johnny, who was as confused as he.

Finally, Colin could take it no longer. "Be quiet! Tell me where my brother's body is, so I can take him home. Of all the blasted times to have a laughin' fit!"

Lydia's laughter ceased at his tone, and she wiped her eyes before answering. "He's in the back," she said. "There's a trap door in the floor under the wood pile. You'll find him down there." She paused, then added, "Guess I'd better tell you before you go on down...the rope broke when they was hanging him. He's got some mighty bad rope burns, Colin. Some, real bad infected. But he *ain't* dead!"

CHAPTER 20

The shout that tore from Colin's throat could be heard all through the cabin! He could scarcely believe his ears, at the words Lydia had spoken. Johnny watched as the color drained from his friend's face, and then as he jumped up, grabbed Lydia and whirled her around, a shout of joy bursting from his lips.

Just as quickly, he loosed his grip on Lydia, and tore through the cabin in the direction of the backroom. Johnny heard the pile of wood covering the trap door being tossed aside, and looked at Lydia. She had sat back down at the table, tears filling her eyes and trailing slowly down her cheeks. He noticed a softness to her expression that he'd never noticed before, and wondered if all the stories he'd heard about her had been the actual truth. True, she was awful thin, and in need of a good scrubbin', and some brushing done to her hair, but she didn't look like the hardened kind of woman that frequented the saloons he'd seen on his travels to find his father. She looked sort of frail, he thought, like she'd needed someone to take care of her for a long, long time. Like she needed a husband and a home, and some decent meals. He thought of the large bruises on her upper arm, and wondered how a man could treat a woman like that. Any woman, even one who wasn't a lady. His thoughts turned back to Laughing Water, as he thought this. He'd kill a man if he put marks like that on her. Any man: white or red. Johnny rose from his chair, and began to walk toward the backroom, then turned back to where Lydia still sat. "Do you have any place to go, when we go back to Hastings?" he asked.

Lydia turned toward him, wiping the tears from her cheeks, a questioning look in her eyes. Pretty eyes, Johnny thought, that looked a man straight in the eye, not deceiving, but straight forward.

"I'll be going back to Hastings, I reckon," she said, her voice filled with a hesitancy and softness that Johnny found quite appealing. "Michael will need a lot of care, I'm sure," she continued. "And I have a..." she lowered her head for just a moment, running her hands over the fabric of the dress she wore, before continuing, "I have a whole lot to make up for. A whole lot to...to answer for, I guess you'd say. Hurt a lot of people when I was young, Johnny. Don't know if they can find it in their hearts to forgive me, or not, but I aim to *try* to..." she hesitated, brushing a straggly strand of hair back from her face, then looked directly into his eyes, as she continued, " I aim to try to set things right. Especially with my...my boy."

Johnny's mouth dropped open as she said this. In all the confusion and excitement that had gone on that day, he had not given a thought to who Lydia was. Suddenly, it dawned on him, and he was more surprised than ever. Lydia was Eli's mother! His *real* mother. She was Lilly Hart's sister who had gone astray, as folks said, when younger. He wondered what Eli would think when he found out that she had returned to Hastings. Returned, and obviously wanted to see him, and set things straight between them. He bit his lip. It would take a mighty strong woman to face the things she had to face. Especially, to face the son she had abandoned at birth. He whistled softly, looking at her with a kind expression. "Eli's a good man, Miz Lydia. My best friend. I wish you all the best."

She smiled at him, a sad, sweet smile. The same smile that Johnny had seen on Eli's face, every so often, over the years. "Thank you," she replied, and then turned away, looking out the one window in the cabin, a worried look upon her face. She wondered if her boy *would* understand. Wondered if he could *ever* forgive her for her past deeds. She doubted it, but had to try. That much she knew for certain.

Colin shouted for them to come and help, and they hurried to see to the business at hand. Getting Michael safely home was the first order of the day. Getting him settled in, and well again, that was what needed to be done now. There'd be plenty of time, later, for facing past deeds. Plenty of time to ask for forgiveness. Right now, her husband, Michael, needed her most.

CHAPTER 21

Michael had never been as happy in his whole life, as when he saw Colin climb down the ladder to the root cellar beneath the old cabin. Tears of joy filled his eyes, blurring the features of his older brother. "Colin," he croaked, the word nearly unintelligible. His attempt to speak caused him pain, his throat raw on both the inside and the out by what he had suffered. The alternative, however, made him shiver. He had come as close to dying as a man could, and had lived only by the grace of the good Lord above, and the well-worn hangman's rope. Still, the jerking motion as the rope broke, nearly broke his neck. It ripped into his flesh before his body hit the ground, causing him to black out. He didn't remember much after that, except a jostling ride in the back of a wagon filled with hay, and the sound of someone crying. It was only later that he realized it had been Lydia who cried, and he wished he could have assured her he'd be alright, but had been too jarred, and too distraught, to offer her any comfort.

He had no idea how many days had gone by since that terrible day. Knew that there had to have been many. Sometimes he slept, dreaming fitful dreams that left him wet with sweat, and shaking, as he dreamt, over and over again, of that day. Sometimes he pictured what had led up to it: the sheriff's friend taunting and teasing Lydia, then grabbing and twisting her arm till she cried out. All the while, the sheriff and his men standing by with smiles on their faces, watching and waiting to see what he would do. He had taken all he could, he remembered. Had tried his best to ignore the cruel things that had been said to her. The look of shame on her face had been the last straw. He remembered jumping up from where he'd been sitting, remembered starting across the room after the man: her boss. Then he remembered hearing a shot being fired, and something slammed into the back of his head. The next thing he knew he was laying on the floor of a cell in the jailhouse. Blood ran from a cut above his eye and soaked the collar of his shirt in back where someone had hit him with the butt of their gun. He didn't know till later that he'd been accused of shooting the fellow who had hurt Lydia, and later still, that he faced the hangman's noose for it. He'd told the judge the truth, as he remembered it, telling him the gunfire had come from somewhere behind him and off to one side. The judge only shook his head, solemnly, looked Lydia over from head to toe, as she sat nearby, sniffling and wiping her tear-filled eyes, and nodded to the sheriff in bored acceptance of *his* version of the events. A few moments later, he sentenced Michael to be hung at daybreak the following Saturday. Michael shuddered, remembering, and bile rose up into his throat, causing his stomach to roll.

"Michael," Colin greeted him, his own eyes wet with tears. "I came as soon as I heard. Are you able to tell me what's going on?"

Michael groaned, sitting up, the purple and red marks of the hangman's noose highly pronounced around his neck. On one side of his neck pus seeped through a cloth that Lydia had placed there, winding the ends of the cloth loosely around his neck above the rope burns. Michael winced as he reached up to hold the piece of cloth in place. "I'll tell you what I know," he replied, each word spoken with great effort.

"Never mind," Colin ordered, seeing the pain his brother was feeling, and noticing the putrid smell from the puss-laden cloth. "Best we get you home." He reached out, helping Michael up, supporting him in the low-ceilinged cellar. "Can you climb up the ladder?"

"Can sure try," Michael replied, taking hold of the sides of the ladder. It wasn't all that far to the room above, but he shook from even the effort of walking, and wondered if he *could* manage to climb up.

It was more difficult than they expected, even though Lydia had come running and reached down to help him. She helped him get his balance as he stepped from the cellar, and then leaned against him to support him while Colin climbed up. Colin noticed the attention she gave his brother, and was grateful for it. Sometimes even a whore has a heart of gold, he thought, and he looked down at the floor in embarrassment at these thoughts. He'd known his share of whores; some good, some bad, some who'd pick your pockets clean while you slept in their beds, some who'd refuse any money just to have a decent man lay with them and hold them awhile. He knew they didn't have it easy. Especially those who had ended up in such dire circumstances through no fault of their own: Orphans, and them who just couldn't find any other way to survive. Times were hard, after all. He knew it wasn't always the bad ones who came to this kind of end. Knew, too, that sometimes a man would come along, needing a wife real bad, and would marry up with one of them. There wasn't always a big supply of women in a town way out here in the west. Sometimes a fellow just couldn't be choosy. He looked at his brother, and at how Lydia stood close beside him, her arm wrapped protectively around him. Maybe even a gal like Lydia, he thought, could mend her ways if the right man came along. She didn't seem as callous as some of the whores he'd met. Why, she even seemed to have real feelings for Michael. And Lord knows, she sure did know how to please a man throughout a long, dark night!

"Where's the others?" Michael asked her, looking toward the kitchen.

"I paid them off, honey. They grabbed the money and lit out of here like they were on fire," Lydia replied, smiling prettily up at him.

"Took all your savings, didn't it?" he asked her, looking down into her eyes, a sad expression on his face.

"It don't matter, darlin'. The only thing that matters is that we get out of here before you get any sicker from those wounds, and before the sheriff shows up."

Michael started then, his head jerking up, as Johnny walked through the doorway. "Johnny! I didn't know you were here."

Johnny walked over to his friend, shaking his hand, noticing the marks on his neck and the smell of infection seeping from the cloth tied loosely around it. He was shocked at the sight.

"It was Johnny, Michael, that heard you were in trouble. He came to Maw's. We got here as fast as we could," Colin interrupted. "If he hadn't come and told us..."

"We best git riding, gents. 'Less you want the sheriff and his men to get to us first?" Lydia said, one arm still around Michael.

"You're right," Colin replied. "We can talk later."

"The wagon's around back, hidden in the woods," Lydia stated. "It'd be faster on horseback, but Michael ain't up to that, as you can see. Best we make him a bed in the back of it, with the straw and any blankets we can stir up from the backroom," she suggested.

"Good idea," Colin agreed, as Johnny hurried toward the back to look for blankets, and Michael started for the door, with Colin and Lydia helping him. Michael's whole body ached, and he wondered if it was from hitting the ground when the rope broke, or from lying around so long in the dark, dank cellar. Whatever the reason, he'd had better days, that was for sure. He pressed his fingers lightly against the infected area on the side of his neck, feeling pain all through it. The only thing he wanted right now was to be home. Not at his home, but at his maw's. He knew she'd know what to do to heal his neck. She had always seemed to know just what poultice to use when he was young and had scraped himself, or gotten some kind of infection. He had to smile, then, remembering how she'd railed at him one day, cause he'd poked around at some old spider's web after she'd warned him to leave it alone or he'd get bitten. And sure enough, it wasn't long before he'd gone running for the house, crying, his finger stinging somethin' fierce. She'd hurried around, making up one of her special poultices, smearing it on the bite and wrapping it securely, then walloped him good with a hickory branch for not listening to her in the first place. When she'd finished, it was a toss-up whether the lickin', or the bite, hurt the worst. He smiled, and climbed up into the back of the wagon.

The next day they forded the river far upstream from Chaska, and north of where Colin and Johnny had crossed. It was shallow, and the current was slight, making the crossing an easy one. Colin drove the wagon, while Lydia stayed in the back with Michael, and Johnny rode alongside. They had seen only one other person: an Indian riding a spotted horse. He was a good distance from them, yet seemed to be skirting them as they headed back toward Michael's farm. Johnny had been the first to spot him, and kept a silent vigil, on the alert for trouble. The whole day the Indian could be glimpsed far off to their right, keeping pace with them, yet never attempting to come closer. Johnny knew it was rare for an Indian to be alone in these parts. He was certain this fellow was part of a scouting party, though why he was trailing *them* did not make sense. All day Johnny kept an eye on the Indian, not able to make out from the distance between them, if he was from a peaceable tribe, or not.

At sunset, Colin pulled up in a secluded spot, close to a spring where they could water the horses and rest a spell. Michael had dozed most of the day, groaning now and then, and it was apparent the ride was hard on him. Lydia jumped down from the wagon and dunked a long piece of material that she had torn from her petticoat, into the cool water, and then hurried back to the wagon. She murmured softly to Michael, removed the old, pus-filled wrappings from his wound, and cleaned the wound as best she could. Then she gently wrapped a clean swathe of cloth around his neck. He kept his eyes closed while she worked, not speaking, which worried her. She knew he needed to rest, but it was clear to her that his silence was far more than that. His forehead felt warm to the touch, and she feared that he was getting a fever. She jumped down from the wagon and walked over to where Colin and Johnny stood talking.

"I think Michael has a fever," she stated, interrupting the men.

Colin turned toward her, a serious look upon his face. "How bad is he?"

"Not too hot yet, but I'm sure he's much warmer than he should be," she replied, biting her lip and looking back at the wagon.

"We've got other trouble, too."

"What?" she asked, a worried look crossing her face.

Colin noticed a tear in the dress she wore that exposed her shoulder and a lot of cleavage. His eyes ran down her, and he took a deep breath before he answered. "Got an Indian that's been trailing us ever since we crossed the river. Don't know what tribe. Don't know his intentions. Didn't want to say anything before and worry you...or Michael. Johnny's been keeping an eye on him."

Johnny spoke up then. "Might not be anything to worry about, but with the way things are now, you never can tell." He glanced around, suddenly sure of what he must do. "I'm gonna ride out, Colin. See if he's alone. See if he's friendly. I think it's best you stay here for the night, but that's up to you. What do you think?"

"Be hard going, with the wagon," Colin said. "Especially in the dark. We're pretty well hidden here. I'd say we stay."

"I can keep putting cool cloths on Michael's forehead, if we stay beside the stream," Lydia replied. "It'll help to bring his fever down."

"Good, it's agreed, then," Johnny said. "I'll be back soon," and with that he turned and rode off.

Colin checked his gun, then walked over to get his coffeepot and cup from his saddlebag. He had enough coffee to make a pot, and knew it would refresh him. He began to gather up a small pile of sticks and twigs, and soon had a pot boiling. As it boiled, he sat down beside the fire, watching Lydia as she dunked the torn pieces of her petticoat into the stream, wringing them out, and then hurried to the wagon to help cool Michael. He was surprised by how tenderly she cared for his brother, surprised by the fact that she knew what to do. The Lydia *he* remembered was only good at *one* thing, and it sure wasn't that! We all change, he thought. Life sees to that. His thoughts went back in time then, to Andersonville, the prison where he had been one of the officers in charge. The prison where he had watched so many of his fellow Yankees die due to the horrible conditions in the camp. Conditions he could do nothing about. Every time he tried to change things, every time he did his best to make his superiors aware of the horrors of the camp, he was brushed aside and given the "run around." Each officer put the blame onto another. Nobody accepted the responsibility. Nobody took the time, or obviously cared, to stop the death and inhumanity that occurred there. There was a time, he thought, when I was proud to fight for the South. He shifted to get more comfortable, as the aroma of the coffee began to fill the air. I used to believe a *whole lot different*, he thought, before Andersonville. Used to be a different man, before I served there. Yes, sir, a real different man, to be sure. He picked up his cup, wiping the rim with his finger. Lydia walked over to the stream just then, and he turned to watch her, his mind still far, far away. Yup, he thought, I used to be *real* different. Maybe Lydia's had a war of her own to fight. Maybe *she's* different now, too. She glanced at him, smiling a quick smile, then hurried back to her husband.

CHAPTER 22

Colin jumped up at the sound of an approaching horse and rider. It was dark, too dark to make out who it was. He glanced at the wagon, knowing that Lydia and Michael were asleep in it, and that he was the only one guarding the camp. He ran for cover behind some brush, where he'd be less likely to be seen, and yet could get off an easy shot or two before he was discovered. His heart pounded in his chest like a drum, and he watched with wide eyes as the horse slowed to a walk at one side of the camp. The rider dismounted and bent low, then began to move toward where Colin crouched. By the remaining light of the fire, Colin could see the flame reflect off the knife the man carried in one hand. He cocked his gun at the same time he called out, "Stop where you are, or I'll shoot."

The figure froze where he was, looking into the darkness in Colin's direction. "Don't shoot. I come in peace," he said, the knife falling from his hand, onto the ground.

Colin stepped slowly out of his hiding place, able to make out the outline of the intruder who stood in front of the flames. His features were hidden by the surrounding darkness, but his figure was distinct. He was a short man, decidedly hefty. Either that, Colin thought, or wearing some kind of cloak. What's your business?" Colin asked, still trying to get a better look at the man.

"I'm heading for a town a far distance from here, got important business there," the man replied.

"I'd be likin' to know that business," Colin stated, and heard some movement from the wagon and knew Lydia had been wakened by their voices.

"And why, pray tell, would it be of any business to you, Sir," the man had the audacity to ask.

Colin's ire was rising. Who was this brash fool, he wondered, who answered his question with a question of his own? "I'm not going to ask you, again," Colin stated. "Tell me your business here."

"Coffee," came the reply.

"What?" Colin asked, totally perplexed.

"'Tis a cup of coffee I hunger for, my dear man. I smelled your good brew from a distance, and craved a cup. 'Tis a hard journey I've had, ya' see. Come all the way from the Irish shores, by fine sailing ship, to me mother's humble abode, only to be turned out into the cold to go on a most urgent journey."

Colin didn't know what to say. He'd heard the obvious accent of his own dear birthplace, Ireland, but had never heard anyone go on and on so. "I fear you've been kissin' the Blarney Stone, my friend," Colin said. "But if it's coffee you're wantin', than help yourself. Just leave your knife on the ground."

"Knife?" the man asked. "What knife?"

"Don't think me the fool," Colin stated. "I saw the glint of steel, as you walked beside the fire, carryin' it."

"'Tis you, good sir, who's been kissing the Blarney Stone, then. For 'tis not a knife I carried, nor a knife I dropped. 'Twas only me tin cup."

Colin scratched his head, not sure whether to trust the fellow, or not. He was certain now that the man was Irish, but though his voice sounded a wee bit familiar, his words were spoken in a very strange manner. As if he were a world traveler, or perhaps an actor from one of the companies who occasionally toured the country, putting on shows for the entertainment of those who enjoyed such as that. "Throw some wood on the fire then, friend, so we'll be able to see each other more clearly, and help yourself to the coffee."

"Thank you," the fellow replied, and bent slowly to retrieve his cup, holding it out so Colin could see it more clearly against the glow of the flames. Colin saw also that it was, indeed, a cloak he wore.

"Are you a world traveler, then?" he asked, still curious as to the man's identity.

"That I am, my good man. That I am."

"And may I ask who it is I'm talking to?" Colin asked, a strange feeling running through him, suddenly.

"You may. Yes, you may," the man replied, then bent to pour himself a cup of coffee. He gave no answer, however.

"Well?" Colin said, wondering if the man was touched in the head. He moved closer, watching the fellow as he bent to put another piece of wood on the fire. As he did, a flash of something silver shown at the man's waist. "Stop right there!" Colin ordered, his gun trained on the man.

The fellow straightened slowly, looking back at Colin. "And what is it that's bothering ya' now, my son?" he asked, disgustedly.

"Don't know what kind of game you're playing," Colin said, walking toward the man. "And I'm *not* your son. Raise your hands above your head, right now, or you'll get a taste of lead."

"That's the thanks I get, is it?" the man asked, raising his hands, though still holding his cup and being careful not to spill it.

"Thanks? Thanks for what?" Colin asked, a perplexed expression upon his face.

"For coming all this way to save your sorry behind. What do I have to do, break an arm, before you recognize me, Colin?"

Colin's mouth dropped open in astonishment. "Patrick?"

"That I am, Brother, that I am," Patrick replied, grinning from ear to ear, though Colin could not see it in the dark, with the light from the fire at Patrick's back.

Colin stood still, completely confused. Why hadn't his brother, if it was indeed Patrick, told him who he was as soon as he rode into camp? Why had he fooled around, taking the risk of being shot? And why the fancy words, and talk of Ireland, and such? It made no sense at all to Colin. "Name your brothers," he suddenly ordered, just to make certain of the fellow's identity. Patrick, he knew, was a prankster, but this whole episode had been downright foolish.

"Ah-h, so 'tis doubt ya' still have, Colin O'Leary," replied the other. "Well, then...there's Michael, James, William, and yourself. All sons of our dear, sweet maw, who sits in her cabin outside of Hastin's, awaiting our return. Does that satisfy ya', then?"

Colin walked quickly forward, holstering his gun, ready to greet the younger brother that he'd not seen for more than ten years. The brother he'd shared a room with when growing up, and watched over every day when younger. The brother whose return they had all been so gladly awaiting. He'd set him straight, later, on how foolish he'd been to enter the camp in the manner he did, and how easily he could have been shot because of such foolishness.

"So, do I shoot him, or what?" Lydia asked, from where she stood hidden behind the wagon. Both Colin and Patrick looked in her direction, surprised to see the woman calmly coming forward with gun in hand. Still ready—as she had been, since she first realized there was a stranger in camp—to shoot the intruder. Both men stood still, their mouths opened in surprise, having not realized that another gun had been trained on Patrick all the time.

"No, it's all right," Colin quickly replied. "It's my kid-brother. You can put your gun away, Lydia." Then he walked over to Patrick, shaking his hand, first, then enfolding him in a hug. It felt like they'd been apart a lifetime.

Lydia holstered her gun, then walked over to where the men were, as surprised as Colin had been that here, of all places, another O'Leary brother had turned up. It seemed a strange place for Patrick to suddenly appear, and she wanted to make sure it was, indeed, him. She had only a vague memory of a younger O'Leary boy when she had lived in Hastings. A troublemaker, she remembered, who was always doing the most foolish things. Colin had complained to her one night, long ago, if she remembered right, of how he had to take time from chores to take his brother into town to the doctor, after he'd fallen off their barn roof while trying to fly, or some other such foolishness. She smiled at the memory. No wonder he'd snuck into camp the way he did, she thought. Must still not have a lick of sense.

"Well?" she questioned, seeing in the glow of the fire, the happy smiles upon the two men's faces. "Is he your brother, then?"

The men stopped talking and turned to her, their smiles saying it all. "That he is," Colin replied, smiling happily. "Brother Patrick, I don't know if you remember the Benedict family that lived outside of town, or not, but this is Lydia Benedict. She was with Michael when we found him. Lydia, this is my youngest brother, Patrick."

Lydia brushed back a strand of hair that had fallen across her face, wishing she looked more presentable. She was very aware that her dress was ripped and dirty, that she hadn't had a bath in days, and to be sure, didn't look like much of a lady. Still she put out her hand to Colin and Michael's younger brother, pleased when he took it. She could tell a lot from a man's handshake, though most men over the years had not been interested in taking time for such as that. She felt the firm, yet gentle, grip of the man who stood before her. His hands were smooth and warm, and she couldn't help notice how he took all of her hand into his. It made her eyes nearly well up with tears, the sincerity and caring she felt, just in his touch. She pulled her hand from his, seeing by the light of the fire that he was smiling at her, a broad smile, joyful, yet boyish.

"'Tis happy I am to meet you, Miss," he said, still smiling.

Lydia blushed, hoping he couldn't tell. "Thank you, Patrick. I'm happy to meet you, too." She hesitated a moment, a strong feeling within her to be totally honest with this man, though she had no idea why. "My name's not Benedict, however. It's now the same as yours."

Patrick's smile never wavered, she saw, but Colin was looking at her in the most peculiar way. "What do you mean?" Patrick asked. "I'm Lydia O'Leary, now. Michael's wife."

Colin's mouth dropped open, no words issuing forth. Patrick, however, reacted quite differently. He reached out, quickly, clasping her face between his hands, and planted a kiss on her forehead. She was so stunned by this, that she stood there, not knowing how to react.

"Welcome to our family, then, Miz O'Leary," Patrick said, his words of welcome sounding more genuine than anything she could ever have hoped for. Colin extended his hand then, hesitantly, and took hers, nodding as he shook hers. She knew what he was thinking, could only imagine his thoughts, in fact. But, well, he'd have found out sooner or later, no time like the present, she thought. So they'd been...what they'd been, in the past. It wasn't like they'd been lovers. Far from it. Not in the sense of really caring, or really loving...not like she loved Michael, anyway. She'd always loved Michael, right from the very first time she ever saw him. And even more, when she knew she was carrying his child. That's why she'd gone away. Why she'd refused to leave town with David, the good Reverend Cole. She'd always hoped, in her heart, that Michael would know what she truly felt, and would come after her. Would forgive her for marrying David, and make a home for her, and their son, Eli. She looked at Colin, still aware of the thoughts he had to be thinking. She'd made a lot of mistakes when younger. Had made a lot of *terrible* mistakes. Mistakes that affected more lives than just her own. Hadn't known how to deal with the feelings that had filled her young body back then. Feelings that had driven her to be what she'd become. Well, she thought, Michael had been the only man she'd ever loved, the only man who'd ever satisfied her. And he'd forgiven her, and still loved her. And only a month ago, had married her. She intended to be the best wife in all the world to him, to stand by his side, no matter what. Yes, sir, she planned to make him proud, that's a fact, and Colin O'Leary, or anyone else, for that matter, could think what they wanted!

Patrick interrupted her thoughts, breaking the silence with a surprising comment of his own. "Seems to me, I'd *best* be setting the record straight, meself," he said, his Irish brogue distinct. "'Tis not Patrick O'Leary I am, now, ya' see," and Colin quickly turned his head, amazed at his words. "'Tis *Father* Patrick O'Leary," he stated, surprising both of them.

"Well, I'll be damned!" Colin exclaimed, staring at his brother.

CHAPTER 23

Lydia mopped Michael's brow as they rode along in the back of the wagon, a worried expression upon her face. Michael had wakened the night before when Patrick called his name, but had been unable to talk to him. He tried, but had been too delirious from the fever, beads of sweat standing out on his forehead. Lydia was terribly worried for him. As old as she was, she could not remember seeing anyone with such a fever. And the stench from the wound on the side of his neck reeked, nearly making her stomach turn. She kept placing cold pieces of fabric on his forehead, hoping to cool him, but it seemed to make little difference. Truth was, she feared it would not be much longer until he died, and the thought of losing him tore at her. She wanted to scream, or cry out in desperation. The water she had gathered at the stream where they had stayed during the night was nearly gone, and she knew if his temperature rose any higher, there was a good chance he would die. What would she do then, she wondered? Where would she go? Had they come this far, finally marrying—as they both knew they should have, long ago—only to lose the chance to start anew? Tears began to flow from her eyes, and she held her face in her hands to muffle the sounds of her weeping. The wagon jostled along, Colin and Patrick riding in front, keeping their eyes on the trail and surrounding land. Johnny had still not returned, and that added to the worry and concern of both men.

Then suddenly, she felt a hand upon her shoulder. She opened her eyes, wiping them on the torn fabric of her sleeve. Patrick had heard her cries, and had climbed over into the back of the wagon. He looked at her, a look of infinite compassion upon his young face. She sniffled; struck with wonder at the immense look of love he gave her. An angel, she thought, and stared, not knowing what to say.

"Let's pray, Lydia. The good Lord hears every word, ya' know, of all our prayers," he said, easing down to sit beside her, noticing as he did the paleness of his brother's face.

"I...I don't know how," Lydia replied, unable to look away from the glow that seemed to shine all around him.

"'Twill please the dear Lord all the more then, dear child, when He hears you," he said, reaching over to take her hands in his, enfolding hers within his own. "We'll pray together," he said, bowing his head. Lydia watched him, spellbound by the aura of sanctity that seemed to surround him. Slowly, she bowed her head, as his words of prayer poured forth. She was no longer aware of the bouncing of the wagon over rutted trail, no longer filled with fear for her beloved husband. Nor did she feel the intense shame that had been so much a part of her life, ever since she had become sorry for what she had done, and for the kind of woman she had been. For the first time in a long, long time, she felt cleansed. Felt pure, and good, and worthy of the life that lay before her now, as Michael's wife. She turned her hands within Patrick's, so that she now held firmly to his. And as tears of joy filled her eyes, Lydia O'Leary felt forgiven for all her sins.

CHAPTER 24

At mid-afternoon the following day, they heard the hoof beats of a horse, racing behind them. "Here comes someone," Lydia called out to the men in front, who glanced back, seeing the lone rider. They watched him approach, glad to see, when he got close enough, that it was Johnny. Colin pulled up on the reins, stopping the wagon, as their friend rode up beside them, his horse lathered.

"We've got troubles," Johnny said, as he slid from his horse and hurried over to the wagon. He stopped when he saw Patrick, a look of surprise upon his face. Then nodded in Patrick's direction, intent on continuing to tell them his news. "That was a Pawnee we saw. Part of a war party. I got close enough to hear some of their talk, and I'm afraid it doesn't look good. Seems they struck a settlement over north of here. They killed most everyone in it, and are now heading the same way we are." He stopped to catch his breath, looking at Lydia, before continuing. "They had three or four children with them; white children. Intend to take them back to their camp as slaves, I'd say, or to trade them, later, for guns."

"Damn," Colin said, knowing what those children must have gone through, and even worse, the awful things that still might happen to them.

"What can we do?" Lydia asked, her concern mainly for Michael. "Your brother's not good. He needs to be cared for, to have medicine, and be in bed," she stated.

Colin shook his head. He was well aware of the condition of Michael, but knew, too, the condition those children might be in.

"There's a cabin ahead," Johnny said. "Might be a good spot to hole up—Michael and Lydia, I mean. Then maybe the three of us could try to sneak in after dark, where the Indians make camp, and steal back the children."

"Don't think that'd work," Colin replied. "Aren't Pawnees known for travelin' for days, when they've got prisoners?"

Patrick had remained quiet through all the exchange, and now he spoke. "Sounds like it'll take a miracle to save those children. What do you think?"

Johnny and Colin turned toward him, willing to listen to any idea, even one of his. What did *he* know, after all, of fighting Indians or making miracles, they both wondered? But they were flush out of ideas of their own. "What have you got in mind?" Colin asked.

"Not a plan," Patrick answered, dashing their immediate hopes. "But let me think on it a moment, if you will," he said, and he jumped down from his seat on the wagon, and walked off into the woods. Johnny looked at Colin, who watched his brother from where he sat, seeing him walk to a fallen log, just out of sight of the others. Then, to Colin's surprise, he saw Patrick kneel and bow his head. Saw him stretch out his arms from his sides, the palms of his hands held upward.

Colin felt moved by what he saw, moved in a way he had not been in many a long, long year. He turned back to Johnny. "We'll give him a minute," he said, and he bowed his head, touched by the sight of his younger brother praying. I, too, had been a man of strong faith, he thought, years back, before the war. Prayed my share of prayers, always believing they'd be answered, or at least, that they were heard. For years I knelt at the side of Maw in church, asking the Lord to guide me in each day's trials and triumphs, to help my family, and to show me the right path to follow to please the Lord. He took a deep breath. Yes, he thought, I used to be a praying man, too, way back before the war. Before I chose to fight on the other side, and ended up at Andersonville. He shuddered slightly at the thought, looking up, just as Patrick walked out of the woods and back to the wagon.

"Well?" Colin asked, looking at his younger brother.

"Nothing yet," Patrick replied, a gentle smile upon his face. "But have faith that an answer *will* come, Colin, when we need it most," he said, and he climbed up onto the wagon seat, a look of total certainty upon his face.

Colin turned toward Johnny, clearly not happy with Patrick's reply. "Guess it's up to us, John. What do you think we should do?"

Johnny glanced to Patrick, knowing he was a true man of God. He had recognized the quiet strength that Patrick seemed to emit. Had seen this same strength many times before, in his many visits to the village of Chief Standing Elk. Had seen it in not only the old chief's eyes, but in the words he spoke. A strength that grew from wisdom far beyond that known by most men. A wisdom that came from his belief in Wakantanka, and repeated throughout the ages, by one generation of the People, and then another. Wisdom that had been passed down from the ancient ones, many, many moons before. "I think we need to keep moving," Johnny said, glancing again toward Patrick. Patrick smiled at his words, knowing his young friend, Johnny—being part Indian—had realized that they did, indeed, have God—the Maker of Miracles—riding with them, and He would lead them in the way they were to go.

Colin flicked the reins, and the horse began to pull the wagon, as Lydia swathed Michael's head with the last of the wet cloth from her petticoat. Michael groaned, not opening his eyes, but his forehead seemed less hot than it had, earlier. She whispered to him, telling him how dearly she loved him, in hopes that he could hear her words. She didn't know what lay ahead for them—for any of them—but given a choice, there was nowhere else she wanted to be. He was her husband, the man she had loved, way back as far as she could remember. That was all that mattered. That, and their son, Eli. The boy she had abandoned so many years before. The boy she had left with her sister, Lilly, for safe keeping, knowing she did not have the means, or the motherly ways, necessary to raise him. Michael hadn't known about Eli. She had never told him that the boy was his, till the day before they married. He had turned on her, furious to learn of her deception, and worse yet, to know that another man had taken his place as father to his son. Lydia thought he was going to hit her, she remembered, as he raised his hand, his fist doubled. Then, just as quickly, Michael had sat back down on the bed in her room above the saloon where she worked. Had held his hands over his face, and wept. Lydia knew then, how deeply she had hurt him, by not telling him. And, by not trusting him to be a man who would have done right by her, and the boy. She had knelt at his feet, feeling the pain she had caused him. Certain that he would walk out the door, slamming it behind him, his anger with her so great. She had been certain he would hightail it out of Chaska, never again looking back, and never forgiving her. Her head against the worn fabric of the knee of his pants, she had begged him to forgive her. But he rose, and as she had feared, walked from her room, never saying a word. She sat there, on the floor, staring at the door; an ache in her heart that she felt could never be healed. She knew that not only could he not forgive her, but she, also, would never be able to forgive herself. She wept then, for not only the wrong she had done him, but *all* the wrongs she had done, to all the people in her life. She wept, till there were no more tears within her, and then she lay down upon the cold, hard, wood floor, and slept.

It was there he found her when he returned. How surprised she was at his return. She would never forget how he had lifted her up into his strong arms, holding her close, telling her, over and over, how much he loved her. Telling her he forgave her, and wanted her to be his wife. He told her about his farm, and how it needed her, how *he* needed her. All that night, he lay beside her, not touching her or making love to her. Just lovin' her with all his heart, and holding her close to him. The following day, they'd been married. No one from town came to wish them well, no one from the saloon even knew. Not even the fellow who ran it, the sheriff's friend, Vincent Jalaco. He'd have stopped her, if he'd known. Lydia, like all the girls who worked there, was afraid of him. He ruled them all with an iron fist, having no hesitation about beating one of them. She'd finish up the week, she told Michael, not going upstairs with anyone, and then they'd sneak away. She shuddered now, wishing it had worked out that way.

CHAPTER 25

The cabin Johnny had told them about was in deplorable condition. It looked about to fall down, and it was evident that a few wild critters had called it home for a vast number of years. Lydia shuddered when she saw it, but rolled up her sleeves, and immediately set about to clear off the one bed. It was covered in dust and dirt, mouse droppings, and even a small skeleton of a mouse. She shook her head. She was used to shabby accommodations, but nothing as bad as this. She worried that Michael would become even more ill, if he had to stay in such a place very long, and hurried to look around for an old bucket to carry some water in, to scrub the place a bit. There was a small stream just outside, and the old fireplace looked solid enough. She rushed here and there, soon finding a dented pail in the bushes beside the cabin. Quickly she went to the stream and filled it. She carried it inside, happy to see that Colin had anticipated her need for hot water, and had started a fire in the fireplace. There was no cook stove, and only one straight-back chair remained, the legs of another lying broken and partially burned, within the fireplace. There was a sturdy table, however, and an oil lamp that looked in fairly decent condition. She remembered one just like it at the farm, when she was young. Lilly used to sit each evening, she remembered, figuring farm expenses, before it. Lydia bit her lip at the memory. I never helped her with anything around the farm, she thought. I hated that old farm with a passion. How I wish now that I had helped, she thought, busying herself with what she had to do to make a comfortable place for Michael, and stopping herself from thinking thoughts of regret. She'd made the choices she had, and knew that was why she was where she was. I have to go on from here, she thought. A fresh start. Just me and Michael...and maybe our boy. She brushed a strand of hair back away from her face, noticing a piece of mirror leaning against the wall, over by an old washbowl. She walked over to it, picked it up and looked at herself in it. She gasped at the sight! She hadn't realized how old she looked, or how...worn. Putting the piece of mirror back where it had come from, she shook her head, sadly. I used to be so pretty, she thought. Everybody used to say so. A tear traced a path down her cheek, and she wondered how Michael could ever have wanted to marry her, the way she looked now. I'll take better care of myself, she thought, when we get settled at his farm. I'll sew me a dress or two, and wash my hair everyday. Maybe even take a bath, once in awhile. Michael told me there was a tub, and a cook stove, and *two* beds. And curtains on the window, and even a big cabinet with lots of clothes in it. Clothes that Sarah Gentry had left when she went back to live with the Indians. Lydia shook her head in disbelief. I'd never go live with a bunch of them savages, she thought. It'd be just like 'em to scalp a person in the middle of the night. She'd heard all kinds of tales from the fellows who stopped by the saloon where she had worked. They said wagon trains were attacked and good folks were killed, left and right, for no reason at all, as they traveled across the country to the lands far to the west. Lands called Californie, and the Oregon territory. Lands where a man could have a new start. Lands of promise and hope. She carried in one armload after another of the straw from the wagon. It had been a kind of bed for Michael on their journey from Chaska. She arranged it on top of the bed, and threw an old quilt she had found, over top of it. Then she mashed it down, hoping to make it more comfortable. "You can bring him in now," she said. And Colin and Patrick walked outside to carry Michael in from the wagon.

Johnny waited till they were inside, and then drove the wagon a short distance from the cabin, hiding it in some tall brush that grew there. Then he led their horses over to the stream to get a drink. He didn't know what lay ahead for the three of them, but was anxious to get on the way. He could track as good as the best of them, but didn't want any surprises. How well he knew the skill of the Pawnee. They weren't the kind to run from a fight. And if they had prisoners with them, especially ones they intended to trade for guns and ammunition, they would not give them up easily. There was a slight wind blowing, and some snowflakes began to fall. Johnny pulled his hat down upon his head, and pulled his coat around him. He wondered what his mother was doing. Wondered, too, if she was ready for the winter ahead. He hoped she was already settled in to her lodge, some heavy buffalo hides to keep her warm as she slept. He knew she was skilled with awl and sinew, and would have made herself a warm buffalo hide coat, and leggings, and fur-lined moccasins. She's probably made some for me, too, he thought, just as Colin and Patrick came out of the cabin.

"Let's ride! You lead the way, Johnny. You know where you saw them last," Colin said, as he mounted his horse. Patrick threw a leg over his horse, his black cloak hanging down on each side, hiding his legs and saddle from view. Johnny swung up onto Buck, racing past the other two men, a feeling of excitement filling him.

Inside the cabin, Lydia loaded her gun, and laid it on the table. She wasn't afraid for herself, but didn't want any surprises. She surely didn't want any visitors that meant Michael any harm. She'd shoot anyone that threatened him, even if it meant the hangman's noose. She'd learned a long time ago to handle a gun. It came in handy in the profession she'd been in, though she'd never had to shoot anyone. A couple of times, just pointing the gun at some rowdy cowpoke had been enough to get him turned around and headed out the door. Usually the ones who'd had too much whiskey, them were the worst ones. They usually had a mean streak, and thought nothin' of knockin' a gal around a bit, if she didn't do what they wanted. She'd been afraid of a few of them, till she got herself a gun, and learned to use it. She smiled at her thoughts, and walked over to see if she could find some soap. Maybe if I wash that pus off his neck, she thought, that wound will start to heal. She'd heard talk of how serious an infection was. How it could kill a fellow, quick as could be. And it didn't take a doctor to tell her that the wound on Michael's neck was bad infected. She could tell that, by the smell. She took a deep breath, sighing.

The Pawnee had traveled fast, leaving few signs in their wake. They were highly skilled warriors, and Johnny knew that though he'd learned to track from his father's friend, Howling Wolf, he was not their match.

He'd lived too many years in the white man's world, not needing to develop such skills. He clung close to Buck's neck, racing along, the other men close behind. There had been no sign for more than a half-mile, now, and he wondered if he'd lost their trail. It would soon be too dark to see the things he looked for: tracks of the Indian ponies, or broken branches, or any such thing. Then he saw it! He pulled up hard, jumping from his horse, hearing Colin and Patrick come to a halt behind him.

"What is it?" Patrick asked, leaning forward, trying to see what it was that Johnny now held in his hand.

Johnny rubbed his hand over the ground at his feet, crouched down to scan the brush for other signs, then stood and walked back toward the others. In his hand he held a piece of blue ribbon. A ribbon they all knew had come from a little girl's hair. Colin swore under his breath, and shook his head, angrily. Patrick reached out for it, slipping it into his pocket. Johnny wondered at this, but said nothing. He knew they were on the right trail now, and that was all he needed to know. He ran to Buck, vaulting up onto the horse's back, and urged the horse on, leaning to one side, scanning the ground carefully, as they moved along. Colin followed, his jaw set, an angry scowl upon his face. Patrick followed behind, silent words of prayer issuing forth from his lips, his boyish face raised to the sky above. The sun was beginning to set, and though the snowflakes had stopped long before, the wind had picked up; it's mounting fury causing Patrick to shiver now and then. He wasn't used to being out in such weather. Had gotten used to well-heated rooms and carriages of quality, not drafty old buggies, or being on horseback traversing the land. As he thought these things, he wondered if the children that had been taken by the Pawnees had any coats, or decent clothing to protect them from the brisk winds. He knew they probably did not, and he felt ashamed for thinking only of his own comfort. I have a lot to learn, he thought, about doing the Lord's will. A man must learn to give up the comforts of the world to do the work of the Lord. He has to set aside his own needs and wants, has to overcome those desires, as he has the desires of his flesh. He'd known these things when he chose to become a priest. It was a choice he'd made, long before he was a grown man. A choice he'd made, long before he'd even known what a priest was.

He could still remember the day he knew, without doubt, that he wanted to give his life to God. How could he forget? It was the day he'd broken his leg falling off the barn roof. The day he tried to fly. Oh, how Colin had yelled at him, when he had to stop doing chores to take him into town so Doc could set his leg. And his maw, she'd come out of the house, a worried look upon her face. He could still see the way she had looked at him: like he was crazy, like he didn't have a lick of sense. He'd tried to explain, tried to tell her why he did it. But with Colin all fired-up, and Maw wringing her hands and shaking her head the way she was, the words just would have made matters worse. Sometimes it was better to say nothing. How well he knew that. And that's just what he'd done. He'd shut his eyes, biting his lip to ease the pain he was feeling, and only once did he look back at the barn. He looked at the highest peak, and across the whole roof, but the lady he'd seen up there—the lady dressed in robes of the most beautiful sky blue and white, her feet bare, except for the roses that surrounded them, was gone. He felt a sense of joy, once again, at the memory of the lady, and whispered a prayer for the little girl who had dropped the blue ribbon. It was the same color as the robe the lady had worn, *every time* he had seen her, in the years that followed.

"Stop," Johnny ordered, his voice a mere whisper. "Wait here." He slipped from his horse, crouched low, and hurried toward the crest of the hill in front of them. Colin slowly dismounted, holding the reins of Johnny's horse. Patrick sat where he was, listening. It was hard to see now, as night had begun to descend around them. Colin realized he was holding his breath, and breathed out, slowly. He could feel his heart beating in his neck, as it had, many times when he'd been in the war. A nervous habit, he thought, and he wished he was home in his maw's cabin, settled around the fireplace with a bowl of her good stew. He couldn't remember when he'd eaten last. As he thought this, he saw Johnny hurrying back toward them. He straightened, anxious to know what he'd seen, if anything.

"There's about fifteen of them," Johnny whispered. "Pawnee, like I thought. Three captives are tied to a tree on the north side of the camp. Boys. Two girls, one about my age and a little one, are huddled together nearby. There's an Indian guarding them, two more Indians over near the horses. The one that was keeping an eye on us is some kind of important fellow. Either that, or what he's telling them is aw-ful important. They're huddled around their campfire, and awful interested in what he's saying. I'm not sure just how we're gonna get in there and get those children out. I've heard stories of the Pawnee. They think nothing of killing their prisoners, rather than having them escape. Any suggestions?"

Colin looked down at the ground a moment, before speaking. "Any chance we could shoot 'em all, before they could get to the children?"

"I doubt it. It'd take a miracle," Johnny answered. "There's too many of 'em. Probably be a lot of them little ones die, if we try to rush 'em. What do you think, Patrick? Patrick?" Both Johnny and Colin turned, quickly scanning the darkness that surrounded them. Patrick was nowhere to be seen!

CHAPTER 26

"He's gonna get himself killed!" That whispered exclamation came from Colin, moments after he and Johnny had discovered his brother, Patrick's, absence. Colin was used to Patrick doing some mighty foolish things, ever since he was a child, but he had no doubt that whatever he was up to now would be the absolute winner. And he was certain Patrick would end up with a lot more than his usual broken leg, or arm. He looked at Johnny, a plaintive look upon his face, then turned and ran back to the crest of the hill. Johnny followed close behind. Just as he sprawled there, looking down on the Indian camp, his worst fears came to pass.

Suddenly, out of nowhere, came a scream from the hillside far below, followed by the Lord's Prayer, in Latin, being yelled as loud as was humanly possible! Not realizing it, Colin quickly crossed himself, drawing his gun, his heart hammering in his chest. Johnny lay beside him, his eyes and mouth opened wide in amazement. At that moment, he didn't know whether Patrick was the craziest fellow he had ever known, or the bravest. One thing he did know, though, was that it was going to take a miracle to keep him alive. His gun drawn, he watched, as the Pawnees jumped up from where they'd been sitting, their voices raised excitedly, as a figure dressed all in black—black hat and black cloak—came riding slowly toward them, screaming out words they had never heard before. The two Indians guarding the children ran over to the others, who pointed excitedly at the advancing figure. The Indian that Johnny believed to be their leader began to stride toward Patrick, his bow drawn, and arrow ready to fly! Colin aimed carefully, hoping as dark as it now was, his shot would hit its mark. He fired, and felt a sense of relief, as the Indian cried out, grabbed his arm, and dropped his bow. Johnny fired at another fellow who seemed to have the same intent of shooting Patrick, and watched as his bullet hit its mark, dropping the man, momentarily. As he got to his feet, another ran to his side to help him, never turning his head from sight of the figure in black still advancing toward them, his words piercing the air. Colin had to smile as he whispered to Johnny, "He's reciting the whole Mass, the darn fool." Then he added, "Let's get down there. If they don't run, he's gonna need us!" And with that, he slipped down the hill, and began to move toward level ground. As he had hoped, he saw some of the Indians turn and race toward their horses. Indians, he knew, were a highly superstitious people. He only hoped the rest would follow. As if in answer to a prayer, he watched in relief, as the others turned, crying out in anger and fear, as Patrick continued to approach their campfire. The shadows the light from the fire threw across Patrick seemed to cast his facial features in strange, dark hollows, giving him a decidedly frightening look. Colin and Johnny both would later agree to that. The only thing they never mentioned, later, was the beautiful, glowing aura that seemed to surround Patrick. From the moment he'd ridden into the Pawnee camp, an unmistakable "glow" of some sort had completely encircled him, giving off ghostly waves of the most beautiful silver and blue light.

In a flurry of activity and shouts, the Indians ran to their horses, mounted, and rode off into the night. Colin breathed a sigh of relief, hurrying over to where Patrick still sat on his horse. As he neared, he saw the shaft of an arrow protruding from his brother's cloak, saw the staring look from his brother's eyes. "Patty, where'd they get you? Of all the damn crazy stunts!" Patrick continued to stare straight ahead, not responding. His eyes had a glazed look to them, Colin noticed, and he feared the worst, as he laid his hand upon his brother's knee. "Patty..." he began, just as Patrick toppled from his horse, into his arms.

Johnny saw Patrick fall, as he rushed to the two girls, untying them and telling them they were safe, to not be afraid. He was, after all, also an Indian, though he doubted they could tell that in the dark. He still felt amazed by the crazy thing Colin's brother had done. And even more amazed that it had worked. He'd never seen anything like it. A whole war party of Pawnee, spooked by a single rider. And one who was shouting at them in Latin, no less. Shouting the Mass at them! It was truly amazing, he thought, smiling. But the outcome looked bad. He watched as Colin knelt, holding his brother to him within his arms, his head bowed. It looked like Colin was praying, though it was hard to tell, as dark as it was. Johnny shook his head, a feeling of sadness filling him. He turned, running over to where the boys were tied. If he knew the Pawnee, there was no time to waste getting out of there. If they got their courage up, or suddenly felt brave enough, they'd be back, and back with a vengeance! "Let's go, boys. Run over there by my friends. We've got to get out of here." He saw the frightened looks on their young faces, and knew what they were feeling, as they raced past him and over by Colin and Patrick. The older gal was holding the little girl in her arms, talking softly to comfort her. Johnny shouted to Colin that he'd go get the horses, and raced up the hill, hurrying as fast as he could. He wanted to stop and see how things were with Patrick, but had heard Colin say, 'Oh, Patty,' as he raced by, and by the tone of his voice he was certain Patrick had paid the ultimate price for his great act of bravery. He grabbed their horses' reins, bolting up onto Buck's back. There would be time for grieving, later. Right now, they had to get out of there as fast as they could. He galloped up to the little group, surprised to see smiles upon some of their faces. Even Colin was smiling, and he wondered what in the world he had to smile about. Then, to his great surprise, he saw Patrick standing beside Colin. He was examining a hole in his cloak, an arrow clasped in one hand, and a huge grin upon his face.

CHAPTER 27

Lydia was pleased as could be, when the cabin door flew open and Colin and Patrick hurried in, followed by two girls, three boys, and Johnny. She had been getting more and more anxious for their return, fearing something terrible had happened to them, as it grew later and later and they had still not returned. She wondered what all they'd gone through to rescue the children, but the men just smiled and told her they wished she had a pot of coffee, that they could all go for a cup. She saw the strange looks they kept giving Patrick, however, and how they'd pat him on the back every so often, smiling at him. It was apparent that something had happened, something they didn't care to talk about.

"We've got to get out of here, fast as we can," Colin said. "We'll head cross country. Don't want to have a second meetin' with those Pawnee, that's for sure."

"I'm hungry," the little girl said, surprising all of them.

Lydia walked over, taking her from the older girl, talking to her in a soft voice, "We ain't got any food, honey. I'm sorry. We're all hungry. Won't be long and we'll be home. There'll be lots of food to eat then, for all of us. What's your name?"

The little girl hesitated, her bottom lip quivering slightly. She looked back at the other girl before answering. "My name's Mary." "She's my sister," the older girl said, as she glanced at Johnny, noticing his darker tone of skin and hair. "I'm Juliana. Juliana Wright. They killed our family," she stammered, her eyes filling with tears. "They never had a chance. We tried to get away, but those murderin' savages were every-where. Everywhere!" She began to sob hysterically. Lydia put the little girl down, and then wrapped her arms around the older girl, crooning words of comfort. The boys sat nearby, watching, looks of sadness and fear upon their young faces. Colin shook his head, as he withdrew his gun from the holster, and began to reload it. Patrick walked over to the boys.

"Are you okay, son?" he asked the oldest boy. He had seen him gri-mace, and noticed a spreading dark stain on the front of his shirt.

"I got hit," he replied, lifting his shirt. The broken shaft of an arrow protruded from his chest. The boy looked down at it, then up at Patrick, a pleading look in his eyes. "I think I'm done for, Mister. Just wanted to see my sisters get safe," he said, and tears began to trickle down his cheeks. It was plain to see the terrible pain he was suffering.

Patrick reached out, taking hold of the boy's shoulders. "We'll keep them safe, son. Don't you worry," he replied, and he felt the boy start to sway, and caught him as he fell forward.

The older girl, Juliana, cried out as her brother fell, saying his name over and over, "Abraham! Abe!" Her little sister ran to her, clinging to her skirt, a look of fright, once more, upon her face.

Colin hurried to clear off the table; hoping one of them had the skill to remove the arrow. He wondered how the boy had been able to bear the pain of his wound as long as he had. "Lay him on the table," he ordered, and Johnny hurried to pick up the boy's feet and help Patrick lift him. Lydia grabbed the oil lamp out of their way, sending a beam of light to where they could better see the wound. Tearing open his shirt, they saw the shaft of the arrow protruding from the left side of his chest, about three inches down from his nipple. Only about an inch of the arrow's shaft remained, not enough to take hold of. Colin shook his head, looking up at Lydia, then Johnny. Lydia turned, walking over to where the two girls stood huddled, crying softly. She sat down on the lone chair, pulling the little girl up into her lap, cuddling her close. She knew what the outcome of such a wound would surely be, and her heart went out to the children. Holding the little one close to her, she began to rock her gently, stroking her hair, as she began to sing to her. It was a song Lilly used to sing to *her*, she remembered, when *she* was little and needed comforting. A song she had not even realized she still remem-bered. The little girl cuddled against her, burrowing her head into the curve of Lydia's shoulder, and wrapping her tiny arms around her neck. Lydia was surprised by this, and at the same time, pleased.

Johnny took his knife from the sheath at his side. "Any chance of cutting it out?" he asked Colin, keeping his voice low so as not to frightened the other children any worse than they already were. Colin shook his head. "Too late," he replied, glancing at Patrick.

Patrick walked to the other side of the table, taking the boy's hand, nearest him, within his own. He bowed his head at Colin's words, and began to pray, his voice the only sound heard above the children's crying. Colin motioned to Johnny, looking at the door, and the two men walked outside into the darkness of night.

"We'll have to bury him," Colin said, his voice sounding gruff.

"I'll look for a shovel," Johnny said, and he walked away, heading toward the rear of the cabin. Colin looked around, able to just make out a slight hill on the far side of the stream. There were no trees close to it, so he knew there'd be no roots to make digging hard. Besides, he thought, it'd be a nice spot for the boy to rest in. Abe, that was his name. Abraham Wright. I'll come back and put a cross on him with his name on it, someday, he thought, first chance I get. Just then Johnny approached, carrying a shovel, the handle broken off at about half its normal length. "This'll have to do," he said, and he handed it to Colin. Colin walked over to the spot beside the stream and began to dig. When he grew tired, Johnny took a turn at digging. Before long, they were satisfied they had dug a deep enough hole to keep any wild critters from disturbing the boy's final resting place, and then walked—weary of spirit—back into the cabin to get the body.

The boy lay on the table where they had last seen him, but now he was wrapped, as best as was possible, in the remains of Lydia's petticoat. The littlest girl, Mary, was sound asleep in her sister's arms over in a far corner, and the two younger boys were curled up in front of the fireplace, all huddled together. Patrick sat on the chair, reading his tattered Bible, a studious look upon his face. Lydia sat on the edge of the bed, stroking Michael's head, and whispering softly to him. He didn't respond, and Colin wondered if they'd be burying him, too, before their journey was over. A shudder passed through him at this thought, and he took a deep breath, wondering why bad things always seemed to happen to good people. Patrick looked up at him just then, seemingly studying him a long time, before he asked, "Is it time, my brother?"

Colin nodded in answer, noticing that Johnny was no longer in the room. "I'll get Johnny," he said, and walked to the door, wondering where he had gone.

Over by the grave, he saw him. Johnny stood looking up, his arms outstretched to the sky. Colin smiled, knowing his friend was praying. He paused a moment, wishing he could find it in his own heart to pray, but he felt too burdened with grief and hopelessness to do so. And besides, he thought, there's enough folks praying, as it is: both a priest and an Indian. That ought to be enough prayers to please the Lord. And with heavy heart, he walked back into the cabin and over to the table, bending to gather the young boy's body up into his arms. It's been a long day, he thought, and an even longer night. I'll do *my* praying later.

CHAPTER 28

The moon was just beginning to peek over the hills as the little group made their way to the gravesite beside the stream. Colin and Johnny had worked together, by light of the moon, burying the young boy. To be certain no wild animals disturbed his grave, they had gathered a bunch of stones and good-sized rocks, piling them on top of the dirt. Colin worked as if driven, anger tearing at him at the senselessness of the boy's death. Johnny, on the other hand, felt totally different. Yes, he was saddened by the boy's death.. But he felt, deep inside, that the boy's suffering was now over, and the joys of the other world that awaited him, were now his. When he'd finished laying the last rock upon the grave he took a small token he had found in the young man's pocket, and laid it among the rocks. He thought of the Indians, and how they put their dead to rest on a tall scaffold, standing their lance, shield, and other personal possessions that spoke of their achievements, beside them. He knew the boy was already in a better place, and unlike Colin, he did not feel anger, just sadness.

The burying done, the small group walked outside in the chill of the morning, the dew on the ground wetting the hems of the girls' dresses. Michael lay inside, his fever once again high. And the littlest girl and two young boys slept, curled on a ragged quilt in front of the fireplace. Patrick had fed the fire with armfuls of wood, making the cabin pleasantly warm, and now he stood before the grave, Bible in hand, ready to say words he hoped would bring a sense of peace to Abraham Wright's sister, and the others. Stillness prevailed, as they gathered there. Juliana Wright stood straight and tall, her head bowed, her eye's glistening from the tears that traced a path down her cheeks. Lydia stood close to her, shivering, one arm around her waist. The men, Johnny and Colin, stood on the other side of the grave, heads bowed. Patrick cleared his throat and began to pray.

As he finished, and those present turned to go back to the cabin, a man stepped out of the trees on the far side of the clearing. Two other men followed. Colin spotted them first, and quickly reached for his gun. Johnny did the same. The women stopped in their tracks, not knowing what to do.

"Hold it right there," ordered the man who approached them, his gun already drawn. Colin knew it was futile to make any moves. It would only put the others in danger, if he did so. He lowered his hand, stepping in front of Lydia and Juliana. Johnny stood where he was, his dark eyes scanning the woods for others.

"What do you want?" Colin asked. "Can't you see we're having a buryin' here?"

"I'm sheriff Townsend, from over in Chaska. I've been trailing you ever since you left there. Don't want no trouble, just turn over the fellow we come after, and we'll be on our way."

"And who would that be?" Colin asked, his heart pounding like a drum, as he tried to stall for time so he could think of a way to protect Michael.

"You know dog-gone well who I'm after," the sheriff replied. "The fellow that gal right there—the one in the torn dress—spirited away when the rope broke as we were hangin' him. Michael O'Leary."

At that moment, just as Lydia was about to run for the cabin, intent on getting her gun and doing whatever it took to protect Michael, she felt Patrick place a hand upon her shoulder. He stepped forward, smiling. "My good man," he said, his voice solemn, yet firm. "Has it escaped yer eyes that we're havin' a funeral, then?" He paused, his hand now upon his Bible, as he shook his head sadly. "We'll gladly let you have Michael O'Leary, if it's sure ya' are that ya' want 'em, as he is." Lydia gasped, and Colin wondered what in heaven's name his brother was up to. Johnny moved slowly, easing his gun from its holster, Colin's position in front of him blocking his movements from view.

The sheriff looked at Patrick, his head cocked to one side, not sure if he could trust this man in the long black cloak. "I want him, all right.

And who are you?" he asked, still keeping his gun trained on them.

"I'm Father Patrick, my good man, a travelin' priest of the Mother Church. Met up with these folks on me way t' yer fine town of Chaska, Sir, where I'm t' look into the possibility of a grand church being built there, in the near future."

The man looked not only surprised, but also confused by Patrick's words. "That's news to me," he said, looking from Patrick to Colin and then to Lydia. "All I want is to git the fella who killed my friend, then I'll be on my way. Where is he?"

Patrick bent his head, opening his tattered Bible. Then he spoke, "'Tis him that I buried, me good man. For the rope that hung him, ya' see, brought him t' justice, after all, infectin' the wound on his neck and killin' him. His little wife here, asked me t' say a few words o'er him, to see him int' the great beyond in proper fashion. 'Tis him, ya' see, buried in yon grave. I give ya' me word."

The sheriff stood there, listening, not at all sure if the priest could be trusted, or not. He had red hair, the same color as Michael O'Leary had, and was obviously Irish. It was obvious, too, that he'd just done a burying, and that saloon gal was grieving. He hesitated, his thoughts abounding. It was also true that Chaska could use a church. There wasn't no denying that. And priests were a different cut of cloth, he'd heard. A preacher might lie to you, but a priest, well, that was a different matter, entirely. They *had to* tell the truth, from what he'd heard, or suffer dire consequences. He rubbed his chin, studying the man who stood before him, his black cloak dwarfing him. He heard the men behind him stir, and knew they were waiting for him to make up his mind. After another lengthy hesitation, he holstered his gun, spitting off into the brush before he spoke. "Alright, Father. I'm taking you at your word. When you get to town, stop at the jail. I'll buy you a cup of coffee."

"That I will, good sir, that I will," Patrick replied, and he smiled broadly at the sheriff, knowing it'd be a cold, cold day before he stepped foot in Chaska. He turned, winking at Lydia, while putting his arm around her to supposedly comfort her, glancing at Colin as he did so. Colin kept a serious expression upon his face for the sheriff's benefit, though he had a hard time doing so, as he couldn't help having noticed the small gun that lay ready for use—if the need had arisen—in the hollowed out pages of Father Patrick's old Bible.

CHAPTER 29

Lilly Hart woke early, as was a habit of hers. Most mornings she was up long before her husband, Jonas. Even long before their rooster crowed. She liked having some time to make herself presentable, and to prepare a hearty breakfast, and have it on the table when Jonas came downstairs. They had gotten into a pattern that worked well for them, over the years, since they'd married.

It had been such a relief to her, when Jonas had gotten his appetite back, long after he'd returned from the war. He'd looked,so pitifully thin the day he returned. She still remembered how shocked she had been at the sight of him that day, seeing not only the horrible thinness, but the look of sorrow that shown in his eyes. She still shuddered, when she thought of his wounds: each step he took leaving a bloody footprint. She hadn't been able to believe her eyes! She hadn't even recognized him till he reached the bottom step of their front porch. She thought it was a stranger coming to ask for a bite of food, or to rest before journeying on to his home. It was only when he smiled and called out her name, that she knew he was her beloved husband.

His mother had been sitting in the parlor when Lilly ran to him, helping him up the steps and into the house. She had cried out when she realized it was her son, pressing a hand to her throat, at the sight of him. Whimpering sounds were the only greeting she gave him. Then she slumped to one side, the shock and grief of seeing him in such terrible condition, too much for her to bear. Lilly tried to rouse her, but had to summon their hired man to help get her up the stairs, and to her bed. Then she rushed back downstairs, doing what she could to get Jonas settled as comfortably as possible. All the while, silently praying she'd have the strength necessary to tend him, without swooning at sight of his wounds. She'd seen how badly he hobbled as he walked, the blood in each footprint, as he took a step. It tore at her heart, knowing how strong and healthy he'd been when he left to go to war.

Once she'd seen to his mother—gotten her settled in her bed, and sent the hired man for Doc Valentine—she rushed downstairs to the kitchen, heating a large kettle of water, while gathering all the clean, soft cloths she could find. Then she carried a basin and the cloths to where Jonas sat, his head laying back against the chair, eyes closed. Garnering every ounce of fortitude, she began to gently unwrap the filthy strips of bloody cloth from around his feet. The cloth stuck to his feet in some places, as if it were his skin, and he grimaced as she did her best to pull it loose, knowing it caused him pain. At one point, the fabric was so rotten that it disintegrated as she attempted to pull it loose, leaving the rest of the fabric not only stuck to the sole of his foot, but embedded into the wound there. Lilly had all she could do not to cry out, as she worked the rotted fabric from his flesh, as fresh blood dripped onto the floor and covered her fingers as she worked. She had never seen Jonas cry before, and it broke her heart as she saw him bite his lip, tears tracing a path to the thick beard he now sported. She stopped what she was doing, seeing the pain it caused him, and lifted his feet, one after the other, into the large basin. Testing the water first, to make certain it wasn't too hot; she knew the soaking would loosen the fabric from his skin. Her stomach rolled at sight of the bloody water, filthy pieces of fabric and residue floating to the top, but she knew the dangers of infection. She knew she had to do all she could, or he'd surely lose his feet to gangrene. And if that didn't kill him, she knew it would kill his spirit.

On she worked, choking back tears, sickened at the sight of his wounds. How he had managed to walk, at all, was far beyond all her imagining. He had lost so much weight that his ribs showed through the tattered shirt he wore, and his cheekbones now protruded above great hollow areas. His eyes were darkly rimmed and sunken. Dearest God, she thought, if this was what the men who had *won* the war looked like, in what condition were those who had lost? How in heaven's name did they survive their wounds, and get back to their homes? It wasn't till much later, when Jonas could finally speak of such things, that she learned how many had *not* survived. On both sides of the war there had been unimaginable numbers of wounded and dead soldiers: husbands, fathers, and sons. The fields had been soaked with their blood, he told her, the water running red with it. She shuddered at the thought, willing her hands to stop shaking, so very thankful that her man had not been among them.

At last, his feet were clear of all remnants of the filthy strips of fabric he had bound them with, hoping to protect them, his shoes having long before worn out. Lilly lifted his feet from the dirty water, wrapping clean cloths around them, then carried the basin of bloody water to the back porch. She poured it out upon the dirt beside the porch, watching as it soaked into the earth. The words "ashes to ashes and dust to dust" came to mind as she stood there, and only then did she let herself cry. Hiding her face in the folds of her apron, she let all the grief and sadness she felt flow free, not wanting to let Jonas hear, and realize how shocked and upset she had been by seeing the condition he was in. Surely, she thought, there must be some other way for men to solve their differences of opinion, besides war. There *had to be* some way for all men to live together in brotherly love, as God intended. She could not understand how war, and all the tragedy it wrought—brothers fighting brothers, fathers fighting sons, man fighting man—could *ever* lead to peace and Godliness. True, she didn't believe a man—no matter his color—deserved to be owned by another. But what did it gain a man in God's eyes, she wondered, to kill another who differed from him because of his beliefs? A woman, she thought, would have found a more sensible way to deal with such things. Women would have met peaceably, letting their feelings of kindness and caring prevail, talking out their differences until an agreeable conclusion could be found. She could not understand the willingness of men to fight and kill. It was as if they could not look ahead to the possible consequences of such actions: the wounds, the deaths, the grief and sorrows that would occur, because of them. A woman was so different. She spent all her time, it seemed, praying for those she loved, taking care of them as best she could, by cooking, cleaning, and nourishing their bodies, and their souls. Wars seemed only to destroy. A woman, perhaps, would have found a much different solution. For though there were men who enjoyed the power war gave them, Lilly was certain there had to be a better way.

In time, with the help of all the healing salves she and Doc Valentine knew of, and the wooden crutches Eli had fashioned for him, Jonas' feet slowly began to heal. He became able, once more, to walk from their bedroom to the kitchen without help, and then to the front porch, where he often sat for long periods of time, staring out across the fields, giving the impression that he longed to be out in them—planting and harvesting—as the seasons changed. In truth, he stared across his fields, seeing only memories of the death and destruction he had witnessed every day of the war. Scenes that would remain forever etched upon his mind—too horrific to forget—kept running through his mind till he thought he'd go mad. And sometimes as he sat there staring silently into the past, a trail of tears would trace a path down his cheeks, soaking an area of his shirt, though he was unaware of it. He felt broken. He felt as broken in both body and spirit, as a man could feel. Even Lilly's tender care seemed unable to mend the feelings he felt, as though his soul—like his feet—had bled dry. Day after day he sat there, grieving for losses incomprehensible to those who came by, shaking his hand and patting him on the back, congratulating him on a job well done for the part he'd played in the winning of the war. He'd stare at them as they talked, seeing only those who had died, hearing their cries, their screams tearing at him from beyond the grave, and he knew—without doubt—that there had been no winning, and no winners.

CHAPTER 30

Jonas Hart bent his back to the plow, tilling the ground in readiness for the crops he would plant in the spring. He felt pleased at the harvest the good Lord had seen fit to bless him with. Every crop had come in abundantly, the wagons full to overflowing from all his fields. He thanked God each morning, as he knelt to pray, for these great blessings: for the good life he now had, for his dear wife, and fine son. Without Eli's help, he doubted the farm would have survived during his absence, when he was far away, fighting in a war he had no heart for. "I'm a simple farmer, Lord," he used to pray as he sat in the camps, so far from all he loved. God seemed not to hear, he had often remembered thinking. Perhaps, he thought back then, God had too many *other* prayers to answer, too many others who needed Him. Or, perhaps God did not answer the prayers of those who fought and killed. Maybe God, too, had a limit to the amount of killing and carnage He could stand. "I'm home now, must remember that," he said, whispering the words so only he heard. His questioning, however, seemed never ending, no matter what he was doing. He wiped his brow, stopping to look around him. No, he thought, I'm wrong. God had to have heard my prayers. I still have my farm and my family. How many others do not? How many others never lived to see their loved ones and their homes? I came home feeling broken in body and spirit, but though it took a lot of time, years, haven't I healed? I can walk the width and breadth of my land now, can hold my wife at night in our bed, can work beside my son, and take pride in the good man he has become. I am truly blessed. Oh, yes, I am truly blessed.

It was only in his dreams that he still heard the cries of the men and boys who had fought at his side. Only in his dreams that he pressed a hand over his mouth to stop his own screams. Nothing, however, stopped the memories. Ten years later, and still the memories haunted him.

Lilly rubbed the back of her hand across her forehead, looking out from the porch across the field to where Jonas and Eli worked. She smiled as she saw them there, bending to the earth, working the soil. Every day she knelt by the side of their bed before Jonas wakened, thanking God for bringing him home to her and their boy. He was home and safe, was healthy and hearty now. She was so very thankful for these blessings. Only at night did she realize how dearly he still suffered, as he rolled and tossed, sometimes crying out, sometimes jerking awake and calling the name of one of those who had fought at his side.

She watched him work, remembering back to the day she'd raced to his farm to tell him she loved him. Remembered how her horse had shied at a rabbit, causing her to fall, knocking the breath out of her. Jonas had been standing on his front porch when he saw her fall, and had run to her, picking her up in his strong arms. He'd held her so close as he ran that she had been unable to get her breath, and struggled to do so. It was then that he had kept repeating "Oh, my sweet, Lilly. Don't die, Lilly, I love you." Once inside his house, however, he'd said nothing, as she finally caught her breath, assuring him she was all right, asking him if he'd meant what he had said. For a long time he stood at the window not answering, she remembered, and she remembered, too, how sad it had made her feel. She had loved him ever since the first day he had come to her father's farm, way back when she was a mere girl. She stood on the porch, thinking back to that day, a smile upon her lips, as her thoughts continued. Finally, after a long silence, he had begun to speak, telling her he wasn't worthy of her, that he, too, had loved her since as long as he could remember, but he had so little to offer. She'd stopped him then, putting a hand across his lips, telling him that all she wanted was him, telling him that she loved him. He'd lifted her up into his arms then, twirling them around and around, the realization of their love for each other bringing both of them great joy. She smiled, waving in his direction, her thoughts continuing...

She remembered how gentle he'd been when they made love, and how sad she'd felt, when, again and again, she'd prayed to give him a child, and it had not happened. Then her sister, Lydia, had come to her with the startling news that she was with child, and it wasn't her husband's baby, and would she and Jonas take the child and raise him as their own? She'd agreed, immediately, knowing Lydia wasn't capable of raising a little one, wasn't settled enough, or responsible enough. To her surprise and immense pleasure, Jonas had agreed, also, with no hesitation whatsoever, saying they had more than enough love to share with a little one. Oh, yes, she thought, he was such a kind and caring man. A gentle soul, this husband of hers. A humble man. A man who had the strength of ten men, and a heart just as big.

She walked back into the house, taking loaves of bread from the oven, the aroma of the fresh bread filling the kitchen. She thought of what a good father Jonas had been. How he'd held the tiny baby boy to him, his large hands nearly hiding the infant from view. There were tears in his eyes, she remembered, as he held him, telling her he'd like him to be called Elijah, that it had been his father's name, and was a proper name for a farmer's son. A biblical name that would hold the boy in good stead all of his life. She'd agreed, happily. As Eli grew, she'd seen how Jonas taught the boy, never raising a hand to him, or even his voice. Explaining with simple clarity how things were supposed to be, and later, the workings of the farm. He taught the boy to sow and reap, explaining how to plant by the cycles of the moon. Taught him all the things his own father had taught him, and more. But the most important thing he taught him was how to be a good man. How to follow the teachings of the good Lord and to always be a Godly man. He taught him to be gentle and kind, fair and honest, to be thankful for all his blessings, and to stand strong in the face of adversity. He taught him to never give up, to listen to his heart, knowing God often spoke to a man through his heart. Taught him to take time not only to pray, but also to listen. He explained to Eli that God often spoke from within a man's heart and soul, but you had to be still, and listen to hear, letting your faith guide you. And not only did he tell him these things, but he taught him by his own example, through the tender love he showed the boy. No man could have been a better father, Lilly knew that for a fact, and no father could have loved his boy more.

She stirred the pot of vegetable soup as it boiled upon the stove, her thoughts continuing. She thought back to the day she had realized she was with child, back in '55. She laughed softly as she remembered how Jonas had looked when she told him. He'd picked her up in his arms, hugging her to him, his eyes filled with a joy like none she'd ever seen before! He told her he wanted her to rest, to take it easy, to not lift or bend. He'd do all the chores he told her, and he sat down in the rocker on their porch, still holding her within his arms. He told her how proud he was of her then, rubbing his hand gently across the folds of the fabric covering her stomach, telling her he'd prayed so hard for another son. She'd laughed at him, asking what she was supposed to do if it was a girl she was carrying. He smiled at her, saying the same thing he'd said when Lydia had come to them, telling them she was with child, and would they please take her baby when he or she was born: "we've got plenty of love to go around, my sweet Lilly. There's always love enough for one more." They'd sat there a long time, she remembered, content in the knowledge that there'd soon be a child of their own.

Lilly got down the dishes from the cupboard, setting three places at the table. There'd been no child born, however. Not then, or ever since. God had given them a wonderful son in Eli. But Lilly had been unable to give Jonas a child of their own. It pained her still. The day she lost the baby still haunted her, too, causing her great sadness. She'd been coming down the stairs, carrying a basin of water that she'd used to bathe Jonas' mother, who could no longer get out of bed because of a fall she'd suffered the winter before. Lilly no longer remembered if she'd slipped on some water on the step, or if she'd caught her foot in the hem of her petticoat. But suddenly, she started to fall, dropping the basin and reaching out to catch herself!

But it was too late, and she had tumbled head over heels, all the way down the stairs. She laid there at the bottom of the steps, feeling the warmth spread around her legs, drenching the fabric of her skirt, and knew even before Jonas found her there, that she'd lost their baby. For days she'd been inconsolable, laying abed, her heart broken by the loss she had suffered. Jonas hovered over her, trying to comfort her, fixing meals she refused to eat, telling her he loved her, that it'd be all right, that there'd be other children. But there never was, and it grieved her.

She took a deep breath, brushing an unruly strand of hair back from her face. Walking back out onto the porch, she felt the chill in the air, knowing she looked forward to the long days of winter ahead, when she'd be inside more, working on a quilt for their bed, and another for Eli's bed. She waved at her husband, and then at Eli, motioning to them that it was time to eat, and watched as they returned her wave, a big smile upon both their faces. The sight of them, as they strode toward the house, filled her with a sense of contentment. She didn't understand why the good Lord had not seen fit to let them have any children of their own, but at least He had blessed them with Eli. How fortunate they were for that. And how like his father he was, she thought, as they walked side-by-side toward her. How like his father he was!

CHAPTER 31

The Blossom sisters, Annathea and Dorothea, were busy as two bees! Between the scrubbing of the walls and floors in Ophelia's big house, and the new curtains to be made for the upstairs windows, it seemed there just weren't enough hours in each day.

Annathea—or Aunt Hilda, as she preferred to be called—chose a small room off what used to be the downstairs parlor, as her own room. There was barely enough room in it for a small bed, an oak ladies desk and matching chair, and her small trunk in which she kept her personal belongings.

Dorothea—called Auntie Belle by almost everyone—took an even smaller room toward the back of the house. At first, Ophelia tried to talk her out of it, saying it was much too small. But Auntie Belle insisted, explaining that it wasn't the size of the room that had drawn her to it, it was the tall window that graced its end wall. From the window, she could observe anyone coming to the house, or leaving it, by way of the back door. Ophelia asked why that pleased her so, to which she held a plump hand over her mouth, and giggled like a young girl before she replied. "Why my darling, Ophelia," she said, at last, her eyes twinkling. "It's the flower garden. I have such a nice view. Can't you just imagine how lovely it'll be, come spring? The scent of those flowers will fill this little room so sweetly."

Ophelia, to be truthful, had not even noticed the view from that window. She had seen the flowers that surrounded the palatial front and side veranda, many times picking a bouquet for the hall table on some special occasion. But in all her walks throughout the spacious home, she had never lifted the curtain in the room that appealed to Auntie Belle, nor enjoyed the lovely array of flowers that grew just outside of it. She bent her head, noticing the many brown stalks and stems, the many bushy mounds, and the wrought iron fence—waist-high—that leaned this way and that, its rails beset with winding vines and other imposing vegetation. "Oh, Auntie Belle," she said, laughing happily, "No wonder you're so taken with this room. I'm certain it will be just beautiful when spring comes."

Auntie Belle smiled happily, and quickly began arranging her few treasures upon the small table beside her bed. She hummed as she did so, carefully laying each thing on a scarf, careful not to break anything. There was, of course, her Bible. Then a book of poetry, a small dish with purple flowers painted along its edge, a gold lady's watch, and a tintype photograph of a dark-haired young man sitting in a straight back chair, with hat in hand, a sad expression upon his face.

"Who is that, Auntie Belle?" Ophelia asked, curious as to the identity of the young man.

For only a moment, Dorothea hesitated, looking at Ophelia and then back at the tintype. "Just a fellow who used to live in our town, years back, that's all." She picked up the tintype, running her finger across it, then opened a drawer and laid it inside.

"Oh, Aunt, why don't you leave it out? If I embarrassed you with my curiosity, I'm sorry," Ophelia said, regretting she'd asked.

"No, it's best it's put away," she replied, the smile upon her face no longer present. "I shouldn't have set it out in the first place," she said, closing the drawer carefully. "You go on now, child, so I can get my things hung in the wardrobe. I'll have to hurry. Annathea will be in a snit if she has to come and fetch me. She wants the large room upstairs all finished by this afternoon. Go. Go on now." She shooed Ophelia from the room, shutting the door quietly behind her. Then she walked over to the small table, opened the little drawer and took out the tintype, once more. She lifted it to her breast, held it there against her heart for a long time, and then laid it facedown, back inside the drawer. Taking a deep breath, she shut the drawer, whispering to herself as she did so, "Silly old woman. You should have known he wouldn't return." Then she hurried from the room, not looking back.

"Well, where have you been?" Annathea Blossom greeted her sister, bustling about as she spoke. "I can't do *everything* by myself, Dorothea. I hope you've gotten all your things put away, though why you'd want that awful room is beyond me." She carried a large bucket over to the far side of the room, her impatience with her sister still her topic of conversation. "I don't know when this room was gone over last. It seems you'd want to help, seeing the work we have ahead of us. Twit's ever to get done, that is. I can't do it all alone, you know, Dorothea, though it's apparent that you keep forgetting that." Auntie Belle picked up a clean rag from a pile of cloths, doing the best she could to shut her sister's words from her mind. It was no use, she found, and she closed her eyes, taking a deep breath. "Are you going to stand there all day, Dorothea?" Annathea asked, looking over at her, and shaking her head, disgustedly.

Suddenly, out the large front window, Dorothea saw Cal Dunnevey walking toward the house, his cane guiding his slow progress. "No, I am *not* going to stand here all day, sister! I'm going outside to greet Mr. Dunnevey. I'll be in to help you, *later*." And with that, she turned and hurried from the room before her very surprised sister could reply.

"Well, I declare..." Annathea said. She could not believe the change that had come over her sister since they'd moved to Hastings. She certainly seemed to no longer be her sweetly docile self.

"Hello, Mr. Dunnevey," Auntie Belle called out as both she and Cal reached the porch at the same time. "Isn't it a fine day?" she asked, and he could picture her smile steadfast upon her face.

"That it is, Miss Belle," he replied, and she giggled with delight to know that already he could tell who she was, simply by her voice alone.

"Have you come to see Ophelia? She's in the kitchen, I believe," she said, reaching out to take his arm as he reached the top step.

Cal smiled, not minding at all that she held his arm and gently guided him along beside her, as they walked toward the kitchen. "How's the cleaning coming along?" he asked, aware of the strong scent of lye soap in the air.

Auntie Belle leaned her head toward him, whispering gaily in the direction of his ear, "Annathea isn't too pleased with me, I'm afraid. I saw you coming, and left her to do the scrubbing by herself."

Cal laughed aloud, certain of the displeasure her sister would be feeling. Auntie Belle squeezed his arm, shushing him, as they passed the room where her sister knelt, scrubbing and fuming.

As they entered the kitchen, Ophelia looked up in surprise, greeting Cal. "Why what a nice surprise. Hello, Cal. What brings you out today? We can use another hand or two with the cleaning, if you're interested?"

Cal smiled. "Well, I have a much better idea, Ophelia, if *you're* interested," he said, looking in the direction she had spoken from.

"Oh, and what would that be?" she asked, straightening her apron, then running a hand through her hair, though she knew—being blind—he could not see how disheveled she looked.

"I thought perhaps you might like to accompany me over to the boardinghouse for a cup of tea," he said, and he felt Auntie Belle squeeze his arm, and knew she was smiling.

"Oh, Cal, I have so much to do," Ophelia said. "If I don't keep at it, I don't know how we'll ever get it done in time for Doctor Valentine's inspection tour, later this week. He's bringing a friend of his, another doctor from back east, no less, to see the house..." she paused a moment, then corrected herself, "the *hospital*, I mean."

He felt disappointed, realizing she was probably right. She had more than enough to do, and sadly, he could not help. He sighed, looking down toward the floor, wondering if there was anything he *could* do to help. He could think of nothing. "Well, I guess you're right," he said at last, and he started to turn away. Immediately, Auntie Belle nudged him, not loosening her grip on his arm. He stopped, wondering what it was she wanted.

"Ophelia, it isn't often a handsome man comes a courtin'," Auntie Belle said, "I certainly wouldn't pass up the opportunity to tarry awhile over tea, if a fellow as handsome as Mr. Dunnevey was so kind as to come all the way over here and ask *me* to tea. There'll be plenty of hours left in the day to finish your cleaning, I'm sure."

Ophelia looked at her aunt, shaking her head and smiling. It was more than evident that her aunt was a romantic at heart, and as she thought this, she remembered the tintype photo of the young man she had seen in her aunt's room. She took a deep breath, seeing that both Cal and Auntie Belle stood looking at her, expectantly.

"Oh, alright. You've convinced me, Aunt. I have to go get presentable, though, Cal. Are you in a hurry?"

"Not at all," Cal answered. "But I must say you look just fine to me, Ophelia," and she smiled at his words, glad to hear he was in such good spirits.

"I'll leave you two alone, then," she said, hurrying from the room and up the back stairs—the servants' stairway—to her room above. She had chosen the largest of the servants' rooms. Like her Auntie Belle, the one with the window that looked out upon the garden below. She had decided it was the room for her because all morning long the sun shone into it, warming it, and filling it with golden light. It cheered her immensely to lie abed early each morning, listening to the rooster crow, just as the sunlight began to stream through the window. She found she was smiling, as she pulled her apron off, and quickly filled her washbasin with water so she could wash her face. She was happy that Auntie Belle had convinced her to go with Cal. She's right, Ophelia thought. How often *did* a handsome man come courting? She thought then of Johnathon. It had been a long, long time since she'd thought of him, of his many kindnesses, and how caring he'd always been to her. Even the house—lovely as it was—would never have been hers under normal conditions. She would never have married him, she knew, even though she had always cared for him. No, I never would have married him, she thought, not after what Pa did to Lea. She shuddered, as she pulled on a clean blouse, and stepped carefully into her skirt. I never would have married *anyone*, till now, till Cal. She straightened her skirt, her thoughts far from being still. Why did it have to be the way it was, she wondered? Why did Cal still have to love Lea, even though she'd left him how long ago? Ophelia counted to herself; eighteen, nineteen, twenty. It was twenty years since Lea had left. Twenty *years*, and Cal still loved her. Ophelia looked down at her hands, noticing the many wrinkles upon them. "Twenty years, and I've loved him nearly the same length of time," she said, softly, "and he doesn't even know it."

CHAPTER 32

The hospital doors were opened, much to everyone's surprise, the following week. Not all of the upstairs rooms were finished, of course—nor were they needed, as yet—but the whole downstairs was set up and ready for use. Doc Valentine had instructed Ophelia on how to arrange and set up the brightest room for his operating room, the two large windows letting in the greatest amount of bright sunshine. In the room that used to be the parlor, he had his desk and file cabinet, his bookcase filled with a great variety of medical books and journals, and of course, a large glass-front cabinet that displayed all the many bottles of medicines, available at once, if needed. Many of the medical books, worn journals, and even some of the older bottles of elixirs were leftovers from Doc Pearson, Hastings original—and previous—doctor.

In the vestibule and main hallway, though they were not very well-lit areas, Doc's wife, Judith, had hung many of his paintings. Most had been done when they had first come to Hastings. The larger and much better paintings, she hung here and there throughout the many downstairs rooms, knowing their lovely colors and peaceful scenes would be a comfort to all who saw them. As she hung them, making certain that they hung straight, she felt secretly pleased to no longer have so many of them at their own home. It had become a joke between her and her husband that they would soon have to move if he painted many more large canvases, their house already brimming with so many. She had to smile as she thought this, wondering if now, at last, she could use the back storage room in their home for some use of her own. A sewing room, perhaps, she thought, or a quilting room. There had never been enough room for her to set up the large loom she'd brought west. She hoped to remedy that, as soon as he agreed. And he would agree, she had no doubt of that, because he had always been most agreeable to any of her whims and wishes. He was a caring man, extremely giving, and not only a fine husband, but also a man who appreciated the beauty of his surroundings, and the beauty of a man's—or woman's—inner nature. He had little patience with those who were surly and short-tempered. 'Life is too beautiful,' he'd often told her, 'to go through it in that manner.'

Judith carried the last picture through the long hallway to the study. It was a painting he had finished, not that long before, of the western perimeter of the prairie. It consisted of a sky of the prettiest blue—a blending of many hues—above a large lake that reflected those many shades of blue in crystalline clouds. And beside the lake, a dark forest before which black-robed Jesuits stood talking to men in curled wigs, and breeches that appeared velvet above their lace and ruffled coats. Beside them, men in buckskin and once brightly colored capotes, guns in hand, and canoes piled high with pelts drawn up to the nearby shore, parlayed with the others. And in the dark shelter of the forest Indians in sparse attire watched, their faces mirroring their amazement and concern at seeing these overly dressed strangers there. Doc had titled this particular work, "Hidden Observers." Judith had never cared for this particular painting. To her it said nothing, even though he had told her that he had come upon subjects, such as these, one day as he strolled through the woods along the lake. At first, he had not noticed the Indians. He'd been so intent upon his art that it was not until one of the men in buckskin began to point toward the Indians, grabbing up his gun and pointing it in their direction, that he became aware of them. They did not seem a threat, though those in buckskin—trappers, he assumed—began to act as though they were, indeed. He quickly began to sketch the Indians, as they looked on, the feathers in their dark hair and their equally dark skin giving them a hauntingly beautiful image against the vibrantly shaded greens and golds of their surroundings. Each Indian looked most elegant and regal, he had thought, as he painted their expressions on the canvas before him. The white men, on the other hand, with their threatening stance, glaring looks, and display of unease, seemed the lesser of the two: frightened and weaker, by comparison. In the painting, Doc had captured all these things, priding himself on doing so.

Judith hung the painting in the study, on the wall across from the many ceiling-high shelves of books. She hoped the many colorfully bound books would draw everyone's attention away from the painting, and direct their interest to the more worthy books. As she stepped back, making certain the painting hung straight, she wiped her hands on her apron, shaking her head at the fact that this was her husband's favorite work. Then she turned and left the room.

She had no idea that three years later, his paintings of life in Hastings would not only draw the attention of people from all over their area, but the painting that he'd titled "Hidden Observers"—the large painting she'd thought so unattractive—would be purchased for more money than she could ever have imagined, by a prominent lawyer from Dodge City, who just happened to see it during his visit to Hastings and brief tour of the hospital. He immediately purchased it for an old acquaintance of his who greatly enjoyed—and had recently begun to collect—paintings of the Old West. An acquaintance who just happened to be a well-known sheriff by the name of Masterson.

CHAPTER 33

It has been said that after the rain, the sun always shines. It was a favorite saying of Auntie Belle, at least, and had been, ever since she was a young girl. But she was beginning to have some doubts about it. The hospital had not been open a full week, when they had their first seriously ill patient. Oh, how it grieved her to see him, as he was carried in, his face flushed with fever, the wound on his neck so infected that it was all she could do to carry in the medicines the doctor required, her stomach threatening to reel at the stench. And the poor mother! Why the poor woman was in such pitiful shape herself, with her hands all bent and twisted. Auntie Belle felt even sorrier for the mother, Mrs. O'Leary, a woman about her own age.

It was late in the day, the day they arrived at the hospital. A tall, good-looking fellow came hurrying in first, asking Ophelia if doc was in. He said his brother, Michael, had been hurt—not really explaining just how—though it didn't take a lick of sense to guess. One look at the rope burns around that young man's throat, and the hideous wound on the side of his neck, and...well...we all had our opinions. And another brother, a priest, no less, rode in with them. Oh, he was a feisty one, he was! He looked me right in the eye, smiling the nicest smile, when I moved the small Bible he had laid on the table by the door. Now I'm not one to gossip, and some things are best left unmentioned, to be sure, but I saw what was in that good book, and I'm not meaning the words to live by. No, Sir! I just saw what I saw, quite by accident, and then I saw that little glint in his eye when he realized what I'd seen, and...well... he was lucky it'd been *me* who'd seen it, and not Aunt Hilda, that's all I can say. Why, she would have thrown some kind of fit, for sure! She didn't hold much faith in them Catholics, as it was, and to find one of them priests, no matter how cute he was, or how nice his smile, having such as he did in his Holy book, why she would have exposed his little secret, sure as can be! But I'm the one who moved his Bible, so the secret was safe with me, and I could tell from that look on his face that he knew it. Cute fella, he was, even in that black cloak that looked way too big for him. Anyway, with him was a young woman, more pitiful looking than the patient's mother, thin—oh, Lord was she thin—and looking like she was about to drop where she stood. Tired, she was, I guess, or just worn out from worrying about the fella with the wound on his neck. She was his wife. Lydia, I heard them call her. Lydia O'Leary. I snuck a couple looks at her, guessing that once she'd been right pretty. Her high cheekbones made me think that, and the way she looked when she bent close to the patient, smiling as she whispered to him that she loved him, and needed him to get well. That their boy needed him, too.

Anyway, we got our patient, Michael, all settled in, and Aunt Hilda rushed on over to fetch the doc. I hurried to the kitchen after getting the older woman—the one with those crippled hands—all nice and comfy in the sitting room closest to the room where her son lay. Well, it was then I got my first glance at an Indian! Oh, he wasn't wearing feathers in his hair, and painted up with war paint, like I'd heard some of them were. No, he was a young lad; about twenty or twenty-five, I'd say, a nice looking young man, to be sure, with them dark, liquid-looking eyes, and the prettiest dark hair. Ophelia told me later that his folks were white, or at least the mother was, and the father had been part Indian, though he hadn't known it till something happened—some "miracle"—she said, and well...I don't know the whole story, but sure intend to ask her, later. Anyway, his name was Johnny. Johnny Gentry. I thought that was a strange name for someone who looked more Indian than white, but there's a lot of strange things in this old world of ours. Oh, a whole lot of strange things, to be sure!

Doc Valentine came rushin' in about then, with Aunt Hilda not far behind, and I saw the concern on his face. He's a real good doctor, from what I've seen. Not hoity-toity, like some of them doctors that came out from the East, but a real down-to-earth fella, who takes his doctoring seriously. And doctoring wasn't even his idea, so I've heard. Seems he had his heart set on being an artist, ever since he was a mere sprout of a lad. But his father didn't think that was a proper choice of occupation, it seems, and so he became a doctor. I'd have to say that, all things considered, he did a fine job of it, too. Don't know as I would have gone against my own grain, if I'd been him, and put my heart into it like he'd done. Even if it *was* my father who'd insisted upon it. Auntie Belle giggled as she thought this. Good thing I wasn't a boy, after all, she thought. A girl wasn't expected to get out there in the world and have some profession. Perish the thought! It was more important that she learn to cook and sew, and do things like that. Things that were necessary to keep the family in good stead.

Thinking these things led to other thoughts. She thought of the family she'd hoped to have, once upon a time, so long ago. In her mind she saw the young man in the tintype that was hidden in the small drawer of her bedside table. She closed her eyes, more able to see his features from memory. Sal. That's what she'd always called him. He'd made her promise not to call him that when others were around. He said it sounded like a girl's name. And it did, but still she called him that. Sal, short for Salvanus. She smiled as she thought of it. It had been his father's name, too. Italian, she thought it was. An elegant name, she'd always thought. She'd met him when his family moved to their area, had been taken with him the very first day she'd seen him. And he had noticed her, too. Followed her home often from school, all the way to the gate leading to her house, even though she was certain he must have had chores to do at his own home. Annathea had teased her because of it, laughing at her. She said she sure wouldn't want one of them there I-talian boys to come courtin' her. Auntie Belle shook her head at these memories, heating more hot water on the stove—another large kettle for the doc, and a small pot of tea so that poor Mrs. O'Leary could have another cup, if she wished. Yes, Annathea had teased her, all right. And the very next day she had dilly-dallied around on the way home from school, flirting with Sal and getting his attention turned toward her. She laughed at things he said, and asked him if he wanted to carry *her* books. Oh, yes, she was much prettier than me, Auntie Belle thought, with her blonde ringlets that shined in the sun like gold, and her cheeks, all rosy and flushed from the flirtin' she was doing. She was smart, too. Not afraid to speak her mind, or go after what she wanted, her being so perfect and all. Auntie Belle hung her head at these thoughts, remembering how sad she had been, back then, as Sal soon started to follow her sister and carry her books, and began to ignore her. And why wouldn't he have paid her more attention, she thought? Hilda had always been the pretty one, the one who was smartest, could run the fastest, could dance, and sing, and even bake the best pies. I, on the other hand, was always the slowest. I stumbled over my own two feet, like they were made of rock when I danced, and my pies tasted like old shoes. She smiled sadly, remembering. Yes, my sister was everything that I wasn't. Me, I was just like our paw used to say: "unlikely to amount to a hill of beans." She sniffled then, and hurried from the kitchen to tell the doctor that more hot water was ready, if he needed it. Then she rushed to the sitting room to see if that dear Mrs. O'Leary wished to have some more tea. If not, she'd sit with her and talk to her, doing her best to get the poor woman's mind off her son who was so ill. Or, if she wished her to, she'd pray with the woman, asking the good Lord to tend to the healing of her son, and the easing of her own mind.

Only once, as she hurried down the long hall, did she think again of the boy she had been so smitten with. The boy who never knew she even existed, once he'd met her sister. The handsome dark-haired boy who'd stolen a quick kiss when he'd come to tell her goodbye, after her sister suddenly lost interest in him, and moved on to her next fellow. It was then he'd given her the faded tintype picture of himself. He'd been her first and only love, since way back then, though she hadn't seen the boy since. The boy who would now be an old man. An old man by the name of Salvanus...Salvanus Pearly.

CHAPTER 34

Johnny walked over to the Mercantile, wanting to pick up both some bullets and some coffee. He could have gotten them at Tommy Dawson's old store, but decided he'd rather drop in on Cal Dunnevey. He figured if his mother had ever visited Hastings in the last four years while he'd been gone searching for some word of his father, it would have been the Mercantile she would have visited. As much as he hated to think of it, he still could not get the picture of Cal, kissing his mother, from his mind. Thinking of that made him more certain than ever that if she had come back to Hastings, it would have been the Mercantile—and Mr. Dunnevey—she stopped in to see. He hoped he was wrong, but the feeling ate at him, and he decided it was time to put such thoughts to rest.

He entered the store, the movement of the door as it opened, causing a bell above it to ring. Cal looked up from his desk at the rear of the store, upon hearing it. Johnny walked toward him, noticing as he did, the graying hair at Cal's temples and the gray mustache he now sported. "Hello, Mr. Dunnevey. It's me, John Gentry," he said, as he came to a stop in front of the desk. Cal reached out his hand in Johnny's direction, a welcoming smile upon his face.

"Well, this is a pleasant surprise. Hello, Johnny. Does your mother know you're back?" he asked, reaching out to shake his hand.

"Not yet. I'll be seeing her shortly, though," he replied.

Cal's voice softened. "Any word of your father?"

"No, sir."

"Sorry to hear it," Cal said. "It's a damn shame. So many of the men lost. So many," he repeated, shaking his head. Johnny looked down at the floor, thinking how true that was. Then Cal smiled in his direction, asking, "Is there something I can get for you, Johnny? We have just about anything you could need, thanks to the train, now." He gestured toward the aisles in the store, and Johnny glanced around. He was surprised by how many items the store now offered, surprised at how the store had grown in just the four years since he'd been gone.

"I'd like some coffee, Sir," he answered, and he turned away, heading over to where a display of rifles stood. He picked up one of the guns, amazed to feel how light in weight it was. Pa would have liked this gun, he thought, and he held it up, looking down the barrel, wishing he could take it home and show his father.

"Those are some mighty fine guns," Cal said, walking toward him, one hand running along the edge of the counter to guide him.

"They sure are," Johnny replied. "Do you know if my mother is well?" he asked then.

"No, can't say as I do," Cal answered. "Silas Haverty came into the store last spring and picked up a pair of the new spectacles we had in stock. Said they were for Sarah. Said he'd been out to Chief Standing Elk's camp, earlier, and she'd been having a problem with her eyes. I hope they helped her."

Johnny was surprised by this news. He couldn't imagine his mother in a pair of glasses. He hoped they didn't hide her pretty eyes.

"I thought maybe she'd been to town, sometime," Johnny said, the image of his mother in Cal's arms, still haunting him.

"Hardly a chance, I'd say, what with things the way they are "tween the whites and Indians now," Cal replied. "I don't know if you're aware of it, or not, Johnny, but there's been some terrible things going on. And it's only getting worse, as time goes by."

"What do you mean?" Johnny asked, giving Cal his undivided attention.

"Haven't you heard the talk?" Cal asked, walking back over to his desk and sitting down in his chair. Johnny followed, taking the chair next to him.

"I heard some talk, Sir, about the massacre near here," he replied, a worried expression upon his face. "But that was before I left to look for my pa. Have there been other ones?"

Cal shifted in his chair, turning to face the young man. "I'm afraid there's been quite a few," he said, a look of sadness upon his face.

Johnny was quiet a few moments, getting his thoughts in order before he spoke, as was his habit. "Was it my mother's people who took part?" Immediately he thought of Laughing Water, and his friend, Brave Foot, and the others he was closest to in Standing Elk's village: Howling Wolf and Chief Standing Elk.

"No, it wasn't, or so I heard," Cal answered, hearing the worry in the young man's voice. "But I don't think it really matters which tribes were involved," he said. "The cavalry has retaliated, repeatedly, wiping out whole villages, they say. Even some who want peace have been massacred." Johnny hadn't heard these things, and he grew more and more worried, as Cal continued to talk. "There were terrible bad massacres...outright killings, they were. And most, as I've heard it, for no other reason than greed. Greed and politics. Massacres committed, more often than not, by the cavalry. " He shook his head, sadly. "I'll tell you what I heard, John, but it's not good," he said, and he reached over, trying to lay his hand, momentarily, on Johnny's arm. Then he began to tell Johnny what he knew, his words chilling Johnny to the bone, and filling him with sadness.

"In the last four years," Cal told him, "so many buffalo had been killed by buffalo hunters that the Indians who depended on the buffalo for their food and shelters, and such, felt more and more threatened by these senseless killings. Not only that, but the lands they had hunted on and lived freely on—even lands considered sacred by them—were getting taken over by the whites. Forts have sprung up all over, for the express purpose of keeping the many wagon trains of settlers safe, John, and more and more, the Indians are getting shoved aside. Not realizing the endless number of our people...I mean the white men..." he corrected himself, "that were coming, looking for a fresh start in the land, the Indians had hopes they could stop them. Instead, the more they fought back, the more the settlers came, and the more the cavalry retaliated. It's gotten to the point that lately even the peaceful Indians are being attacked. Whole villages, as I said before: women, children, and the old men, all killed. I can understand the Indian side of it. They only want what they've always had: their rights, and their freedom. That's understandable." He paused, shaking his head. "But that's not how most white folks see it. They blame the Indians. White men, as you know, have a different concept of life. They want to *own* their own piece of land, whereas the Indians can't understand how the land *can* be owned." He paused, his thoughts continuing. "I'm sure you know all this already, being the way you were brought up and all. You're lucky to have the knowledge of both peoples, son. It's too bad others aren't that knowledgeable. The way things are now, though, there just doesn't seem to be any way we can learn to live together under the same sky." Cal shook his head, clearing his throat before continuing. "Anyway, I...I hoped you'd get back before very long. I hoped, too, to get this chance to talk to you." He cleared his throat, again, not quite sure how to say what he felt so strongly in his heart. Above all, not wanting Sarah's son to misunderstand. "I...I'm worried about your mother, Johnny. I know she's happy with the Indians. She told me a long time ago how she felt about them, and how deeply she cares for them. But it's not the best place for a woman to be, all things considered now. I'll speak plainly. It's not the best place for a *white* woman to be. I don't mean to offend you, son, but I...I care for her. I promised your pa, before he left for the war, that I'd look after you and your mother. I can't help but think it's my duty, as his friend, to say these things to you."

Johnny looked down at his boots, noticing how worn they were, and made a mental note that he'd be needing a new pair in the near future. Cal's words rested easily upon his mind, knowing there was no offense to be taken by them. "I appreciate your...your concern for my mother, Mr. Dunnevey. I'll be heading to see her soon. I'll pass on what you've said. You know how she is, though. It probably won't change her mind one bit. She's always been happier with the Indians than she ever was here. Except, of course, when Pa was with her. She understands the Indian ways, and has taken many of them as her own, as I have. To be honest, I don't think *either* one of us..." he paused, gathering his thoughts, "has much chance of finding happiness in a white man's town. I mean no offense. It's just the way things are."

"I'd say you're right," Cal replied, but still he was worried about Sarah. "I hope you'll convey my concerns to her, son. Tell her that even though she might not be happier, she might be safer here."

Johnny looked at the man who sat before him. Cal's concern for his mother wrinkled his brow. He felt sorry for Cal. He was old, Johnny thought, but still had his strength. And he was an intelligent man, wise to the way of things. It was apparent, by the things he'd said, that he didn't accept things at face value, but looked for the deeper meaning behind the actions of others. And it was evident that he did seem to have genuine feelings for Sarah. Johnny's feelings toward his father's blind friend, softened. If he'd had his sight, Johnny thought, I guess then there'd have been something to worry about. But, if he'd had his sight, he wouldn't have fallen in the creek in the first place, giving himself an excuse to kiss her. Johnny rose from where he'd been sitting. He reached out, placing a hand upon Cal's shoulder. "I'd best get that coffee, and a box of bullets, and be on my way, Mr. Dunnevey. My friend, Michael O'Leary, is in a bad way. He's at the new hospital. I want to go over and check on him." He picked up a box of bullets, and small container of coffee, told Cal what he owed, and paid him for them.

Then Cal rose, reaching out toward Johnny. They shook hands, Cal asking Johnny if he minded if he walked along with him. Johnny said no, not at all, and the two men made their way to the front of the store. Cal locked the door behind them, and they walked side-by-side down the street toward the hospital. When they reached the hospital, Cal took hold of the railing, slowly going up the many steps, asking what had happened to Michael. Had he had an accident, or taken sick?

Johnny hesitated for just a moment, lowering his voice before he spoke. "He's got a bad infection, Sir. It's not looking good. He has a real bad wound on his neck that's gotten infected."

"I'm sorry," Cal replied. "I hope Doc can heal him. He's a real nice young man. I've known the family for years."

They parted then, Johnny heading for the sitting room, and Cal making his way, slowly, toward the kitchen. He hoped to surprise either Auntie Belle, or Ophelia. He'd made up his mind to ask both of them to join him for tea at the boardinghouse, if they had the time. He'd had a fine time, when Ophelia had gone there with him, and he was sure Auntie Belle would be beside herself with joy at getting his invitation. He felt his way down the hall, hearing voices ahead of him, off to his left. Carefully, he edged his way along, trying not to eavesdrop, but found himself unable to do otherwise, as he neared the room the voices were coming from. He hesitated, wondering if he should just turn back the way he had come. But it seemed foolish to do so, so he waited a moment, and then proceeded. Then, to his surprise, he heard words that caused him to stop in his tracks! He froze, his heart beginning to pound wildly! Had he heard wrong, he wondered. But no, he was more than certain he'd heard right. The man who was speaking had said, most clearly, "Did he kill him? Did he kill Jalaco?"

Cal turned, fear suddenly filling him. The only person he had *ever* told about Jalaco was Moses. Yet he knew that it was not Moses he'd heard mentioning Jalaco's name. It could mean only one thing, he thought, as he turned and hurried, as fast as he could go, down the hallway, feeling the walls as he rushed along, his breath coming in short gasps. He stuck his hands out in front of him when the wall ended, moving straight ahead, hoping he'd soon feel the front door. As they suddenly hit the glass oval of the front door, making a loud sound, he heard Johnny ask, "What's wrong? Mr. Dunnevey? What's wrong, Sir?" He found the knob, throwing the door open, his pulse pounding in his temples as he rushed ahead, not taking the time to answer. Suddenly, to his dismay, he felt himself begin to fall, his feet finding nothing but air beneath them! He put out his hands, trying to protect himself, though he knew it was too late. He yelled out, just as he felt himself slam into first one step, then another, his body rolling—head over heels—as it twisted and turned, coming to rest on the bottom step, as the side of his head hit the railing a glancing blow!

He groaned, as severe pain-worse than any he'd ever felt before—seemed to explode all through his head, shattering his thoughts. Then all was silent.

CHAPTER 35

Blurry images in a myriad of colors hovered before him, a din of confusing sounds—muffled and unclear—cut through his momentary consciousness, making little or no sense. Cal Dunnevey closed his eyes, not certain where he was, or what was happening to him. He wasn't even sure if he was dead or alive. He listened, trying once again to open his eyes and focus, but the shapes that hovered before him now seemed to have vanished, leaving only a bright, white "nothingness" in view. He took a deep breath, though he was unaware of doing so. The shapes were there again; as were the many sounds that he could not distinguish, try as he might. Then suddenly, a flash of golden light caused him to clench his eyes tightly shut, as a severe pain caused his head to whirl. He began to feel nauseous, and felt like he was reeling, uncontrollably. He flailed about, desperately trying to get the spinning sensations to stop. The sounds he'd heard before, pierced his consciousness...voices, that's what they were...but he couldn't understand them, couldn't separate one voice from the other. It seemed as if there were ten or more voices reverberating in his ears: some soft, some loud. He opened his eyes again, or thought he did, only to discover that the bright light, the color of gold, was all around him. It was as if he was...he tried to think...as if he was in a great bolt of lightning. As if it was all around him, drowning him in its brilliant, golden light. He tried to call out, aware that his mouth felt cottony and dry. He shut his eyes, suddenly aware of feeling as if he were drifting like a leaf upon the wind. Then the noises quieted, and he slept.

Doc Valentine sewed up the gash across the side of Cal's head, worried because he had not yet gained full consciousness. He worried, too, if the fall Cal had taken, and the deep cut he had received, would have any adverse effect on him. It was on the same side of his head where a bullet had grazed him, years before, in a gunfight. It was bad enough that he'd been blinded then; he could only guess what further damage had occurred, due to the fall. What in the world was he running from, Doc wondered. He'd seemed all right when he and Johnny had come inside. Then Johnny had walked into Michael's room, talking a bit with James O'Leary, and suddenly Cal had come rushing down the hall like the devil, himself, was after him. He shook his head, continuing to stitch the long gash. At least the bleeding had finally stopped. That was good. But he couldn't help wonder what had caused the whole thing in the first place. He hoped there'd been no irreparable damage done to his friend and patient.

In the sitting room, Ophelia wrung her hands, sniffling, as her Auntie Belle paced back and forth before her. "I just don't understand it," Auntie Belle said, shaking her head so fast that her gray curls bounced back and forth. "It doesn't make sense, Ophelia. I saw him start down the hall, heading for the kitchen, then suddenly he looked like he'd seen a ghost..." She stopped talking, and began to cry. When she gained control of herself, she stopped crying, wiping her eyes with a handkerchief she had pulled from her apron pocket, then started explaining again. "The poor man, he looked..." she searched her mind for just the right word..."He looked terrified! That's what he looked like. Oh, Ophelia, I'll never forget the look I saw on his face, if I live to be a hundred!" she exclaimed, continuing to pace before her niece. "I can't imagine what it was that frightened him so, I just can't! Did either of you see any reason for it?" she asked, turning to where Colin sat beside Lydia.

"No, Ma'am. We were sitting here talking, and just as he reached this room, he turned and bolted, fast as he could for the door. I don't understand why. I can't imagine what possessed him."

Lydia shrugged, saying, "The poor fellow. I hope Doc can stitch up that gash on his head. Bad enough he's blind. It would be really terrible if he got an infection, too, like my husband."

"I'm going to check on him," Ophelia said. "It doesn't make any sense to sit here worrying when Doc might need some help." She got up, patting her aunt on the shoulder, then hurried from the room.

Colin got up and walked over to the window. He wondered just why Cal Dunnevey *had* looked so upset. He and Lydia had just been sitting there, discussing all that had gone on that led to Michael's getting the wound on his neck. She'd been telling him how Michael started for her boss, Vincent Jalaco, and then she'd heard a shot and Jalaco had fallen forward, dead as could be. Colin watched as a buggy pulled into the lane leading to the hospital. As he stood there, he again thought back to the conversation he and Lydia had been having. I'd just asked about Michael, he remembered, had just asked if he had killed him. Yes, that was it. I'd just asked if he had killed Jalaco. He bit his lip, as he remembered, and ran a hand through his hair, wondering even more what it was that had caused Cal Dunnevey to react so. It had to be what he'd overheard. Colin was sure of that now. Well, he thought, when you get back on your feet, Mr. Dunnevey, I think we'll have to have us a little talk!

CHAPTER 36

By mid-week the new Clark Hospital of Hastings was filled—downstairs, at least—to near capacity, much to the surprise of Ophelia Denton. In one room, Michael O'Leary laid, his neck swathed in clean strips of cloth, the infection in his neck no longer reeking. In another room, Cal Dunnevey laid staring into the dark, now conscious, but no longer the talkative fellow that everyone thought so highly of. In the next three rooms, a saloon gal, a cowpoke, and storekeeper, Heinrich Yeager lay, each one suffering from a bout of pneumonia. And in a small room nearer the back, Mary Wright struggled for breath, as coughing spell after coughing spell wracked her small body. Her sister, Juliana, sat beside her bed, stroking her arm, and laying cold, wet pieces of cloth on her forehead, hoping to bring down her fever.

Doc Valentine, his wife, Judith, and Ophelia rushed from room to room, as needed, seeing to their charges, while both Aunt Hilda and Auntie Belle scrubbed sheets and towels, hanging them out on the line in the backyard, in spite of the heavy snow that had begun to fall.

In the waiting room, Colin O'Leary paced back and forth, waiting for his mother to finish her bedside vigil beside his brother, Michael. He knew it was a good thing to have prayers spoken for one so ill, and had even prayed a few of his own for Michael, but there were things to be done around their farm—chores to tend to—and he paced back and forth, anxious to be on his way. With James just barely recovered from the effects of the war, and Father Patrick busy at the new Catholic

Church, and visiting the many patients at the hospital, it left him to see to the chores. The fact that he would have preferred to *not* do chores, at all, was now not a matter of choice. It fell on his shoulders to do them, and that was that. He'd fixed the broken gate, mended the many fences that needed it, and had done what he could to fill the cracks and crevices around the barn walls with a mix of straw, grass, and mud, hoping to keep the animals a bit warmer through the winter. He'd done all that, and still managed to drive his mother into town, daily, to sit at Michael's bedside and keep her tireless vigil over him. Colin knew what it meant to her to be there. He understood how she felt about her family, and was glad to carry his share of the load at the farm, and see that she got to the hospital every day. With her hands all bent and twisted like they were, he knew she couldn't have driven their old horse and buckboard by herself. He continued to pace, going over to the window and looking out at the heavy snow as it drifted beneath the window, the grass already completely covered. He shook his head, wondering if he'd ever get the chill out of his bones, and hoped he wasn't coming down with a cold. Ever since he'd served at the prison at Andersonville, he just couldn't seem to get warm. He'd heard others talk about the cold weather, and how it was a different kind of cold: the cold in the North and the cold of the South. He shivered, aware of the fact that ever since he'd arrived back in Hastings, he had not been able to shake the chill from his bones. Hearing a noise behind him, he turned then, surprised to see a lovely young woman enter the room. She had hair the color of gold, and the ringlets that escaped from beneath her blue bonnet seemed to bounce as she walked.

"Oh!" she exclaimed, as she realized someone else was in the room. "I'm sorry. I didn't mean to intrude," she said, her voice easy on the ears, her eyes lighting up with surprise.

"That's alright, Miss" Colin said. "I was just waiting for my mother. She's in with my brother."

"Then I'll keep you company, if you don't mind," she said, settling herself on one of the small chairs, across from the fireplace. She liked the way he looked at her, the tenderness that shown in the man's eyes, easing some of the worries she felt for her father.

"Please do," Colin stated. "Are you warm enough? I'll add another piece of wood to the fire, if not?" He couldn't help but notice the way her eyes seemed to twinkle when she spoke, and the lovely curve of her cheeks, as she turned to look directly at him. She was a vision of loveliness, and all of a sudden, he hoped his mother would not rush her visit with Michael. In fact, he hoped that she would stay at least an hour, or more. Colin liked the soft voice of the young woman, the way she tipped her head when she spoke, the tiny nose that seemed to tilt upward at the end, and those lips, he thought, suddenly wondering if she had ever been kissed.

She folded her hands in her lap, glancing out the window as she did so, shivering slightly at the sight of the heavy snow that fell there. Only once did she steal a quick glance at him, noticing his broad shoulders, and strong facial features. What she could see of them, that is, that his thick, dark beard didn't hide. She liked the way he looked at her, and his deep, rich voice when he spoke. He was a handsome man, she couldn't deny that, and she wondered who he was, and why she hadn't seen him around town before. Finally, her curiosity getting the best of her—even though she knew her parents would be appalled at her doing so—she asked if he was new to town.

He smiled at her, not in a condescending manner, but with genuine delight at her having asked. "No. My family has been here for many years," he replied. "I was away for awhile, the war, you know."

She smiled shyly, "Yes, the war," she said, adding, "It breaks my heart to think of all those we lost."

Colin felt an uneasiness fill him. He hoped she wouldn't say more about the war. He'd seen, all too many times, how people turned away from him when they found out he'd fought for the South. He hoped she wouldn't end up doing the same. He walked over to the fireplace, turning his back to her, shoving one of the larger pieces of wood into the flames. Then he straightened, going to sit in the large chair that faced hers. He glanced up, pleased to see that she was smiling at him. Colin smiled in return, wishing he knew who she was, and where he might see her again. He didn't want to ask, though, and possibly make her uncomfortable. Glancing down at his boots, he tried to think of something to say. He'd never been tongue-tied around a gal before, always knew just what to say. But she wasn't just any gal. She was the prettiest gal he'd seen, in a long time. And she was a lady, a *real* lady, he was positive of that. It was apparent she wasn't one of the saloon gals that he was used to spending time with, on occasion. He looked up, just in time to see her glance away, again.

"We're sure getting a lot of snow," he said, at last, feeling like a total fool, because he was at such a loss for words.

"Yes, we are."

"Do you live..." he began, getting up his nerve to finally ask her if she lived near town. But just at that moment, to his dismay, Auntie Belle came into the room, a happy smile upon her face.

"Your mother wanted me to fetch you, Colin, right away," she said, and then noticed the young woman sitting across from him. "Oh, hello, Katie. How's your father, dear?"

Katie smiled at the older woman, as Colin picked up his hat, excusing himself, and left the room. He'd wanted to ask her where she lived, wanted to tell her he had enjoyed talking with her, anything... but it was too late now. He smiled, as he hurried down the long hall. He knew her name was Katie. He'd heard Auntie Belle call her that. There couldn't be that many gals in the area named Katie. There'll be another time, Miss Katie, he thought, hurrying into Michael's room. There'll be another time, and that's for sure.

Michael O'Leary lay in his bed, his eyes open, and one hand resting in the hand of his wife, Lydia. "Brother," he croaked, as Colin approached the bed. He smiled, grimacing slightly, his voice weak.

Colin reached out to take his brother's other hand, squeezing it gently. He saw the dark circles beneath Michael's eyes, and his sunken cheeks, but he was conscious now, and that was all that really mattered. The medicines Doc had given him had done their job, apparently, and Colin felt relieved. Their mother sat on the other side of Michael's bed, a look of both happiness and relief on her face. "So you're on the mend, are you?" Colin asked, shaking his head. "I'm happy to see it."

"I never thought I'd make it back to Hastings," Michael said, his voice barely a whisper.

Colin glanced at him, and then at their mother, not wanting her to know all that they'd gone through to bring Michael home, and certainly not what Michael had gone through, before that. "It's best not talked about, Michael. We've got plenty of time to talk, later, when you're all healed," Colin said, hoping Michael would take the hint.

Michael looked at him, understanding his meaning, and closed his eyes, exhaustion overtaking him. "I'll rest a bit," he said, not opening his eyes, but squeezing Lydia's hand, a weak squeeze.

"You do that," Colin said, smiling. "Are you ready to go home, Maw? I've got chores to do, you know."

Mrs. O'Leary rose from her chair, looking even more tired than usual. She looked smaller, Colin noticed, as she stood there. Her dress seemed to dwarf her. He noticed, too, how faded it looked, and worn, and wondered when she'd last had a new one. As long as he could re-member, she'd put her children's needs, and her husband's, before her own. He remembered how she had often stayed up all night to finish a blouse for his sister, Mary, or to mend a pair of pants for one of the boys, back before her hands were so bad. I should buy her a dress, Colin thought. A pretty dress in a soft shade of blue, or green. He held her coat out for her, helping her get her arms into the sleeves. He felt a sense of sadness, noticing, for the first time, how difficult it was for her. He remembered how she used to sit before their fireplace, every evening, stitching pieces of fabric together, making them into the most beautiful quilts. He wondered now just how many she had made, over the years. I should have helped her more, he thought. As her oldest son, I should have seen to it that she had some things: some new frocks, and a decent coat. Hers looks all threadbare. I should have gotten her a pretty bonnet, like the ladies in the South wear now, with fancy bows and ribbons, and flowers on the brim.

He was surprised when his mother brushed past him, just then, in-terrupting these thoughts. "I saw Katie Yeager go down the hallway awhile ago, son. I want to step into the sitting room, and say hello, if she's in there," she said. "Her father is very ill, I'm told. A kind word might be of some help to her." And with that, she turned toward the sitting room, her steps small, but quick. Colin nodded at Lydia, glanced quickly at his brother, then hurried after her. He didn't want to miss the chance—a truly golden opportunity—he thought, to be formally intro-duced to the lovely young woman he'd spoken with earlier, in the sit-ting room. He'd had a run-in with Mr. Yeager, once before. Not a happy one. But that no longer mattered to him. Nothing mattered, beyond the feelings he felt for the lovely, Katie Yeager.

CHAPTER 37

Colin found that evening's chores the easiest he'd ever done. He'd finished them, in fact, in record time, catching himself singing as he slung pitchforks full of manure out the back door of the barn, and slopped the hogs. Every moment was filled with the vision of the young woman he'd met at the hospital, Miss Katie Yeager. He'd seen the slight hesitation, on her part, when his mother had first introduced him, and knew she'd already heard of him. He knew, too, that what she'd heard had not been favorable. But, as they said their farewells, she'd reached out to once again take his hand, saying how happy she was to finally meet him. Her words were like music to his ears, as he felt her gentle touch, and saw the look of interest in her lovely eyes. Oh, yes, she was interested, all right. He had no doubt about it, though he also realized she had made it a point to hide that fact from both his mother, and Auntie Belle, who had looked on, a twinkle in her eyes, showing that she was hoping romance was in the air. Colin laughed aloud, shaking his head, as he hung the pitchfork up on the wall on the one nail there.

"And what is it, my brother, that's set a gleam to yer eye?" he heard Patrick ask from behind him.

"Wouldn't you like to know," Colin answered, smiling.

"It can not be the manure you're pitchin', I'd guess, nor the hogs you've just slopped, then. It must be a lovely lass that's touched yer heart. Am I right, Brother?" Colin grinned at Patrick, wishing he was not in his priestly garb, for if he wasn't, he would have grabbed up the pitchfork from where it now hung, and quickly pitched a fork of fresh manure at him. Patrick smiled at him, knowing him so well. "Remember, son, I've my priest's robes on," he said, and he shook his finger at Colin, giving him fair warning. Then they walked toward the house, noticing that the snow had stopped, but the wind continued its fierce blowing.

They entered the small cabin, smelling the delightful aroma of bread baking in the oven, and the smell of soup cooking on the stove. The fireplace gave off an inviting warmth, and they were happy to be inside. Their brother, James, was reading a book, over in the rocker in the corner, and looked up, momentarily, as they entered. He nodded at them, and then turned his attention back to the book. Their mother stood at the stove, trying to get a thick towel around her hands so she could lift the pans of fresh sourdough bread from the oven, when they were finished baking. The look on her face was one of frustration.

"Here, Maw, let me help you," Colin offered, taking the thick towel from her and opening the oven door. "You make the best bread," he said. "It sure smells good. My stomach's growling, just from the smell of it." She smiled up at him, pleased with his words.

"Go wash up, Patty," she said, as she saw Patrick start to sit down at the table. "The soup will be ready in a minute. Soon as the bread's cooled a wee bit."

James looked over at Patrick, grinning. It didn't matter that he was now a well-liked priest. To their mother he was still her little boy, and that tickled James, no end. Patrick smiled at him, rolling his eyes, well aware of what he was thinking. He rose, walking toward the washbasin in the corner, and as he passed the rocker where James sat, he cuffed him on the back of the head. A gentle cuff, but nonetheless, a cuff that caught him squarely on his head and caused the book to fall from his hands, the page James had been reading, lost.

"Patty, mind yer manners," his mother said, adding, "or do I have to take you to the wood shed?" All the O'Leary sons grinned broadly at her words, knowing they'd *all* visited the woodshed on occasion, over the years, but it had been *many* years earlier. The idea of their mother taking a switch to the bottom of their brother, the *priest*, soon had all of them laughing loudly, including Mrs. O'Leary, who—as she thought about what she'd said—just couldn't help herself.

Later, their stomach's full and bodies warmed, James went back to his book and Colin and Patrick sat at the table, a cup of coffee being enjoyed by both. Mrs. O'Leary, a contentment filling her at the sight of her three sons all gathered close by, washed the dishes, trying not to drop and break any.

"I'm afraid that little girl, Mary, isn't going to make it," Patrick said, breaking the silence.

"She's that bad?" Colin asked, seeing in his mind again, how frightened she had looked when they rescued her from the Pawnee.

"It doesn't look good," Patrick replied, taking a swallow of his coffee, and looking into the flames of the fireplace a long time.

"Maybe you can...you know...make another miracle," Colin suggested, meaning it in earnest, not in jest.

Patrick looked over at him, deciding that Colin meant what he said, and had not meant it in an unfavorable way. "No, I can't do it," Patrick replied, a sadness to his voice. "It takes *God* to make a miracle, my brother. Not me."

Colin looked at his younger brother, seeing his tousled red hair, and the many boyish freckles that still covered his nose. He wondered when it was that his brother had become the man he now was. Wondered what it was, that caused such faith to fill him, that it seemed more than sufficient, not only for him, but for so many, many others. He took a long sip of coffee, turning to stare into the fire.

"The church is comin' along just fine," Patrick spoke, not looking at Colin, but continuing to also look into the flames. "You might want to come, sometime," he suggested, softly. "It can't hurt, you know," he said.

Colin didn't answer, nor did he look at his brother, he just nodded, knowing how he felt inside, knowing he lacked the words needed to explain. "I...might...someday."

"So, son, what did you think of Katie Yeager?" Colin's mother asked then, coming over to the table to refill their cups of coffee.

Colin felt his face flush in embarrassment, and looked up to see a wide smile break forth upon Patrick's face. He shook his head, warning him with a look, not to say anything. But Patrick laughed, glancing at their mother. "So, 'tis love that's given you cause to sing, as you muck out the stalls in the barn, my brother," he teased. Colin hung his head, well aware that he'd be making a trip to the woodshed, for sure, if Patty wasn't a priest.

CHAPTER 38

Johnny was alone at his old family homestead when he heard a horse and rider approaching. He'd been doing all he could around the place to get it in better shape for Michael, if and when he came home from the hospital, and for Lydia, and Juliana, and her siblings. He'd carried a month's supply of wood up to the house, stacking it in a manner that he hoped would prevent it from getting snow-covered, and wet. Then he'd split and filled the wood box inside the house, near the stove, so there'd be plenty of starters for both heating and cooking. He had also carried in three pails of water, knowing that Michael wouldn't be able to do it, and as thin as she was, in all likelihood, neither would Lydia. He didn't know that for certain, though, admitting to himself that she might be thin, but she sure had some kind of strength to her. He'd been surprised to see how well she handled a gun, and had no doubt that she'd use it, if the need arose. In a way, she reminded him of his mother, which surprised him. Her unending determination, he thought, that was what it was that they seemed to have in common. Once his mother made up her mind about something, there was nothing that could stand in her way. How many times had Johnny seen this proven true? He stopped what he was doing, as the rider got close enough to recognize, and was happy to see it was his best friend, Eli.

"Hello, Eli. How are you?" he asked, walking over to him as he dismounted.

"Fine," Eli replied. "What are you doing here? When did you get back? Any word of your father?" His questions came one after the other, because of his surprise at seeing his friend whom he'd not seen in over four years. He reached out, grasping Johnny's hand, more than a little glad to see him.

"No word of my pa, I'm afraid," Johnny replied, sadly. "Let's go in. I've got a fresh pot of coffee on the stove. I came to help Michael," he answered, heading with Eli, toward the house.

The two men took off their coats, hanging them near the door. Johnny took a cup down from the cupboard, filling it for Eli, then filled his own that sat on the table. "What are you doing out here?" he asked, straddling a chair, as Eli took the chair across from him.

"I got tired of sitting at home," Eli said. "Thought I'd come see if Michael was around. I came by about...I don't know...a month, or so ago, and he wasn't here. The place looked deserted. The more I thought about it, the more concerned I got. I knew it wasn't like him to just run off somewhere. Is he here?"

Johnny wasn't sure just what he could say. He didn't feel it was his place to tell about Lydia being back in town, and all. And yet, Eli was his best friend. How would *he* feel, if Eli kept silent, knowing what *he* knew? He shifted in his chair, studying his friend before answering, getting his thoughts in order. "As it turns out, Michael made a trip west of here," Johnny said, "and got into a whole passel of trouble. I won't go into it, best he tells you about it, himself, if he wants to. Anyway, I heard about it, and hightailed it over to the O'Leary place. Then Colin and I set out to... ah... to see what we could do to remedy the situation. Michael was in bad shape when we found him. He had a serious infection on the side of his neck, and we weren't sure he was going to live. It was that bad. To make a long story short, we had a run-in with the Pawnee before we could get back here. They had attacked a settlement to the west, killed some folks, and grabbed some children. Three boys and two girls, to be exact. One of the boys was shot clear through with an arrow, and died right after we rescued them. The rest are staying here with Ly..." he stopped speaking so abruptly, that Eli looked at him, wondering about it. Johnny knew Eli had noticed his abrupt hesitation, and tried to cover it, by continuing.

"They're staying here with *Michael*," he said, emphasizing Michael's name. "He's at the new hospital in town, under Doc's care."

Eli took a couple sips of his coffee, looking steadily at his longtime friend. He let all Johnny had told him sink in, before speaking. Then, after a long period of silence, he spoke. "And what is it that you're *not* telling me, John?" he asked, knowing him so well.

Johnny looked Eli in the eyes, knowing how strong their friendship had always been, and how deeply he liked and respected him. He looked down at the brown liquid in his cup, then up at his friend. As he did, the cabin door opened and Lydia O'Leary stepped inside, stopping, her mouth dropping open in surprise as she saw the red-haired young man, sitting at the table. He was the spitting image of his father, though younger: same eyes, same lips, same frown, as he turned and looked at her. She stood transfixed; staring at the son she had not seen in twenty years, the son she had given away without the slightest backward glance. Silence filled the cabin, as the many things she'd planned to say to him floated away, and all she could do was stand there, returning his stare.

CHAPTER 39

Johnny saddled his horse and headed for town, giving Lydia and Eli privacy, so they could talk. He didn't know if mere words could heal the many questions and doubts his friend had felt over the years. He only knew that Eli was a kind and caring man, who had been raised by fine folks. Folks who had instilled in him a sense of purpose, and a sense of understanding. Eli knew that life wasn't always fair, true, but he handled disappointments with fairness, as he'd been taught, and had faith that all things worked out for the good. Over the years, whenever he'd asked Jonas and Lilly why his real mother had left him, not caring enough to take him with her, they had explained that she had been young, and that she'd left him with them because she wanted the best for him. They had always tried to assure him that she loved him, loved him enough to see to it that he was in a home where he would truly be part of a family, and where he was not only wanted, but also needed. As the years came to pass, and time after time they hoped to have a child of their own, and could not, he was even more deeply loved, and needed. Both Lilly and Jonas had long before stopped thinking of him as Lydia's son, delighting in the man "their" son had become. They could not have loved him more, if he'd been their own, in fact. Eli knew this to be true as he grew from child to man, and felt secure in knowing. He no longer asked about his mother, no longer questioned his beginnings. He was loved, and knew it, as surely as he knew the rains helped the crops to grow. It gave him a strong sense of confidence, knowing the man he had become was all because of the parents who'd been there for him. Every day of his life, they'd been there: loving him and guiding him, nourishing him and supporting him in all he did. Sometimes he wondered if Jonas and Lilly had any idea how very grateful he was, and how very much he loved them.

Now, as he sat in Michael's cabin, staring at the woman who stood before him, her hair windblown, her face pale and bone-thin, her dress worn, he found himself filled with regret that he'd come to the cabin to see if Michael was all right. He had no idea what to say to this woman, this stranger who stood before him. And just as obviously, she had nothing to say to him. He pushed his empty cup aside, and stood. Then slowly he walked toward the door. "Don't go," she whispered, plaintively, reaching out with both hands, laying them on his arm. He stood still, looking not at her, but at the floor, taking a deep breath. He heard Johnny ride off, and wished *he* was going with him. In his mind, he heard the words, "be kind, be kind," repeated over and over again, and remained still. Lydia let go of his arm then, and just stood before him, looking him over. He looked into her eyes, seeing that they were his eyes; the same color, the same shape.

"I don't know what to say to you," he said at last, his words sticking in his throat and sounding strange to him.

Lydia took a deep breath, glad to have heard his voice. She began to reach out to him again, but stopped, folding her hands together as if in prayer. "I...I had so many things to say to you," she whispered, her voice shaking as she spoke. She took a deep breath to calm her a bit, and then smiled an ever so slight smile at him.

His eyes, so like her own, continued to gaze into hers, and she felt her heart fill with so much love for him that she was afraid she was going to faint. She shivered, a look of hope and love filling her eyes, and he saw it, and looked down at the floor. Then he stepped around her, and started for the door. "Eli..." she said, her voice filled with pain.

He turned back to her. "I was only going to shut the door," he explained, and he walked to it, reaching out and closing it against the cold winds that blew outside, buffeting the cabin. Then he turned back to her, still unsure of what he would say. He'd known this day would come. Had *always* known it would come. He'd dreaded it, as long as he could remember. Now it was here, *she* was here, staring at him as if she cared. Staring at him as if she loved him. He cleared his throat, his gaze dropping once again to the floor. He jumped when she reached out and touched his arm, stiffening at her touch. Then she reached up and gently touched his face. He looked at her, wanting to tell her to stop. Wanting to tell her to get away from him. That she'd given up the right to touch him, a long time before, when she'd walked out of his life with nary a look back. But he saw that her eyes were closed, as she ran her hand over his cheek, and tears ran down her face, dripping upon the fabric of her faded dress. He felt his own eyes fill with tears, and as he did, he remembered as a young child how he had lain awake so many nights, wondering where she was, wondering if she ever thought of him. And as he had done then, he whispered softly, "Mother."

CHAPTER 40

The following day when Lydia visited Michael at the hospital, he was sitting up and looking much better. She was so glad to see that, but she was even happier to see the look on his face as he saw her. She had on the light blue dress that had once been Sarah Gentry's, and had fixed her hair, tying it back and covering it with a lovely bonnet she had discovered on top of an old cabinet, at the cabin. The bonnet looked old, but hadn't been worn much, she was sure. She thought, perhaps, that it had belonged to Sarah's mother, judging by the style of it. But Lydia liked hats, and knew it looked nice on her, once she had blown all the dust off of it. And Michael had looked so pleased.

She had thrown more than enough wood on the fire the night before, and carried in four full pails of water, heating them on the stove till they were nearly boiling. Then she filled Sarah's old tub almost to the brim. Making certain that the cabin door was securely locked, she undressed and stepped into the tub, soaking till the ends of her fingers wrinkled. Then she scrubbed and scrubbed her body, and washed her hair, rinsing it in a pail of clean water that she had brought in for just that purpose. When she was finished, she dried her hair, happy to notice a silkiness to it, once more. She brushed and brushed it, to get out all the snarls. It had been a long time—longer than she cared to remember—since she had enjoyed the luxury of a good long soak, or a hot sudsy bath. She found herself smiling because of it. Then she quickly dried herself, and hurried to the large bed where an old, but soft, flannel gown of Sarah's lay. She pulled it over her head, smoothing it over her stomach and hips, enjoying the warmth it provided. Then she hurried into the small bedroom, and pulled open the doors of the large pine cabinet that stood in one corner, anxious to look at all the pretty dresses Michael had told her it held. She took out first one, then another, deciding to wear the light blue one the following day when she went to see him. It looked pretty against her skin, and the color even made her eyes appear brighter, she thought. She was sure that Michael would be surprised, as well as very pleased. I'll look like a lady, she thought, a *real* lady. She smiled, laying the dress on the small bed in that room, being careful not to wrinkle it. Then she blew out the oil lamp and dashed for the big bed. As on the two previous nights, Juliana and the boys had been staying at the hospital, in a spare room on the second floor, not wanting to leave their little sister who was so ill. Lydia wasn't afraid to be alone at Michael's farm. Far from it. It was her home now, and she felt safe and secure there. It was a feeling she hadn't felt in years. Funny, she thought, I hated the farm I grew up on. I couldn't wait to get away from it, in fact. But Michael's farm is so different. She snuggled down beneath the lovely old quilt that adorned the big bed, smiling. No, she thought, it's *me* who's different, and she closed her eyes, enjoying the softness of the bed.

She thought then of Eli, her tall, handsome son. She was too tired to remember all the things they had talked about the day she had first seen him at the cabin. The only thing she knew for certain was that he didn't hate her, as she had so feared he would. He had stayed, talking long into the evening, drinking coffee, and telling her of his life: of his childhood, and of his parents, Lilly and Jonas. She hung her head when he called them Maw and Paw. It was painful to know they held this place in his heart, and she didn't. She'd thought only of herself when she left him, she knew that now, and felt deeply sorry for having done so. She'd told him this, later that evening, when she could find the words. Choking back tears, she'd asked him to please forgive her. He hadn't answered at first. He'd just sat there, looking at her. She knew what he saw; knew how unkempt she had looked that day. It was when he got up and poured them both another cup of coffee, that she noticed the dampness of tears on his lashes. She got to her feet, reaching out to him. He stood still, looking at her, not saying a word. She took a step forward, and reached up, her arms encircling him, hugging him to her in warm embrace. She was afraid he'd push her away, or tell her to leave him alone. She was even more afraid that he'd turn and walk out the door, and out of her life. But he didn't. Instead, Eli let her hug him for the longest time, his heart beating in tune with her own. Then he eased away, telling her he had to go home, that his folks would be wondering where he was. It was then he spoke the words that warmed her heart, "I'll come back...soon, Mother." And in her heart, Lydia O'Leary knew she was home.

Yes, there were still so many things she needed to tell him. So many things she hoped to explain. But somehow, she felt like the worst of it was behind them. He hadn't stormed out angrily, nor had he called her names. He had reacted in a way that proved the good choice she had made when she'd asked Lilly and Jonas to take him. They had taught him to be kind and caring, and above all, forgiving. She didn't know how they'd feel about her coming back. Or how they'd feel when they learned that she and Eli had met, and talked. By now, she thought, they've probably got a whole lot of children of their own. It shouldn't hurt them that I'm back, and want to spend all the time I can with my son, she thought. I'll go see them. I have to thank them for the wonderful job they've done, raising my boy.

CHAPTER 41

Lilly looked up as the buckboard came up the lane. She could tell that a woman was driving it, but was not certain who she was. The buckboard looked similar to one Michael O'Leary had, but there was no woman at his place, to her knowledge. She rubbed a hand across the middle of her back, trying to rid herself of the niggling pain that pulsed there. Every day it seemed to get worse and worse, though she wished it would go away. Sometimes it felt like a little "catch" in the middle of her back, other times it was a deep, relentless ache, like a bad tooth-ache. It always got worse, she noticed, when the cold weather arrived. In spring and summer, she could tolerate it, though it did seem to be persistently worse even then, now. It must be from the fall, she thought, and in her mind she remembered how hard she had landed, the day she lost the baby. She rubbed her back again, going to the door, as the woman stepped down from the buckboard and walked up the steps onto the porch. Lilly glanced toward the window, noticing the blue dress the lady wore, and the blue bonnet. A heavy shawl circled her shoulders, and Lilly wondered who it was that would stop by on such a blustery day. The dress looked strangely familiar, but she couldn't place it. She saw that the woman had neither boots, nor mittens on, and wondered about it. Answering the knock, she opened the door, asking, "Yes?" And then she gasped, and stared in disbelief, as she realized it was her sister who stood there. Lydia smiled at Lilly, who continued to stand speechless before her.

"Lilly..." Lydia said. "Can I come in?"

Lilly backed up, opening the door wider, still not saying a word. Her expression was one of total bewilderment. Lydia looked around, noticing how much the room reminded her of the one at their farm when they were young. She noticed, too, the graying hair of her sister, and the way she looked at her. Lilly opened her mouth to say something, still staring at Lydia, the silence seeming to go on forever. Then in a mere whisper she asked, "What *are you* doing *here?*"

Lydia was surprised by her question, having not expected Lilly to react in such a manner. "I...I wanted to speak with you, wanted to see you again," she replied. "Perhaps I was wrong to come, but..." she hesitated, as Eli walked into the room, stopping abruptly when he caught sight of her.

The silence was unbearable, and seemed to go on and on, no one saying anything. Then Eli spoke, "Are you alright, Mother?" and *both* sisters answered in unison, "Yes, son." The clock upon the wall ticked loudly, and outside a dog barked, but inside the house there was a pall similar to that when death occurs.

"I'd better leave," Lydia said, noticing her hands were shaking, and she turned to go, her heart heavy. She pulled open the front door, one corner of her shawl dragging on the floor. She felt the sting of tears as they started, quickly filling her eyes, and running down her cheeks. In her hurry to leave, she nearly ran into Jonas, who had seen the buckboard and thought it was Michael's, and had come up to the house from the barn to say hello.

"Well, my goodness!" he exclaimed. "Hello, Lydia. How are you? When did you get back to Hastings?" He saw then how upset she was; saw the tears that coursed their way down her cheeks, and put a hand out to stop her. "What's wrong, Lydia? What is it? Stop. Come back in the house."

She tried to smile at him, but whispered instead, "I can't," and ran past him, almost falling in her attempt to get up onto the seat of the buckboard. Her shawl caught in the wheel of the buckboard, and as she snapped the reins, it pulled from her thin shoulders, and fell beneath the wheel into the slush and snow. Much too embarrassed to care, or to even notice the cold, she snapped the reins a second time, turning the horse and buckboard in a wide circle, and went racing off down the lane as fast as she could go.

Jonas called after her to stop, then hurried up the steps, intent on getting to the bottom of the problem. He could not understand why she would have left so quickly, or why she had been so upset. But just as he reached to open the door, it was yanked open by none other than Eli, who went racing down the steps, taking them two at a time. He looked in the direction of the hastily fleeing buckboard, and then ran across the yard toward the barn. As Jonas watched, a look of total surprise upon his face, Eli raced from the barn on his horse, trying to catch up with Lydia. When the boy was well out of sight, Jonas shut the door, turning to see Lilly still standing near the doorway, her face wet with tears. "What is it, Lil?" he asked her, holding her shoulders within his large hands. "What's happened, honey?"

Between sobs, barely able to speak, Lilly choked out the words he'd always feared hearing, "We've lost him, Jonas. We've lost our son." Jonas wrapped his large arms around his wife in an attempt to comfort her, but he'd seen the look on Eli's face. He'd seen, too, how he raced down the steps, and to the barn, how he'd spurred his horse, heedless of the slippery snow, his mind on only one thing: on catching Lydia. He corrected his thought: on catching "his mother." He held Lilly close, trying to comfort her, trying as best he could to ease her pain. But in his heart he knew that they had done all they could. The way things turned out would all depend on Eli now. Eli, and God. It was out of their hands, no matter how much they loved the boy.

CHAPTER 42

As Johnny rode through town he was well aware of the looks of dislike on the faces of some of the people. Even some of those he had known since he was a young child, glared at him. Well, he thought, let them look and point their fingers, this town wouldn't be the way it is today if my father was still sheriff. Pa saw to it that it was a place where law-abiding folks could live, safe and free from the lawlessness that's so rampant here today. Johnny couldn't help but notice the drunks and derelicts staggering down the street from the many bars, or hear the gunfire, as two men faced each other in anger, further on down the street. No sir, he thought, it wasn't like this when my father was sheriff.

As he rode by the house that had belonged to his grandparents, Rosie and Angus MacGregor, he glanced at the elegant carriage and two fancy horses, tied before it. "High-steppers," that's what he had always called them, much to the delight of his Scottish grandfather. They were some kind of fancy breed: their coats shiny black in color, their necks arched and heads held high. They were the same kind of horse he had seen in the South when he was traversing that part of the country, searching for his father. He'd heard that one of the more prominent citizens now owned his grandparents' home, and he wished he could go inside, just once more, before he left town. But he knew that was not possible. Fancy folks weren't likely to welcome a man who looked Indian into their home, regardless if he'd been in it many times before when he was growing up. How time changes things, he thought, wishing it still belonged to his grandparents. He could picture his Grandma Rosie at the front door; her apron covering her dress, her lovely, soft white hair—like cotton—encircling her head, her joyful smile as she waved at him, so obviously happy to see him. He pulled his coat tighter around him against the cold wind that blew in from the north, and reached down to pat Buck's neck. It seemed nothing was the same anymore, and it saddened him.

Dawson's old store now sported a big sign that read, "Yeager's General Store," and the bank no longer had the long row of large windows across the front. Now a wood wall faced the street, with only two small windows, and those were behind heavy iron bars. Only the Mercantile seemed to have stayed the same, with it's two large front windows still displaying merchandise of all kinds: tools, oil lamps, a variety of household necessities, and all sorts of gear. He noticed a quilt in the window, its off-white background seeming to bring alive the red, blue, and yellow flowers that graced it, here and there. He thought of the quilt his mother had given Michael O'Leary when she returned to Chief Standing Elk's tribe. This quilt looked a lot like it, and he shook his head, his mind filling with memories. How many times his mother had wrapped him in that old quilt, against the cold chill that—in the worst of winters—seemed to penetrate their cabin when he was a small child. He smiled, remembering.

As he came abreast of the cemetery, he looked out to where the old birch tree once stood, then to the place grave markers now stood, marking the graves of all three of his grandparents; John Bruce, and Rosie and Angus MacGregor. No need stopping, he thought, I've already said my goodbyes. It's best to just get on my way. He had come back into town to see how Michael was doing. After that he planned to stop and see Colin at the O'Leary's farm on his way out of town. Unless, of course, Colin was at the hospital visiting Michael. Once he'd told them goodbye, he'd leave for Standing Elk's camp to see his mother. Heavy snow was already late in coming, though the brisk winds gave strong evidence that it could arrive any day now. He hoped to be comfortably settled within his mother's tepee by the time the worst snows came. She'd be happy to see him; he knew that for a fact, even though he'd not found his father. And truth was, he'd missed her terribly on his long and arduous journey. He had often thought of her, wishing he could be with her. She was no longer young, and he hoped she still had her health. He smiled as he remembered Cal Dunnevey saying that she now wore spectacles. I'll have to get used to seeing her in them, he thought, smiling. Oh, well, as long as they helped her see, that was what mattered. He couldn't help remembering the day when, as a mere child, she had shown him a picture in one of her books, of a woman in spectacles, and had told him in no uncertain terms that *she* would *never* wear them. She'd told him she thought they were terribly unbecoming, especially on a woman, and she hoped her sight always remained sharp and clear. Times change, Mother, he thought, oh how they change! And he urged Buck on, anxious to get on his way.

In the middle of the street, a group of men were arguing, as he approached, their voices raised. He heard their words, filled with anger and righteous indignation about "dirty redskins" and that "they should all be killed." One of them said, "justice *will* be done, just wait and see," and more than once he heard the word, "reservation." Johnny guided Buck over to the far side of the street, hoping to pass by unnoticed, but it was not to be.

"Look! It's an Indian!" exclaimed one of the men, pointing in his direction. The others turned angry faces toward him, fists raised, and began to curse him. He glanced at them, knowing what a mob was capable of, then urged Buck on, his back straight and chin raised. He was proud of his Indian heritage, and it showed in his posture. Seeing that, intensified the anger of the men who shouted even more hate-filled threats at him. He knew these men were like so many now, spewing hatred everywhere they went. Men, who banded together with others of the same ilk, believing themselves to be on a righteous path.

Suddenly, one of the men ran toward Johnny, his fist raised as he screamed slurs at him. Another stepped down from the walkway on the other side of Buck, grabbing his halter. Johnny tried to urge Buck on past the men, who had clearly now become a gang, set on violence.

"Get him!" one of the men yelled, and Johnny knew he was in trouble, as the group surged forward, hatred upon their faces.

"Kill the dirty injun," another screamed, and hands pulled Johnny from his horse, a fist slamming into his stomach, knocking the breath out of him. Johnny felt the blows of many others against his body, his coat softening some of them. Then a large fist hit him on the side of his face, feeling like a rock against his cheekbone. He fought back valiantly, more than aware that a group so riled, might easily kill. Knowing this seemed to give him added strength, and he lashed out, his fist connecting with the fellow directly in front of him. The man crumpled at his feet, but another took his place, screaming angry words as his fist slammed into Johnny's jaw, dropping him to his knees. Johnny tasted the warm gush of blood that suddenly filled his mouth, as he struggled to get back on his feet, and then another fist caught him under the chin, and all went black.

The next thing he remembered was waking up in a cell at the jail, his head and jaw aching something fierce. To his surprise, Eli lay on the cot in the corner, and on the floor in the far corner another figure lay groaning. Johnny got to his feet, going over to Eli. He bent, touching his friend's shoulder, surprised when Eli struck out at him, and jumped up off the cot. "Hey, it's me, Eli!" Johnny exclaimed, blocking Eli's attempt to slug him. "How'd you get here?" he asked, totally confused by Eli's presence in the jail.

"I came into town, saw the fight," Eli said, sitting back down, rubbing his jaw where it was bruised. "When I saw it was you they were tearing into, I jumped in and rescued you," Eli said, attempting to smile at Johnny.

"Some rescue," Johnny said, sitting down beside his friend, running his hand across his sides, wondering if any of his ribs were broken. It was then he remembered the other fellow over in the corner. "Who's that?" he asked, nodding toward the inert figure who still groaned, but was now trying to sit up.

"Your first rescuer," Eli answered. "Don't you know him?"

Johnny got up, walking over to the man sprawled in the corner. He squatted down, reaching out a hand to turn the man toward him so he could see who it was. As his hand touched the man's shoulder, he jerked his head around, yelling, "Git yer hands of'n me!"

"It's all right," Johnny said. "I'm the fellow you tried to help." The man closed his eyes, wiping bloody drool on the sleeve of his torn shirt. His growth of whiskers and unkempt hair made it hard to tell just who he was. He looked old as all get out, Johnny saw, and that surprised him. "Can you get up?" Johnny asked, reaching out to try to help the old fellow to his feet.

"'Course I can get up. I'm just restin' a bit. Let me be," the man answered, the strong smell of stale beer and whiskey on his breath, causing Johnny's stomach to lurch. Johnny stood, one hand upon his stomach in hopes he wouldn't heave. He tasted the blood from the cut on his lip, and eased back down onto the cot, sitting shoulder to shoulder with Eli.

"Is he gonna be all right?" Eli asked, moving his jaw from side to side, hoping to ease the pain that flooded his face.

"I don't know," Johnny replied, looking over at the man. "Some great shape we're all in," he said. "I wonder if we won."

Eli laughed, which caused him to groan, and quickly put one hand over his chin. "We're still alive. I guess that's in our favor."

"Yeah," Johnny replied, and he wondered why they were the ones in jail, and not his attackers. As he thought this, the old man in the corner struggled to his feet, wobbled a bit, and then fell with a resounding thud onto the floor.

Johnny stood, hurrying to the man's side. "I think he's really hurt," he said, looking at Eli.

"We're all hurt," Eli replied, still rubbing his jaw.

"He's in pretty bad shape," Johnny said, and he felt for a pulse in the old man's neck. He knew the old fellow was alive. He could see his chest raising and falling as he breathed, and worst of all, he could smell the booze upon his breath. Johnny stood, and walked to the door of the cell, yelling for the sheriff.

In a few moments, Sheriff MacKay entered the room, walking nonchalantly over to their cell, a big grin upon his weasel-like face. "Well, you boys look like you should give up fightin'," he said, grinning even more.

"I was attacked," Johnny replied. "Apparently my friend...my *friends*," he amended his words to include the old man, "jumped in to help. Don't know why *we're* locked up. We didn't start it." Then he added. "But that's not important right now, Sheriff. That old fellow over there looks bad. I think he needs a doctor," Johnny said, pointing toward the inert figure in the corner.

The sheriff looked over at the man, a look of disgust crossing his face. "Just for the record, boy," he said, "you and your friends would be dead if me and my deputy hadn't stepped in. You're in here for your own protection. The door to yer cell ain't even locked. Try it, you'll see." He swore under his breath then, still looking at the man on the floor. "Darned old drunk. Guess I'd better go get Doc. I'd hate to see the old fool die in my jail," and he turned and walked out into the room where his desk sat. As the door to the cell area swung shut, he yelled, "yer gun belts are hung on the wall by my desk."

Johnny shook his head, looking over at Eli. "I guess we're free to go. Why'd you say you were in town?"

"I didn't," Eli answered, rising to his feet a bit unsteadily. Johnny knew by the tone of his voice that Eli had something chewing at him. They'd been friends too long for him to not recognize his friend's reaction to things. "I've got some unfinished business at the hospital. I decided to stop off at the Mercantile before going there. That's when I saw that bunch of no-accounts pounding the devil out of you." He smiled slightly, and then jokingly added, "I waited to see if you could handle all of them, but after awhile it looked like I'd better jump in and rescue you."

"Thanks," Johnny replied, a trace of sarcasm in his voice, the blood from his split lip still leaving a disagreeable taste in his mouth.

"Any time," Eli replied, glancing over at the prone figure in the corner. "I never thought we'd get other help. He's got to be as old as my pa, if he's a day," Eli said, shaking his head. "*My pa...*" he said again, snorting disgustedly. Then he grew silent. He sat back down, resting his head in his hands, as he did so.

"You okay?" Johnny asked, wondering what was bothering Eli.

"I will be, when I get a few things said to an old "friend" at the hospital," Eli replied, rising again. "Let's get out of here."

"No. I'd like to thank the old fellow," Johnny said. "Think I'll wait and see what Doc says. I want to see if he's gonna be okay."

At that moment, Doc Valentine entered the sheriff's office, hurrying back to their cell. "Hello, Johnny...Eli. Are you two all right?" Doc asked, kneeling beside the old man, feeling for a pulse.

"We're fine, Doc," Eli replied, "fine as can be expected."

"You look pretty rough," Doc said, looking at Johnny and Eli, while opening first one eye and then the other of the old man, all the time leaning away from him to avoid the smell of his breath. Then he stood, waving one hand in front of him to clear the air. "I can't really tell how much damage he's suffered, and how much he's suffering from all he's drank. I think I'd better get him over to the hospital. I never knew him to be a fighter, but he's been a drinker all his life, from what I've heard."

"You know him, Doc?" Johnny asked.

"Sure do," Doc replied. "He lives alone out the other side of town. He usually keeps to himself. Not the friendly type, from what I've heard. His name's Pearly...folks call him 'Old Man Pearly.'"

CHAPTER 43

Between the two of them, Eli and Johnny managed to get Old Man Pearly over to the hospital, and into a bed. To save any of the ladies from having to come in contact with the filthy condition he was in, the men undressed him down to his drawers, so Doc could see the extent of his wounds. He was a wiry old fellow, ancient—in his late seventies, if he was a day, Doc figured—who'd seen more than his share of hard years. His hair and beard reeked with the smell of all he'd drunk, and what he hadn't kept in him. Doc found himself nearly overcome by the smell, and knew that only the old man's need for a doctor kept him there at his side, checking him out, and doing the job he was trained to do. He found himself grimacing with disgust at sight of the old man, and it was all he could do to make himself touch him. Probably sporting a whole passel of bugs in his hair and beard, he thought, and he tried to avoid much contact with either. His body was ravaged with sores and bruises, and signs of the life he'd led, and Doc wondered just what it was that would cause a man to choose that life. He shook his head, stepping back from his patient, taking in a deep breath of fresh air from the nearby window. Then he began his inspection in earnest, listening to the old fellow's heart, looking at the pupils of his eyes, and seeing how badly infected each and every sore was. As he worked, he thought back to all he'd been taught about what a lifetime of drinking could do to a man's body. How Pearly had lasted as long as he had, amazed him.

He knew the old man had a daughter. Someone had mentioned that, awhile back, and he wondered if she was nearby. He'd seen the signs and heard how the old fellow coughed, as they carried him over to the hospital, and was pretty sure he was consumptive. Wouldn't last long, if he was, Doc Valentine mused. He'd lost many a patient to consumption, in spite of all his efforts to save them.

After a lengthy examination, he stitched up a long cut on the old man's shoulder, aware that there was no reaction from his patient, other than a series of racking coughs. It didn't look good. He couldn't tell how much blood he'd lost from the cut, though what was left of his shirt had a large, dried stain across most of the back of it. He shook his head, feeling a sense of complete hopelessness. He knew if the old man *did* pull through his present afflictions, he'd probably be right back in a saloon as soon as he was able to get there. Doc shook his head, and called to his wife, Judith, who came hurrying in to aid him.

"Don't get his clothes against you," he said, smiling slightly at her, "carry them out to the back, and see if the aunts can wash them, please. Better check the pockets before they're washed. Might be something in them of importance to the old fellow." He looked over at his patient, who continued to lie still, only his continuous wracking coughs causing him to stir. "If you'll bring me in a pail of hot water, I'll do my best to wash him up, some. Who knows what we might find under all that shock of hair and filthy beard?" He laughed softly as he said this, hoping Judith couldn't smell the rank scent of the old man from where she stood.

"I'll help you," Judith replied, a slight smile upon her face. "He's not the first fellow I've helped you with, you know, who was in such poor condition."

"That he isn't," her husband agreed, and he grew concerned, as his patient was besieged by another long coughing spell, and there was a trace of blood in the drool that ran into his beard, afterwards. "He's in rough shape, I'm afraid. Probably not much I can do for him, all things considered," the doctor said, looking at his wife. "Don't know if his kin are near. He has a daughter, I believe. I'll check it out, and see how he is when he regains consciousness. If he does, that is. But I'm afraid the poor chap has about had it." He shook his head again, feeling sorrow for the old man. "Call Johnny, would you? See if he'll come give me a hand," the doctor asked his wife, then he went to the pile of books that lay on a nearby table, intent on finding other cases of the same nature, and how they were best handled. In all his years as a doctor, he never got used to the patients like this one. Men who had literally thrown their lives away, as far as he could tell. Men who had as many reasons to live and to enjoy family, and yet they chose this heartbreakingly destructive path. Chose the saloons and their kind of inhabitants, because of the intense craving that ate away at them for just one more bottle of spirits. It was a terrible thing, an addiction to which there seemed no cure. And Doc Valentine wished with all his heart that he could find a way to warn men away from the devastation, and downright destructiveness, that excessive drinking caused.

"How can I help, Doc?" Johnny asked, walking quickly into the room, noticing as he did, that the old man had still not regained consciousness. "Is he gonna be all right?" he asked, a look of concern upon his face.

"I hope so. But I can't really say," Doc replied. "Will you give me a hand, Johnny, cleaning him up? We need to shave off his beard. Heaven knows what's growing in it," he smiled, glancing at the patient to see if he might have heard.

"Yeah, I'll help," Johnny said. "Eli's gone in to see Michael, so I'll be glad to help. I knew the old man was in bad shape as soon as I saw him fall at the jail."

"Did he happen to hit his head on anything when he fell?" Doc asked, getting out a straight razor and some towels from a nearby cabinet.

"He just fell flat on the floor, far as I could tell," Johnny said, remembering the fall the old man had taken. "He never came to, after that," Johnny added.

"I don't like the sound of his cough," Doc stated. "It sounds consumptive. I hope the old fellow doesn't have a concussion, too. Let's get this filthy beard off of him."

Johnny nodded, wondering why the old man had jumped in to help him when he was attacked in the street. He wished now that he hadn't. It was obvious he was way too old to be fighting. He was way too old to be drinking, too, for that matter. But that was the choice a lot of men made nowadays, what with all the troubles and grief that seemed to exist. It was the ruination of many a good man. He'd seen plenty of proof of that on his travels to find his father.

CHAPTER 44

Angry voices could be heard all through the downstairs of the hospital, causing Ophelia and both of her aunts to rush down the hall and into the room they were coming from. They were surprised to see that the offenders were Michael O'Leary and young Eli Hart, two men who were not known, in the least, for such outbursts.

"What's going on?" asked Ophelia as she entered the room, one hand raised to her throat. "We can't have such a commotion going on," she said, as she looked back and forth at the men. "We're not a saloon, you know. We're a hospital."

Both men looked embarrassed by her words, and said they'd keep it down. Eli apologized, his face fire-red. Ophelia wondered if it was because of how angry he was—which was obvious—or because she had embarrassed him. Michael's face was also much redder than normal, though not as red as Eli's. He, too, apologized to her, while looking at the young man who stood before him. There seemed to be something...Ophelia thought...a similarity of sorts to the two of them: a resemblance. She had never seen them together before, and so, had never noticed it. They seemed to have a likeness, of sorts, to their features. Their lips, she thought, or the eyes...yes, it was in their eyes that they looked so alike. And in their red hair.

"Well, I don't know what the problem is," she said, keeping her voice firm. "But we'll have no more such outbursts, do I make myself clear?"

The men nodded in reply, the younger of the two staring down at the floor, the older, staring at his young visitor. Ophelia turned then, nearly running into the two aunts, whom she hadn't realized were standing directly behind her. "Oh, excuse me," she said, stopping abruptly, until they, too, turned to leave the room. She glanced back at Michael and Eli, giving them a look, then left the room.

Once out in the hall, she motioned to her aunts. "I have more wash to hang out. If there's another outburst, would you please come and get me immediately?"

Both aunts agreed, Aunt Hilda looking back toward Michael's room with a disgusted look upon her face, and Auntie Belle smiling her usual angelic smile. "Oh, I forgot to tell you, there's a new patient in the front room. He's an old fellow in quite serious condition, from what Judith said. Doc has enlisted another fellow's help to get him cleaned up a bit, before we can even see to him. A drinker, you see. And the little girl, what's her name? Oh, yes, Mary...Mary Wright. She needs a complete change of her bed and gown. Would one of you give her sister a hand with that, please? I'll give the pot of soup a thorough stir, ladies, on my way out to finish hanging the wash, if you will tend to those things."

"You know how hard the stairs are on your knees, sister, so I'll go on up and help Juliana with Mary. You can tend to our other patient when Doc's done seeing to him," Aunt Hilda said, turning and heading up the stairs before Auntie Belle could even reply.

Auntie Belle had intended to see to him, anyway. She'd heard that he was a fellow at the mercy of "John Barley Corn" and figured if she got the chance, she might talk to him about the Lord, and His forgiveness, and maybe turn the fellow onto a more Christian pathway. It wouldn't be the first time she'd come across some poor soul who so badly needed a slight push, as she liked to think of it, toward a more righteous life. It was, after all, her Christian duty to help those who had slipped off the "true path," and fallen into the devil's lair. She smiled, as she thought of the welcomed task before her, and turned on her heel, heading down the hall toward the fellow's room.

"So when did you know?" Eli hissed, trying not to raise his voice. "Was it some kind of joke to you, knowing all along that I was your flesh and blood, and not telling me?" Anger flashed in his eyes, as he glared at Michael, giving him no time to answer his questions.

"Eli, calm down," Michael ordered, hoping he'd say the right things to the boy. "I didn't know, Eli, till just recently. I never knew before, or I wouldn't have let you be raised by Jonas—or by *anyone else—for* that matter. I thought we were just friends, too. I was happy to be your friend. I had no idea that we were anything else." Michael kept his voice low, so as not to offend others in the vicinity.

"I don't understand it," Eli stated, pacing over to the window of the room, clenching his fists as he did so. "I *liked* you. You were my friend. Other than my friendship with Johnny, *you* were the friend I felt closest to, felt I could trust! How could you break that trust? I don't understand how it could have meant so little to you!"

"I didn't know, Eli. I liked our friendship, too. It meant a lot to me, too, to spend the time we did; hunting, and tracking, playing cards, and just sitting, discussing things like we did. I never betrayed your friendship, son, not once."

Eli whirled around when Michael called him "son." "I'm *not your* son," he said. "I'm *nothin'* to you, Michael O'Leary! I'm not your *son*, and not your *friend!*" Eli stated, glad to see the look that crossed the other man's face at the words he spewed at him. Then he turned and walked from the room, anger filling him because he felt so betrayed. He entered the hallway, almost running smack into Johnny, who had just finished helping Doc with the old man.

"Eli, what's wrong?" Johnny asked, hurrying to catch up with his friend, as he slammed out the front door of the hospital, and was now taking the steps two at a time, in his hurry to be far away from whatever it was that had upset him so. "Eli, wait a minute," Johnny implored, hurrying to catch up with him. Eli swung up onto his horse, never looking back, nor answering, and raced off down the road, as Johnny flung himself up onto Buck's back, and raced off in pursuit. He'd seen Eli mad before, but nothing like this. There had to be some way to help him, he thought. They'd been friends since childhood. Had always talked to each other about their problems. He spurred Buck on, noticing that Eli wasn't heading home to the Hart Farm, but was taking the road that led away from it, instead. Well, he thought, I don't know what's riled you, my friend, but whatever it is, I'm going with you. We'll get it all straightened out, if there's a way to do so, once you've had a chance to calm down.

Back at the hospital, Auntie Belle passed Doc in the hall, getting the nod from him to go in and see to their patient. She could hear him coughing as she entered the room, and knew he was very ill, indeed. She walked softly into the room, not wanting to wake the poor man if he was asleep. Going over to the bed, she stared in total disbelief, at her childhood sweetheart, Salvanus Pearly.

CHAPTER 45

"Auntie Belle," Ophelia said, as she entered the house, awhile later, noticing her aunt sitting at the kitchen table, her face pale and tears showing upon her cheeks. "What is it, dear?" she asked, hurrying to her side. "Are you ill? Has something happened?" Auntie Belle shook her head, sniffling loudly, and then blew her nose on a hanky she pulled from her apron pocket. "I'm all right, Ophelia," she said, and promptly burst into tears. She covered her face with her hands, trying to gain her composure, knowing she could never explain to her niece, or anyone, for that matter, why she was in such a state. "It's nothing, dear," she whispered, choking back more tears with great effort. "I'm just a silly old woman, that's all. Go about your work, dear. Forget about me. I'll be fine."

Ophelia was just about to question her further, when Aunt Hilda entered the room, stopping in her tracks when she saw that her sister was crying. "What in tarnation's gotten into you, Dorothea? My word, we can't have the patients see us crying. Whatever is wrong?" she questioned, an almost blameful tone to her voice.

"I'll be...I'm fine now," the usually happy sister replied, and she hoped she wouldn't burst into tears again. She stood; wiping her eyes once more on her handkerchief, then shoved it back into her apron pocket. She attempted to smile at Ophelia, to assure her that she was now in control of herself, but had to quickly look away, as she saw the sympathetic look on Ophelia's face. "I'd better get back to my patient," she whispered, and hurried from the room and down the hall.

Salvanus lay as he had before, his breathing labored, his head and one shoulder bandaged. He'd been in a fight, Doc had explained. It looked like he'd gotten a concussion during the melee, and if he didn't regain consciousness soon, it was doubtful he'd regain it at all. That's why she'd been crying. But, of course, she couldn't tell anyone that. She knew what Aunt Hilda would say. She'd chide her for being so foolish. She'd tell her to straighten up, to come to her senses. He was, after all, just an old drunk. Worthless. Hopeless. Despicable. She could hear her already, and felt ashamed of her, for her inability to see the good in a person like him. Like Sal.

She pulled a chair up beside his bed, and took his hand into hers, stroking the scarred and wrinkled skin. It looks like life has been so hard on you, she thought, watching him closely, hoping he might open his eyes and notice her sitting there beside him. Of course she was no longer the young girl he had once walked home from school. Far from it. He probably wouldn't even recognize me, she thought, and she reached up with her other hand to smooth her white hair into place. He coughed then, a series of raucous coughs that sounded terrible. She covered her mouth with her hand. You poor dear, she thought, smiling down at him. Then, looking around to make certain they were alone, she began to tenderly stroke the side of his face.

He groaned then, and stirred slightly, as another coughing spell wracked his body. "Don't stop," he whispered, never opening his eyes, and raised one gnarled hand up to cover hers, much to her surprise. She gazed at him, not seeing him as he was now, but seeing him as the young boy she had cared so deeply for, so many years before.

Without a word, she continued to stroke the side of his face. His beard having been shaved off by Doc, the skin beneath looked so pale, the rest of it, deeply tanned. She heard the rustle of movement behind her, and turned her head to see Father Patrick standing in the doorway, smiling at her. She began to rise, but he called softly, "I'll be back," and turned away, not wanting to disturb her. She felt Sal gently squeeze her hand then, and settled back in the chair beside his bed, a feeling of contentment filling her. Sounds from out in the hall did not bother her. Nor did the coming and going of others. She stayed with him, long into the evening, her heart filled with tremendous peace. Then, just before dark, his hand dropped from hers, and she knew he was gone. She took a deep breath to gain her composure and slowly reached to pull the blanket up to cover his face. Before she did so, however, she bent her face to his, whispering, "Goodbye, my love," and kissed him softly upon the cheek. Then she walked slowly from the room and down the hall, looking for either Doctor Valentine, or Father O'Leary. Sal was theirs now. She had shared her special time with him, and knew she would never forget it as long as she lived.

Father O'Leary walked from Cal's room as she approached. Seeing her face, he did not have to ask what had occurred. He wrapped his arms around her, knowing she was deeply affected by the death of Old Man Pearly. He didn't know the man had been anything, other than just a patient of hers, till he looked into her eyes and saw the love and pain the old woman was feeling. "'Tis a blessin' to go home t' the Lord," he said, hoping to cheer her.

Auntie Belle rubbed her eyes, tears running down her cheeks, and smiled at him as best she could. "He won't be sufferin' anymore, will he, Father?" she asked, her voice close to breaking.

"No, that he won't," Father Patrick replied. "Did you know him, then, Miss Belle?"

"I knew him...yes...and I loved him," she said, surprising the young priest. Then she walked slowly down the hall toward her room.

CHAPTER 46

As Father Patrick finished praying over the body of Salvanus Pearly, a loud commotion began in the hallway. He could hear the sound of women crying, and feet running, and words that he couldn't understand. German, he thought. He hurried out into the hall to see what was going on. To his surprise, a large, older woman, dressed all in black, ran past him, her hands raised up toward the ceiling, her face flushed, and eyes wild. He had hugged the wall, certain she was going to run him down, and felt relieved that she hadn't. He began to walk down the hallway in the direction she had gone, and before he knew it, another woman squeezed past him, hurrying in the same direction. They looked so odd, bringing the thought to his mind of a story he had read when much younger, of a pair of banshees that wreaked havoc on a countryside village in some foreign land. Banshees, he thought, smiling, and then—just for good measure—he crossed himself. It was foolish for a man to believe everything he read, he knew that. But, a little superstition might not be completely bad, he thought, remembering how the Pawnee war party had run away, allowing Johnny and Colin to rescue the children, all because the Indians had been so superstitious. I guess "everything in moderation" is excellent advice, he thought, and just then he saw Aunt Hilda hurrying toward him, a strained look upon her face.

"Well, we got another one," she said, in greeting. "Better go do your thing, Sir." Then she rushed on by him, explaining no further. I guess we've had another death, he thought, hurrying along the hall to where weeping could be heard from the two women who had nearly run him down. He entered the room, knowing it was the room of Heinrich Yeager, and the two distraught women were his wife and mother. He walked to the bedside, looking down at the deceased, and began to pray. The older woman wailed louder and louder, the more he prayed, and he found himself wondering if the good Lord could hear his words of prayer above her hysterics. Oh, well, he thought, we all react to death in our own way. This just happened to be her way, he supposed. He continued to pray, and the woman continued to wail, getting louder still. When he finished, to his surprise, both women grew silent. He wondered at this, but figured it was probably just a strange custom from the Old Country, not realizing that they were Lutheran, and upset by having a priest pray over their beloved. He turned to leave the room then, having said a few words of sympathy to the women, happy to escape the older woman's baleful looks.

Once in the hall, he breathed a sigh of relief, and strolled to the parlor to sit before the fireplace. It was bitter outside, even though the snow had been slow in coming this year, and he knew the warmth of the fire would be most welcoming. He sat before it, reading his Bible in silence, and meditating on the events of the day. One death had given him a sense of comfort, as he saw the love in an old woman's eyes. The second death had wreaked upset, in its wake. Funny, he thought, just how different folks are.

It was then he heard his name called, and turned to see Katie Yeager standing in the hallway to his right, tears running down her lovely young face. He rose quickly, and went to her.

"Ah, Katie, me child," he said, his Irish accent strong, as was his habit when he was under the least stress. "'Tis sorry I am, about yer dear father," he said, and she flung herself against him, weeping softly. He held her, noticing the highlights the fire threw across her golden locks, and how the sweet scent of her seemed to envelop them, as if they stood in a field of flowers. So this was the girl who had stirred his brother's heart, he thought, and no wonder. She was a lovely young thing, both pretty and sweet. All the things a normal man could hope for, he was sure. A normal man. That thought ran over and over in his mind, as she clung to him, wetting the shoulder of his garment. And I'm *not* a normal man, he thought. I'm a man of God. And with that thought in mind, he gently extracted himself from the sobbing young woman, telling her how sorry he was about her loss, and then he walked her down the hallway to where her mother and grandmother wept beside the body of her father.

When he returned to the parlor to get his Bible, he was more than a little surprised to find Aunt Hilda sitting in the chair he had vacated, his Bible held within her work-worn hands. "I see you've found my book," he said, unsure of what else to say.

"Yes, Sir," she replied, looking up at him, a wary look upon her long-boned face.

He laughed softly at her calling him "sir," and reached out to take his Bible. To his surprise, she held it tightly against her bony chest, looking at him questioningly for the longest time, before speaking. "I need to know if what I've heard about you is true," she said at last, never taking her eyes from him.

He sat down upon another chair facing the fireplace, studying the woman, wondering what it was she had on her mind. "I'm afraid I don't know what you mean," he said, smiling slightly.

"Oh, yes," she said. "You know what I mean, all right, Sir."

Patrick cleared his throat, "Why do you call me 'sir'?" he asked, seeing her eyes light up, momentarily, at his question.

"'Cause that's what I figure you are," she said, her cheekbones encased in dark shadows, as she turned toward him and away from the fire's glow. "I seen what's in this here book of yours. Can't say I know many preachers who carry a book like that. You're a hired gun, I figure. One who masquerades as a man of God, am I right?"

Patrick laughed aloud, suddenly enjoying the exchange they were having. So this old aunt thought he was some kind of gunslinger. He slapped his knee, wondering if he should play along, or set her straight. He didn't want to offend her, but felt maybe some harmless shenanigans, on his part, might ease the tension between them. He leaned back against his chair, trying to look the part of her imagined "hired gun". Then slowly he smiled, making certain he looked like a villain who'd just been found out. "I don't know how you found me out, but you've got me dead-to-rights," he said. "I'm the lowest, meanest gunslinger in the whole territory, Lady. Can I trust you to keep my secret? Or am I gonna have t' shoot ya'?" he asked.

"That's what I thought," she said, handing him back his Bible and getting up from her chair, all the while, shaking her head.

"What do you mean?" Patrick asked, not understanding.

"The rumors of that "miracle" you done to get them children away from them Injuns was too hard for an old woman like myself to believe, even if them girls swore it was true. So you see, I figured only a holy fella could do what they said. Now I know the truth."

"Now, wait a minute," Patrick said. "I was just fooling with you. I know you saw what's in my Bible, but I was only fooling. I really *am* a priest, not a gunslinger, by trade," he said.

"Sure you are," she said, edging past him. "Sure you are." Patrick stood there, wondering how he could convince her that he'd only been playing a joke on her, when she turned back to face him, saying, "Goodnight, Gunslinger. Oh, and while you're at it, would you see to a miracle, *Sir,* for that nice fellow my niece thinks so highly of; Cal Dunnevey?" Then she turned and headed down the hall. And as he tried to figure how he'd convince her that he truly was a priest, he heard her call out, "Goodnight, Sir."

CHAPTER 47

Cal Dunnevey knew that something was different, the moment he woke. He didn't realize it right away. He simply heard some birds chirping outside his hospital room window, rolled over, opened his eyes, and wella! The dreaded black he was used to finding himself in had been replaced by an odd shade of yellow. At first, he just lay there in his bed, not sure if he was imagining it, and afraid to hope. He lay very still, not moving even the slightest. He was afraid the strange color would vanish, if he moved. Lying there, still as could be, he heard movement in the hallway, and knew the ladies were going about their business, busy as usual. Any moment now, Ophelia would come into his room, a cheery greeting upon her lips. Then she'd set his breakfast tray down on the little side table by his bed, and hurry over to open the curtains of the large window that graced his room. Returning at once, she'd ask how he was feeling, if he'd had a good night, and if he needed a few moments to himself—which of course, he did, after the long night. Then she'd see to it the small table was right where he needed it to be, so he could manage to feed himself the breakfast she'd fixed for him. The other ladies had always insisted on feeding him when he first entered the hospital, but Ophelia had told them, in no uncertain terms, that there'd be none of that. He remembered how definite she'd been about it, and had to smile at remembering. "He's not an invalid, ladies," she'd told them. "Mr. Dunnevey is a full-grown man. He is neither an invalid, nor a baby, and we shall treat him with the respect due him, because of it." Cal wouldn't have minded a little babying, but even he had been set straight by her words. These few days in the hospital had made him realize how strong Ophelia was, and he admired her for it, more than he could say. She dealt with the ladies who helped care for her patients, decisively, in a firm, yet caring manner, letting them know exactly how to deal with each patient's individual needs. He noticed, however, that it was *she* who tended him. He hadn't realized it, at first. But it soon became evident to him that he was completely in her care alone, each and every day. Even when Doc came to check on him, Ophelia was right there, asking what he needed, making certain she was doing all she could for him. He'd been a little embarrassed by all her attention, at first, knowing there were more and more patients to be looked after, as each day went by. But still she came. Not Auntie Belle, though the old dear always dropped in to say hello, now and then, throughout each day. Not Aunt Hilda, though he'd hear her footsteps as she came in to gather up his bedpan, or dirty bedclothes. He could tell it was her, by this way she had of wheezing a slight bit when she breathed. She was a strange one, she was, he thought. If he didn't know better, he'd think underneath that tough exterior, she actually liked him. But far be it, he thought, for him to try to befriend her. She'd just as likely tear his head off, as be friendly. He laughed aloud, turning his head slightly and opening his eyes, again. The yellow haze was all around him, just like when he first woke up. He'd have to tell Doc, the minute he arrived. Don't get your hopes up, Dunnevey. It might not mean anything. Just be thankful the headaches have stopped, and the pain over that eye has let up. These thoughts ran through his head, as he rolled over and sat slowly up on the side of his bed. Still yellow. He looked in the direction he knew the window to be. Lighter yellow.

The sound of the front door opening, caused him to feel for his blanket, and check quickly, as best he could, to make certain he was decently covered. Footsteps—a man's—stopped in his doorway, and he guessed by their sound that it was Patrick O'Leary. "Hello, Father," he said, smiling.

"Good morning, Cal. Can't put one over on you, can I?" his friend replied, walking over to his bed. He put one hand on Cal's shoulder, in greeting. "And how are you this fine morning, my friend?"

"I'm fine," Cal replied. "Yourself?"

"Fit as a fiddle," Patrick replied, and Cal could hear the joy in the young man's voice.

"I didn't expect you to be here so early this morning," Cal commented. "After all, you didn't leave here till nearly morning, wasn't it? It must have been dawn when you looked in on me, just before you headed out?"

"That it was, my friend," Father Patrick replied. "I stayed a bit longer last night, at the bedside of Miss Juliana's little sister, Mary. She's not expected to recover, I'm afraid, and I hoped my presence would bring a bit of comfort to her sister. They've been through so much, you know, with the Pawnee thing, and now the wee girl being so ill. On my way out, I stopped in to check on you. Didn't know you were awake. I'm sorry if I disturbed you."

Cal smiled. "You didn't disturb me. I...well...I guess it might sound odd, but I felt comforted, too, knowing you were here. I felt like there was a sudden warmth—I can't think how else to explain it—in the room. Do you know what I mean?"

Patrick patted his friend on the shoulder before answering, smiling at his words. "'T'was the Spirit of the Lord, my friend. Have a good day now. I've a hankerin' for a cup of Auntie Belle's coffee, and think I smell it. I'll see you later," and with that, the young priest left the room and walked on down the hall to the kitchen, to wheedle a cup of coffee from his favorite aunt. He wondered if Aunt Hilda would also be on hand, and would have anymore of her insinuating ideas to share with him. He hoped not. I'm too tired, he thought, to try to placate the old woman this morning. Let her think me a gunslinger, a priest, or the king of France, for all I care. I'm too tired to care just what she thinks this morning. And he entered the kitchen, happy to find only Auntie Belle there.

He was halfway through his cup of coffee when a shout could be heard from down the hall, and Auntie Belle hurried off to see what had happened. He was just too tired to race off at the sound of every loud noise, he decided, and planned to finish his coffee first. Then he'd go to see what the excitement was. After all, he thought, it hadn't been a shout of anger, or pain. It sounded like a happy shout. Surely someone else could see to a happy shout, he thought. He took another swallow of his coffee, then rubbed a hand across his eyes. He yawned, stretching his body a bit, hoping to get some of the tiredness he was feeling to leave him. He had a big day ahead: another visit with the sisters, Juliana and Mary, paperwork to tend to at the church, and a sermon to prepare before the next Mass. He groaned at these thoughts. If he had time, he also hoped to have a word or two with Michael. There were some questions he had wanted to ask him, ever since they'd come back to Hastings from Chaska. It wasn't that he wanted to stir up any problems; he just wanted to make sure that there'd be no further trouble because of the events that had taken place there.

As he picked up his cup to take another sip of coffee, Auntie Belle rushed into the kitchen. The look on her face told Patrick, without asking, that something wonderful had happened. The lovely old woman positively beamed!

"They want you, Father, down the hall," she said, a wide smile crossing her face.

"In which room?" he asked, taking a final swallow from his cup, emptying it.

"You know which one," she said, and she turned and hurried from the room, heading back down the hall.

Patrick shrugged, getting up from the table, and walked down the hall. As he neared Cal's room, he could hear many excited voices. He entered, surprised to see Doc Valentine bending before Cal, using some tool to look into his eyes. Ophelia stood to one side, her hands clenched tightly together. By the door, Aunt Hilda stood, her back straight, her chin held high. She looked over at him, studying him a few moments, then whispered, "He's getting his sight back." She paused a second, her eyes welling up with tears, then added, "I knew you could do it. Thank you ...*Father.*"

CHAPTER 48

Eli finally pulled up, stopping to rest his horse, a fair distance from town. Johnny knew he had to stop, sooner or later, and was glad when he saw that he finally had. He rode up to his friend, dismounted, and waited to see if Eli would tell him what was wrong. Something had angered him, and Johnny was curious what it could have been. He knew Eli to usually be levelheaded, unshakable, and considerate of other people's feelings. The way he had stormed out of Michael O'Leary's room at the hospital had been anything but those things. He had never seen him so mad, in fact, and had been totally surprised by his friend's actions.

Eli tied his horse's reins to a small lower limb of a young tree and walked off into the woods, not saying a word to him, however. Johnny tied his horse beside Eli's and walked off in another direction. When both men returned, Johnny asked if they were going to ride, again, or if he planned to sit a spell, and tell him what it was that was eating at him.

Eli looked long and hard at him, then spoke. "When did *you* find out? Did *you* know all along, too?"

Johnny was confused by his friend's questions, and had not the slightest idea what he was talking about. "Did I know what?"

"You know darn well *what*," Eli said, pacing back and forth.

"I'm afraid I don't," Johnny answered, watching his friend.

"If I find out you knew, too, all along, I'll beat the tar out of you, Johnny. Friend or no friend," Eli threatened, glaring at him.

"Well, if it's a fight you want, it's a fight you're gonna get," Johnny replied, having had just about enough. "So maybe you better tell me what's riling you, and then we'll take it from there."

Eli walked over to a large fallen limb and sat down upon it, studying Johnny, before speaking. "Did you know that he was my father, my real father?" he suddenly asked, watching Johnny closely.

"Did I know *who* was your real father?"

"You know darn well who," Eli stated, getting back up, and pacing back and forth like a caged animal.

"You better tell me," Johnny said, sitting down on the same limb Eli had been sitting on, "before we have that fight you're aching so bad for." He stood then, facing Eli.

Eli came to a halt, still furious, still feeling betrayed by the truth, as he now knew it. "Michael! Michael O'Leary's my father! Tell me you didn't know, John. I'll never trust you again, if you did."

Johnny sat back down, shaking his head, thinking no wonder Eli was so upset. He knew *he* would have been just as upset, if he was in his place. "No, I didn't know. I understand now why you're mad."

"All this time, Johnny. All these *years*, and I thought he was my friend. The only friend I felt close to, you know, except for you," Eli said, pacing again. Johnny kept silent, hoping Eli would talk his anger out. "We hunted together. He taught me to track, taught me to whittle. We used to play cards in winter, when the chores were done. I'd be glad to get away from the farm, you know. I'd ride out to his place, and help him with *his* chores, then we'd go in, and talk, or play cards." He sat down beside Johnny, shaking his head sadly, at these memories. "Do you have any idea how many things I talked to him about? I told him...all kinds of things...how I felt about Ma and Pa," he said, and he groaned at re-membering. Johnny held his tongue, knowing it was good for Eli to talk through the things that upset him. "I told him how I felt about...about my real ma...Lydia. I told him how I hurt when I learned she just left me and walked away. I even told him about the...the girls I liked. And he'd give me advice; tell me how to treat them. He taught me how to *dance* before I went to my first dance. We laughed about it." He stopped talking; his cheeks afire, and then covered his face with his hands, groaning.

Johnny sat beside him, not seeing it as Eli did. He thought on all the things that Eli had said, and then spoke. "Eli, you said that Michael hunted with you, and taught you things, and that you two talked about all those other things, right?"

"Yeah," Eli said, still holding his head in his hands. "So?"

"You talked about your feelings, right? And about the good things—and bad—that were going on in your life, right?"

"I just told you that. So what?" Eli asked, looking over at Johnny, wishing he'd just make his point.

"Did you ever talk to Jonas about those same things? Did you ask him how to dance, or tell him about the girls you liked?"

"No," Eli replied, shaking his head slightly, in response.

"Eli, I never had the chance to go to my pa and ask him all those things. I'd give *anything* to have had that chance. Maybe I'm not seeing things clearly, my friend, but don't you see...you and Michael have had a father-son relationship, all along. You just called it by a different name. It seems to me that you owe him an apology. Does it really matter *how* you were close to him...as a friend, or as a son? I think the main thing is, you two have been close, all along."

Eli was staring at Johnny, having not thought of these things in this way. He let Johnny's words run over and over in his mind, seeing the foolishness of his actions, earlier, at the hospital. Johnny was right; he did owe Michael an apology, a *big* one. He looked over at his friend, smiling sheepishly. "I guess you're a lot smarter than I give you credit for," he said, and Johnny reached over and was about to pat his shoulder, when they heard a horse approaching, and wondered who it was, so far from town. "Do you know who he is?" Eli asked, as the rider came into view.

Johnny stood, a funny feeling settling in his gut, as he saw Jubal Cade riding toward them. "Watch your back," he told Eli. "That fellow was at Michael's, awhile back. He's the one who told me Michael was in trouble over in Chaska. I don't trust him."

Eli stood, feeling for the holster at his side, undoing the strap that held his gun in place. It never hurt to be cautious, he thought. The man riding toward them had a look to him: the look of trouble.

Jubal Cade reined in his horse in front of Johnny and Eli, looking uneasy. "Well, look who I run into," Jubal said, spitting off to one side, smiling down at Johnny. Johnny saw that the old fellow was looking him up and down. "What you boys doin' way out here?" the old man asked, still smiling.

"Nothing that's any business of yours," Johnny replied. He was more sure than ever that Cade had been an integral part of the trouble Michael had found himself in, over in Chaska, and wanted no part of the old man.

"Who's your friend?" Jubal asked then, spitting again.

"Just a friend," Johnny replied.

"Did you manage t' get that O'Leary fella home for burial?" Jubal asked then, and Johnny saw Eli perk up at mention of the O'Leary name.

"That we did," Johnny answered, not wanting to let him know that Michael was still alive, since he wasn't sure what part Cade had played in the trouble Michael had in Chaska. He was more certain then ever that Cade, and the men he'd been with at Michael's cabin, had somehow been involved.

"Darn shame," the old fellow said, and he spit again, much to Johnny's disgust. "He was a friend o' mine. We was "business partners" once, sort o'..." he said, clearing his throat. Then he rode closer to where Johnny stood, and reached out his hand. "Take care, boy. I hope you give my regards to your pa. We was drinking buddies, way back years ago, when he was grieving so bad. Take care now, ya' hear," and as he leaned forward to shake Johnny's hand, Johnny saw the medallion that hung from his neck. The round deer bone medallion that belonged to his father, Moses Gentry.

Johnny stood frozen in place, shocked at seeing the medallion. The old man's hand remained extended toward him, but Johnny could only stand there, staring. When at last, he found his voice, he reached for his gun, drawing it, pointing it at the old man, who stared at him in surprise. "Where'd you get that medallion?" Johnny asked, his words barely a whisper.

"What the hell? What medallion? What's riling ya'?" Jubal said, sitting back in his saddle, adding, "You better know how t' use that gun, boy, if'n you plan t' point it at me fer much longer." He spit, his face now flushed with anger. "I'm tellin' you, son..."

"Shut up! Give me my pa's medallion," Johnny ordered. "I want to know where you got it."

"Hell, son, if'n you want this old thing, it's yours. I got no fight with you," Jubal said, and he pulled off the medallion and tossed it toward Johnny, who caught it in mid-air.

"Where'd you get it?" Johnny asked, anger filling him.

Jubal Cade hung his head, shaking it back and forth a few times, an odd look upon his face. He looked at the young man who stood before him, hating to answer, but not wanting to get shot. At last he spoke. "I took it, boy. Took it off'n a dead Yank. Couldn't make out his face, it was...messed up. I took it off him where he lay, stone cold, after the battle o' Gettysburg. I thought it looked Injun. I liked it." He looked at Johnny, continuing. "I swear on my maw's grave, son. The fella was dead. It took me a whole lot o' scrubbing, that night, jest t' git all his blood off'n it."

Johnny holstered his gun, glanced quickly at Eli, and then walked away. Clenched tightly in his hand was his father's medallion. He'd heard about the Gettysburg battle. He'd heard that more than half of the 300 men from the 1st Minnesota had died there, as they crossed an open field, charging into the Confederate lines against tremendous odds. In all his travels, searching for word of his father, he'd been told that Gettysburg most likely was the place he had died. He'd gone there many times, never finding proof.

Johnny walked off into the woods, no longer caring about Jubal Cade, wanting only to be alone. Far enough into the woods, he leaned against the trunk of a tall oak tree, and cried.

When he walked out of the woods a short while later, Eli was sitting on the large fallen limb waiting for him, and Jubal Cade was nowhere to be seen. Eli rose and walked toward his friend. "Are you all right?" he asked.

"Could be better," Johnny replied, looking out across the land, his eyes giving evidence of the tears he had shed.

"I'm heading home," Eli said. "I have to set things straight with my folks...all my folks," he added, a slight smile upon his face.

"Good idea. I intend to do the same. I'm going to see my mother at Standing Elk's village." Johnny reached out, taking Eli's hand within his own, "May Wakantanka ride with you, my friend."

"And may the good Lord watch over you, Johnny Black Hawk, wherever your path takes you," Eli said, grasping his friend's hand, his grip strong and firm. And as the two childhood friends shook hands, they couldn't help wondering if they'd ever meet again.

CHAPTER 49

Cal Dunnevey had been back in his small room just over a week, when he realized how unhappy he was, in spite of having his sight almost totally restored. He caught himself pacing back and forth through the store during days that seemed unbearably long and dreary. And at night, he'd pace even more, unable to sleep. He couldn't put his finger on it, but something was...missing. That was it; that was the way he felt, like something was missing.

He'd always been a man who was content with his life, before he was blind. A man who was content in his surroundings. Now, hard as he tried, he just couldn't understand the strange unsettled feeling that crept into both his day and night, even invading his sleep.

Maybe it's from being in this small room again, after being in the more spacious room at the hospital, he thought. Thinking that, he suddenly remembered the treasured plans he had long ago drawn out: plans of the house he had hoped to build on the beautiful piece of land he owned outside of Hastings. He hurried over to the kitchen cupboard and pulled open the drawer where he'd kept the long ignored plans. There was a time, a moment really, when he'd been so discouraged that he was tempted to rip them to pieces. But somehow he found himself unable to do so, and was so glad now, that he hadn't.

He pawed through the many papers in the drawer, shoving papers and pens, this way and that. Making a mental note to clean out the drawer, first chance he got. He hoped he could find the papers. He was sure that finding them would cheer him.

At the very bottom of the drawer they lay, and he pulled them out, not picking up the other papers that spilled onto the floor, or even shutting the drawer. He carried them into the store, spreading them out across his desk, searching each page to see what order they should be in. When he got them all in order, he bent low over them, squinting as he studied each line, each detail, his eyesight still not completely clear. He was so intent on what he was doing, that he failed to hear the bell above the door, as it opened, and an old man entered. He stood just inside the door, gazing around at the inside of the store, not speaking. Only as he turned to leave, did Cal become aware of him. "Can I help you?" Cal asked, wishing he hadn't been interrupted. The old man turned slowly, looking back at him, his head cocked to one side as if to hear better, but gave no answer. He had snow-white hair that hung well beyond his shoulders, and a thick white beard to match. He wore dark blue pants and a coat that looked threadbare. His hands were red from the cold, Cal saw, though the sleeves of the coat covered them most of the time, and a dark felt, wide-brimmed hat was pulled down upon his head. Around his neck, a red scarf was wound, and Cal could plainly see that one end of it was unraveling. "Can I help you?" Cal asked again, a little louder, not certain the man had heard him the first time.

Instead of answering, the old fellow turned, pulling the door shut behind him, and as Cal watched, he started to cross the street toward Yeager's General Store. He walked slowly, with a shuffling gait, Cal noticed, and he wondered who the man was, and where he'd come from. Probably just some saloon patron, he thought, and he turned back to his papers.

That evening, as Cal sat on his bed in the back of the store, he couldn't help hearing the sounds from the saloons further on down the street. The piano music reminded him of his childhood, of his mother, Maggie, and of Victor Jalaco. It reminded him, too, of the conversation he'd overheard from the hallway at the hospital. The conversation that had caused him to turn and rush out of the hospital and fall, head over heels, down the front steps. The conversation that had ultimately led to him getting his sight back. He wasn't certain who the man was who'd been speaking. But he'd clearly heard him say, "Did he kill Jalaco?" There was no doubt about that. He'd heard him loud and clear. Cal felt a nagging fear spread all through him, as he remembered. I spent twenty miserable years in total darkness, he thought, twenty years I wouldn't wish on my worst enemy. Could I regain my sight now, only to end up hung for a crime I committed when I was nine years old? Jalaco deserved to die. Anybody would have shot him for what he'd done. But nobody *had* shot him, or even stepped up to help. Everyone in the saloon that night had sat there, simply watching, as Jalaco beat Maggie to death. I was the one, Cal thought. I was the one who killed Victor Jalaco. He took a deep breath, rubbing his hands together, fighting the uneasiness inside him. Well, no need worrying about it right this minute. If they want me, they'll come and get me. I can be sure of that, he thought, and he pushed aside the papers, unable to keep his mind on them, and walked to the front of the store to lock the door, then walked to his room in the back.

He was overjoyed to have his sight back. Even the way it was now; slightly blurred and tinted that odd shade of yellow. He was sure it was fading, little by little, the yellow. It seemed like it, anyway. He remembered how he had prayed and prayed to get his sight back. But every day that went by made him feel more and more helpless, and more and more hopeless. He remembered the anger he'd felt, too, and how it had burned all through him. It had been so hard being blind. Now his prayers were being answered. He was getting his sight back, no matter how blurred. Would the fact that he'd killed Jalaco come back to haunt him now, after all he'd been through?

He stepped out of his boots, and his pants, and pulled off his shirt, then lay down upon his bed, resting his hands behind his head. Looking up at the marks upon the ceiling above him, he noticed again the piano music from the saloons. He wished he was still at the hospital and Ophelia was by his side, talking softly to him, her voice easy on his ears, and filled with hope and caring. Ophelia, he thought, that's what I'm missing. I'm missing Ophelia. And he smiled into the dark, wondering why he hadn't realized it sooner.

He dreamt that night of Lea. He'd had no word from her since she'd left town, but that night he dreamt of her. She stood before him, her hair in soft golden ringlets, wearing a dress of shimmering white. She smiled at him, happy it seemed, and he tried to close the distance between them, but could not. The dream seemed to go on and on, but had lasted only a few moments he realized, as he woke from it, and looked at his watch. He wondered why he'd dreamt it. He lay there, staring into the darkness, thinking. As he did, he realized he no longer felt any pain because of her absence. Truth was, he couldn't remember when he'd thought of her last. That surprised him. *I felt so hurt when she left,* he thought. *Felt like I had no reason to go on. Without her, I didn't want to live.* And now, he thought, *she's just another person.* He closed his eyes, surprised by these thoughts.

And as he lay there, thoughts of Ophelia entered his mind. Ophelia as she'd looked that last day of his stay at the hospital, unruly ringlets pulling loose from the ribbon she'd tied her hair back with, her sweet smile so full of caring and kindness. Ophelia in her soft dress, her waist the size a man could wrap his hands around, her skirt billowing out, swaying when she moved. He opened his eyes, still envisioning her. As clear as if she was there beside him, he saw her delicate chin and upturned nose, her lovely hands, and long and slender fingers, always busy, always helping, always so eager to help... him. He wished he could hold her, could hear her voice, could take her into his arms and kiss her. Not Lea. He knew now it was Ophelia he wanted by his side!

The next morning, bright and early, he procured a horse and buggy from the livery stable, dressed in his "Sunday best" clothes, and rushed to the hospital. He was careful not to disturb any patients as he let himself inside, and hurried on down the hall to the kitchen. He was certain Ophelia would be hard at work, as she always was, cooking or beginning some of the other day's chores.

To his great disappointment, however, the only two occupants of the kitchen were the aunts, Belle and Hilda. He stopped at the doorway, his hat in hand, looking from one to the other, not certain how to explain his early morning visit.

"Oh! Good morning, Cal," Auntie Belle greeted him, as she stirred a large pot of gruel at the stove.

"Good morning...ah...ladies," he replied.

"Are you all right? Do you need the doctor?" Auntie Belle asked, wiping her hands on her apron, a concerned look upon her face.

"No. No doctor," He answered, wishing he could think of an explanation, his mind suddenly blank. "I...ah...I wondered if Ophelia might... ah...might be around?" he asked, feeling foolish for asking. Of course she's around, he thought. She's always around. Where else would she be this early in the morning?

"So...it's Ophelia you're wanting," Aunt Hilda said, stopping whatever it was she was doing to turn and look at him, her tone stern. "It must be pretty important, the way you're all "gussied up." It being barely morning, and all," she said, raising her eyebrows, her hands upon her hips, while she continued to study him.

Cal felt his cheeks begin to burn with embarrassment. "I...ah...I just came to see if she...ah...a *picnic*," he blurted out, suddenly having thought of an explanation. "I just came to see if she wanted to go on a picnic," he said, taking a deep breath and smiling.

"A picnic?" Aunt Hilda said, "I see."

"Yes. Yes, a picnic." he repeated, clutching the brim of his hat within his hands.

The two aunts were staring at him now, Auntie Belle twittering softly, and hiding her rosy cheeks behind one plump hand, her eyes twinkling. Aunt Hilda was looking at him as if he'd just stolen her finest apple pie off the windowsill, where she'd left it to cool.

"Well...just what would you be wanting our girl for?" she asked, squinting at him, a terribly stern look fixed upon him.

Cal was completely rattled by her question, and to everyone's surprise, including his own, and Ophelia's—who had just come down the hall behind him—he blurted out, "I'm wanting her to be my wife!" He heard a gasp, and turned, just as Ophelia walked into his arms, returning the kiss he now gave her.

And behind them Aunt Hilda said, "Well, it's about time!"

CHAPTER 50

Colin O'Leary rushed through chores, finishing them long before noon. Then took himself down to the far side of the barn. Gritting his teeth, he stepped out of his clothes, and stepped into the frigid water. He groaned, feeling the horrible chill of it, then soaped himself from head to toe. "I'll catch my death," he said, between blue lips, his teeth chattering like castanets. He rinsed quickly, then grabbed the towel, and dried, shaking badly. No courtin' is worth this, he thought. I'll probably end up in the hospital with Michael. It was then he remembered that Michael had left the hospital, the day before. Well, I'll take his place, he thought, and he pulled on his socks, pants and boots, rubbing his hair with the towel. Dashing to the house, he hurried in, glad to feel the warmth. His maw looked up as he entered.

He smiled at her, his teeth chattering too much to try to speak, then headed into his room. Grabbing up his best clothes, he quickly changed from his dirty pants to a clean pair, and then hurried back into the main room to finish dressing by the fireplace. James smiled at him, asking what he was up to.

"I'm going to pay my respects to the Yeager family. They're the ones who bought the old Dawson store. The old man recently died," Colin said.

"I don't remember them," James stated, scratching his head. "I don't know as I ever met them."

"I only met him once," Colin said. "Once was enough."

James looked at him questioningly. "Then why are you going to his house? Seems an odd thing to do, if you didn't like the fellow."

"I like his daughter," Colin replied, winking at his brother. James shook his head in understanding, and walked over to the stove to pour himself a cup of coffee.

An hour later, Colin dismounted outside the Yeager house, wondering if he'd been right to come. He really had nothing against the old man. Nothing, that is, except what had happened not long after he'd returned from the war. His maw had asked him to ride into town and fetch her a bag of flour and some sugar. He'd walked into the store, noticing an older woman over to one side, folding material. He'd tipped his hat at her, and she had smiled at him. Then she'd asked him what she could get for him. Just as he began to answer, however, a burly man with mustache had hurried from the back of the store, shouting at him to "Get out! Get out! Get out of the store of Heinrich Yeager. I don't want any business from the likes of you!" He kept yelling, his voice rising more and more with every word.

Colin felt his face flush with renewed embarrassment, as he remembered back to that day. Miz Yeager had followed them outside, saying, "Hush, Heinrich. Hush, hush." But still he continued to yell, as Colin got on his horse and rode on down the street to the Mercantile.

Now, months later, he stood beside his horse, looking up at the Yeager house, a doleful look upon his face. "Damn!" he exclaimed, pulling his reins loose from where he'd just tied them. Then he again mounted, and began the long ride home. He belittled himself as he rode along, blaming himself for being so stupid: first by going to the Yeager's, then by not going in. How hard would it have been, he asked himself, to just stop in, say a few words—real respectful-like—and then leave? Oh well, that wasn't the reason I was going, anyway. I was going to see Miss Katie and have a few words with her. Ever since the day he'd met her at the hospital, he hadn't been able to get her out of his mind. Even in his sleep she tormented him, slipping into his dreams, waking the desire in him. But maybe it was best this way, he decided, dark thoughts filling him, of the time he'd served at Andersonville. The carnage he'd seen flashed once more across his mind: the disease, the deaths, and all the rest of it. As an officer, he was to blame, regardless of the efforts he'd gone to, hoping to make things better for the prisoners. No wonder Heinrich

Yeager hated me, he thought. No wonder he ordered me out of his store. He was right. His daughter deserves better. Colin pulled his hat down further on his head, hating the man he had been, and not giving credit to the man he had become. He rode slowly down the street, his heart heavy.

In front of Gilhaney's Saloon an old man leaned against the hitching rail, the holes in his coat visible even from the distance that separated them. Colin shook his head sadly, wondering who he was, and where he was from. He saw the old fellow hobble up to the door of the saloon then, but he merely stood outside, shaking from the cold. He turned his head as Colin got closer, and Colin couldn't miss the look of confusion upon the old man's face. He also saw the crusted mucus in the corners of his eyes, and that his nose had run down into his beard. He pulled up on his reins, stopping beside the man, and reached into his pockets, pulling out a pair of gloves his maw had given him only the day before. She had knitted them for him, years before, while he'd been away in the war, and saved them just for him.

Colin had noticed the old man's hands; how stiff and chapped they looked from the cold. He saw the cuts and scrapes on them, and the dirt. "Here, friend," he said, reaching out to hand them to him. The man stared at him the longest time, a questioning look upon his face, then he shuffled over near enough to take the gloves, mumbling some words Colin couldn't understand. "You're welcome," Colin said, straightening in his saddle. He watched as the old man pulled on the gloves, almost frantically, rubbing his hands together and smiling. He nodded, and urged his horse on down the street toward home.

The old man stumbled back over to the door of the saloon, not knowing where else to go. He was shaking with cold. All he wanted was to curl up where it was warm, and sleep. He didn't know when he'd slept last, or when he'd last been warm. His body had ached so long now, that he no longer noticed all the aches and pains. Only the cold seemed to penetrate his consciousness. He had to get warm, he knew that, and stumbled on down the street, unable to remember where he was going, or where he'd been. He'd been walking now, as long as he could remember, trying to find something...or someone...he couldn't remember just what or who he'd been looking for. On days his mind was clear, he'd remember little things: a ladies' small, gold watch with ornate fob, and sometimes, a woman's face.

"Warm," he whispered, as he saw the lights shining in the large old house down the road. "Have to get warm," he whispered, as he climbed the steps, one by one, barely enough strength in his arms to hang on to the railing and pull himself up. He looked through the oval window in the door, seeing the inviting interior, knowing there was warmth inside. No one stirred within the long hall as he watched, shivering badly, his nose pressed against the pane, leaving a smear. He turned the knob, his fingers—even in gloves—so very cold he could barely bend them.

At last he managed to open the door, and hobbled inside, not noticing the tears that rolled down his face at the welcomed warmth. He shuffled down the hall, peering into the darkened rooms, listening for sounds, afraid someone would come and find him, and send him out, once more, into the cold. Then he saw the fireplace with its blazing fire, and walked over to it. Wrapping his coat around him and tucking in his scarf, he laid down upon the floor in front of it, his gloves still on, and whispered, once more, "Warm," and then he slept.

Katie Yeager had seen the horse and rider stop outside her house. She'd thought perhaps it was Father O'Leary; never dreaming it would be his brother, Colin. Colin O'Leary, she thought, as she peeked from behind her curtains, watching him as he stood outside. For some reason, unknown to her, he didn't come to the door as she hoped, but stood there, looking up at the house, a sad expression upon his face. She waited, whispering silent prayers that he would come to the door. Then she might get a chance to talk to him, or if not, at least to smile at him. But he remained where he was, then mounted his horse and rode away, much to her dismay.

She watched him go, her heart still skipping beats at the mere thought of him. "Colin O'Leary," she whispered softly, "how am I going to get you to notice me, if I never get to spend a moment with you?" Pouting, she walked downstairs, wondering why he had ridden off, and if she would ever have another chance to speak with him.

All that day, she watched the door, hoping he'd return. By late afternoon, she had plotted and planned many ways to meet him—quite by accident, of course—as she could imagine. She had finally given up on him returning, when there was a knock at the door. She opened it to find Mrs. O'Leary standing there, accompanied by another son, James.

"Hello, Katie darlin'," Mrs. O'Leary greeted her. "'Tis sorry I am about your father's passin'." Katie ushered her and James in, taking their coats and hats. "I wanted to pay my respects, but was not able to come, till now. When things are not so sad, Katie dear, come to our house, if you'd like, and I'll show you my quilts," she said, hoping to cheer her.

To her surprise, the young woman went to her, hugging her, and said, "Oh, Miz O'Leary, I'd *love* to come. I'd just love to." Mrs. O'Leary couldn't help noticing how happy her invite had made Katie, and smiled, knowing Katie wouldn't be the *only one* who was happy when she came to visit!

CHAPTER 51

Colin O'Leary wondered how Michael could have been so stupid. There was no excuse for the things he had done, the mistakes he had made. As he walked to his horse, anger raged inside him. I guess I'm not the only O'Leary who's made mistakes, he thought, not by a long shot. Oh, well, there'd be no more. Michael had assured him that. He had no need for "involvements" like in the past. He shook his head, disgusted with his younger brother, then turned his horse and headed back toward town. Michael had sworn to him that he hadn't been the one who shot Vincent Jalaco. Had sworn on their pa's grave. He hoped it was the truth. He stopped, looking back at Michael's spread, shrugging his shoulders. Well, I guess I'll just have to believe him, he thought. Lydia, too, had sworn that Michael had started to rush to her defense, and the shot had sounded from some place beside him. After that, things had all happened so fast, that neither she, nor Michael, was positive how they had transpired. Michael had been hit on the head, they both agreed, and to everyone's dismay, Vincent Jalaco had fallen forward at about the same time, shot dead. Colin urged his horse along, upsetting thoughts his only company on the long ride back to Hastings.

He thought then of the day at the hospital, when that fellow from the Mercantile, Cal Dunnevey, had run out of the hospital like he was on fire after he'd overheard him and Lydia talking. There was something nagging at Colin about the whole incident, something just wasn't right. He was more sure than ever now that Dunnevey had overheard their conversation. And more sure than ever that Dunnevey had heard him mention the name Jalaco, asking who had killed him, and *that* had caused Cal to bolt for the door. He'd tried and tried to figure what else might have caused his actions, but nothing else made any sense. Well, I intend to find out what's at the bottom of it, he thought, knowing he'd have no rest, until he did. I'll find out what Dunnevey knows, he thought, if I have to tear into him to do it.

Michael had made some bad decisions, that was for sure. He shouldn't have gotten involved with that group of no-accounts, like he had, just to get the money to buy the Gentry place. And shouldn't have gotten involved with their Chaska plans, letting them use his place as a place to hole-up. But by then, he'd felt indebted to them, and had found out where Lydia was. Having her in his head, fillin' his mind the way she was, well, he wasn't thinking clear, that was for sure. And it had almost gotten him killed! They were a bad bunch; no doubt about it, that Cade fellow and them others. But Michael had known that when he went with them. He'd already seen how he could come up with some fast and easy money, riding with them on one of their earlier jobs, just so he could purchase the Gentry place. When he found out Lydia was in Chaska, he lit out for there, fast as could be. They showed up about the same time, checking out some of the towns in the vicinity, for some unsavory reason, Colin was sure. They made themselves to home at Michael's place, since no one was around to stop them. What they'd done—or not done—in Chaska, neither Michael nor Lydia had known, but it was certain they were up to no good. And Michael had ended up near dead, because of it, or because of his own foolishness. Colin shook his head, pulling his coat tighter around him, seeing his breath before him, as he exhaled into the cold, crisp air. It'll surely snow today, he thought, glancing up at the sky, and he shivered slightly, wishing he'd not taken that bath in the creek the day before. Well, he thought, I'll just go see Dunnevey, see what his story is, then head for home, and a good, hot bowl of Maw's vegetable soup.

Cal was stocking shelves in the Mercantile when the bell above the door sounded. "Be with you in a minute," he said, not bothering to look around.

"Take your time," came the answer.

Cal finished what he was doing, quickly, and turned to see a tall, red-haired man standing to one side, patiently watching him. He smiled, asking, "What can I do for you, Sir. A bit cold out there today, isn't it?"

The man was looking at him, studying him, it seemed, and it was a moment or two before he replied. "A little too cold for my likin'." The man looked around the store then, as if checking to see that they were alone, and then turned back. Cal wondered at this, a niggling feeling settling upon him. For just a moment, he wondered if the fellow had come to rob him, but who would be so foolish, he thought, to do so in broad daylight, with townsfolk passing just outside? Then the fellow said the words Cal had long dreaded hearing, and beads of sweat broke out upon his forehead. "We need to talk about Jalaco."

Colin saw Cal's reaction to his words. He saw the sweat that suddenly appeared on Cal's brow, and the way his eyes widened at the mention of Jalaco's name. He saw, too, the momentary look of fear that crossed Dunnevey's face, and knew he'd been right to confront him.

When he could find his voice, Cal replied, trying his best to keep the fear he was feeling, out of it. His hands were sweating and his heart had begun to pound like a hammer in his chest, as he looked at the man who stood before him, waiting. "I...I didn't think anyone would find out," Cal said. "It's been so long." He paused, and then added, "He deserved to die, you know."

Colin was totally taken aback by the fellow's words. He'd just admitted to killing Jalaco. Hadn't hedged around, denying it, or trying to hide it, as he had anticipated. He'd just come right out with it, like he was getting a weight off of his chest that had been there a long, long time. Colin looked at Cal, remembering how he'd heard good things about him, over the years, from Patrick. He'd never heard a bad word about the fellow, in fact. He knew how he'd lost his sight, years back, in a gunfight, protecting Ophelia Denton's sister. And he knew that he'd gotten it back, when he'd rushed out of the hospital and fallen the day he'd overheard the conversation about Jalaco. Well, Colin mused, this sure explained things. Or did it? How could a blind man get to Chaska and shoot someone? "How'd you manage it?" Colin asked, not taking his eyes off of Dunnevey.

"What do you mean?" Cal replied. "I just...ah...grabbed the gun when no one was looking, and...ah...pulled the trigger."

Colin studied the man, still not sure he understood. "But how did you get to Chaska? And how did you see well enough to shoot him and not hit anyone else in the crowd?"

Cal was confused. "What do you mean? It wasn't in Chaska. Chaska's to the west. I don't understand."

It was Colin's turn to be confused now. "You just admitted to shooting Vincent Jalaco, didn't you?" he asked, eyeing the man who stood across from him.

"*Vincent* Jalaco?" Cal said, surprise showing upon his face. "I don't know any Vincent Jalaco. I meant *Victor* Jalaco. I shot him when I was nine, after he beat my mother to death in his saloon."

"They must have been brothers," Colin said. He looked at the man who stood across from him, then reached out his hand to him, "I'm sorry to have caused you any upset, Dunnevey. Your secret's safe with me. You can rest easy about it, I give you my word. I'm Patrick's brother, by the way. Colin O'Leary. I hope you'll forgive me for any worry I might have caused you about this matter," and he shook the hand Cal now offered him.

As Colin turned to leave, Cal spoke, "I owe you a lot, Colin. If I hadn't overheard your conversation that day, and rushed from the hospital like a fool, I never would have fallen and hit my head, and never would have gotten my sight back. I can't tell you what that means to me."

"Then some good has come from all this," Colin replied, and he smiled at Dunnevey, tipped his hat, and walked from the store, leaving a very relieved Cal Dunnevey standing there, a prayer of thanks upon his lips.

CHAPTER 52

After he'd watched his friend Johnny ride off, Eli started his own journey home. Stopping first at the hospital to apologize to Michael, he was surprised to learn that Michael had left earlier to return to his farm. He felt disappointed at missing him, felt it was of the utmost importance to set things right between them. Johnny was right; it really didn't matter whether he thought of Michael as a friend, or as a father. The important thing was that they had shared a great relationship—a close relationship—since as far back as he could remember. He saw now that no matter how much he cared for Jonas, he'd shared things with Michael that—for one reason or another—he just couldn't share with Jonas. It wasn't that he didn't respect him enough. He respected him more than anyone else he knew. And it wasn't that he couldn't talk to Jonas. They had often talked late into the night about chores, and crops, and other such things. It was just that he felt different toward Michael. I'll ride on out to his spread, Eli decided. I want to tell him how sorry I am, right away.

He strode down the hall at the hospital, hurrying, not really watching where he was going. He was so intent on tending to his business with Michael that he ran into Juliana Wright, as she walked out of the parlor to go sit with her younger sister. To his dismay, she lost her balance and began to fall. "Oh!" she cried, as she started to fall, and Eli reached out, grabbing her around the waist, catching her.

"I'm sorry," he said, when she had regained her footing, realizing he still had his arms around her.

"Let me go...please," she said, her eyes suddenly wide with fright, cheeks flushed. She pressed her hands against his chest, trying to push him away, in an almost frantic manner.

"I'm sorry," he repeated, noticing her long lashes, and lovely green eyes. He couldn't help notice the fear in her eyes, and wondered why she was so frightened. He released his hold on her.

"I'm Eli Hart," he said. "I should have been more careful."

She straightened her skirt, running her hands across it, and then ran a hand nervously along one side of her face, brushing back a few strands of hair. Then she stepped around him, not answering, and hurried on down the hall.

Eli watched her go, his thoughts no longer on Michael. "What's your name?" he whispered, hoping she'd turn and answer. But the young woman continued on her way, as if she didn't hear him. He watched until she disappeared further down the hall, and then turned on his heel, again intent on finding Michael to apologize. I'll find out, later, who she is, he thought, and why she looked so scared.

He rode out to Michael's farm then, though he felt a bit uneasy doing so. Having not completely thought out what he would say to the man he now knew to be his father, he hoped his words could mend things between them. He wondered if he'd be welcome, in fact, after the harsh and cutting remarks he'd made earlier. Tying his reins to the fence near the barn, he walked over to the cabin and knocked on the door. In a few moments, he heard it being unlocked, and Lydia stood before him, a look of surprise upon her face. "Eli," she said, opening the door wider to let him enter.

"I stopped at the hospital. They said Michael had gone home. I wonder if I could see him, please," he asked.

"He'd like that," she said, smiling.

Eli stepped inside, glad to feel the warmth from the fireplace, and took off his coat, handing it to Lydia. She hung it on a nail over by the door, then ushered him into the small side-room, calling out softly, "Michael. Look who's come to see you."

Michael was lying on the small bed, and raised his head to look; smiling when he saw it was Eli. He was still weak from the infection he'd had, and had been resting—his neck still bandaged. Eli walked over to the side of the bed, looking down at the man who had been one of his best friends for as long as he could remember. "I...I came to apologize to you...ah...sir," he said, his voice low.

Michael looked up at him, seeing the sincerity in his eyes, seeing the red hair and fair skin—so like his own—of the boy, *his* boy, and he felt a mixture of gratitude and relief fill him. He smiled at the younger man, asking, "What's this "sir" stuff? You and I go back too far to have you suddenly start calling me "sir.""

Eli looked at him, seeing the genuine affection Michael felt for him. "I don't know what I'm supposed to call you, now that you're my...my pa, and all."

"I guess we can just go on like we've always been," Michael said, smiling at him.

Eli returned his smile, a look of relief upon his face. "I just want you to know, I'm sorry for the way I acted at the hospital. I was mad, and didn't take time to think. Our friendship meant a lot to me. I didn't know what to make of...you know...of everything changing, of being your...son. Guess I was afraid I'd lose that friendship." He hung his head, feeling vulnerable.

"Well, I'm just sorry we didn't find out sooner, son. Do you mind if I call you that? Your friendship has always meant a lot to me, too. They were good times, those times we had together. I don't want to lose our friendship either, Eli," Michael said.

The two men shook hands then, just as Lydia peeked into the room, asking Eli if he'd like a cup of coffee, or a bowl of soup. He said no, he had to get home, but as he turned to leave the room, he turned back, saying, "There aren't as many chores in winter. I'll get mine all done, then come out and help you with yours, till you get your strength back. If that's okay?"

"You bet," Michael replied. Lydia had to wipe the tears from her eyes, knowing in her heart that God had truly blessed her. He'd not only given her back her husband from the brink of death, He'd given her back her son. She knew she'd never be able to thank Him enough.

When Eli rode up the long lane leading to Jonas and Lilly's farm, just after dark, the most important thing on his mind was to set things straight with the two people who had raised him. He felt shame and remorse at how he had ridden off, chasing after Lydia. It wasn't because she was his mother—his real mother—that he had gone tearing after her. Well, at least not the *only* reason. It was because of a whole lot of different reasons. He'd thought about things, all the way home from Michael's, trying to understand just what he had been feeling. Now, still unsure about what he'd say, he ran up the steps to the house, hoping they'd hear him out, and understand.

When he opened the door, Lilly was sitting in the old rocker, mending a pair of his work-pants, and Jonas was sitting by the fireplace, reading some papers. They looked up as he came in. The silence that greeted him was so thick it could have been cut with a knife. Eli looked from one to the other, aware of the look of hope on Lilly's face, and the quiet, questioning look on Jonas's. He took off his hat, holding it in his hands, suddenly at a loss for words. Clearing his throat, he took stock of all he'd meant to say, having gone over and over it on the long ride from Michael and Lydia's. He cleared his throat a second time, and then began to speak. "I guess I worried you, running off like I did, and all. I didn't think about it at the time, my reason, I mean. Just seemed it was... something I *had* to do, and I did it. There were a lot of reasons." Jonas laid down the papers he'd been reading, glancing over at Lilly who sat looking at Eli, her hands now resting quietly in her lap. "You taught me to be the...the man I am. You raised me to be honest and fair, and to always try to do my best." Turning to look at Jonas, he said, "You taught me how to farm, and more important, you showed me how to be the kind of man that you are; a good, decent man. The man who taught me about praying and believing, and what love and family is all about. You took me in, not hesitating, or thinking of me as just another mouth to feed. As long as I live, you'll be my pa. I hope you know that," Eli said, still holding his hat.

He cleared his throat again, looking over at Lilly, continuing. "I couldn't have had a better home, or more loving parents, and I'm grateful to you *both* for that. But all my life I felt like something was missing...do you know what I mean? It was like there was a part of me "out there" somewhere, no matter how much you cared for me, or loved me." He shifted his weight from one foot to the other, searching his mind for just the right words. "When I saw Lydia rush out the door and race down our lane, I felt that piece of me, that *missing* piece, leaving me. Just like she did right after I was born. It wasn't *her,* so much, that I was chasing. It was the missing piece of *myself.* Anyway, I caught up to her this side of town and we did some talking. I won't go into that right now, but part of what she told me was that Michael... Michael O'Leary... is my real pa." Jonas looked down at the floor, as Eli said this, and Lilly raised one hand to her mouth in surprise. "Lydia thought everything was all right, cause I held my true feelings in, not letting her know how that news upset me. And she went on along home to their place. Michael and I have always been friends, as you know. I thought he'd known all along, and had been acting like my friend, when he knew I was really his son. As it turned out, he hadn't known till just before he and Lydia got back to town. I guess he was as surprised as I was." Eli took a deep breath, getting his thoughts in order. "Anyway, I lit out for the hospital, ready to settle a score with him for how he'd betrayed my trust, and, well, I said some pretty terrible things to him. It's all cleared up now. I apologized and he accepted my apology. I've given it a lot of thought, and have told him that after my chores are finished here at home, I'll come out and help him with his, at least until he's over the infection he's had. That way I'll get to spend some time with them, and see what they're like. I'm not doing it to hurt you. It's just something I've got to do, to get that lost piece of myself back. I hope you understand."

The silence seemed to go on forever, and then Lilly asked, "So you're going to live with them, part of the time?"

"No, Ma. This is my home, and always will be, if that's all right with you and Pa. This is where I belong, and *have* belonged, all my life. This is where I want to stay. Here, with my *real* family."

Lilly looked at him, her eyes filling with tears. "There's a pot of stew on the stove. I'll heat you a bowl," she said, as she hurried from the room, so he wouldn't see the tears of joy that ran down her face.

Eli walked over to Jonas. He stood before him a few moments, then stuck out his hand, saying, "Pa?"

Jonas took Eli's hand within his own large one, replying, "Welcome home, Son."

CHAPTER 53

John Black Hawk Gentry arrived at the winter camp of Chief Standing Elk about noon. It had begun snowing the day before, and he was chilled clear through. He wore his buckskin shirt and pants, his old boots that were tight on his feet, and the frock coat that had been his father's. His long black hair hung loose, gracing his shoulders and down his back. To anyone watching, as he entered the village, he looked like any one of the braves who'd made their home there all their lives. Even in his skin tone, he resembled the other young men. And he rode, as they did, with his back straight and head held high, looking proud.

He had left Silas Haverty's five days earlier, having stopped there to tell Nancy of how her father had helped him. He knew that Nancy and his mother had been friends for as long as he could remember, and thought it the considerate thing to do. He'd also told Silas that he'd found no trace of his father in all his travels, though now and then, he'd heard that possibly a man of his description had been spotted. Every time he had gotten such a lead, he'd followed up on it to the best of his ability, he'd told him. Sadly, to no avail. Then he'd come across an old man named Cade, who was wearing Moses' medallion, claiming Moses had died at Gettysburg. Silas was sorry to hear it, and they had sat together, sharing memories of Moses.

Later, Silas had insisted Johnny spend the night, and he agreed, though now more anxious than ever to see his mother. And, if truth be known, anxious to see Laughing Water. He had tried to keep thoughts of her from his mind, but it had been impossible the past long months. And even more impossible, the closer it came to his arrival at the village.

Long into the night, Silas and Johnny had talked, topics spoken of that were disturbing to both men of the many attacks and battles between soldiers and Indians throughout the land. Silas spoke of the Indian uprising in '62, mostly. It had been one of the bloodiest massacres; 400 or more whites having been butchered in their homes and settlements, along with some soldiers at nearby Fort Ridgely. In the end, he said, nearly 40 Indians were hanged, and all because of the many broken promises given by the whites. Promises of training and supplies to make the Indians self-sufficient—given in exchange for prime hunting land—had never materialized. And worse yet, promises of food from local Indian agents had not materialized, or were denied, though the Indians were starving due to the fall harvest having been blighted by a terrible cutworm infestation. This followed a bitterly cold winter that left the Indians desperate. To Silas' way of thinking, this caused the battle that had wreaked the most havoc in the area, though they'd both heard of other battles, more recently, and as deadly.

The Sand Creek massacre, as it later came to be called, they also spoke of, where a colonel and former Methodist minister by the name of John Chivington, and his Colorado Volunteers, attacked and wiped out the village of a peaceful tribe of Cheyenne on Big Sandy Creek. The bloodthirsty volunteers had mutilated, scalped, and tortured not only the Indian men, but also *all* the women and children, even though Chief Black Kettle had a flag flying in front of his tepee, clearly showing that his were a peaceful people. Silas shook his head, saying it seemed like there would be no end to the fighting and anger, or the attacks and acts of retaliation on the part of both the Indians and the whites, and he felt as bad about it as Johnny did.

"Why did so many whites have to come?" Johnny asked. "This has been the land of the Indian for many, many moons. I used to think the day would come when we could live in peace together, but I'm not so sure anymore. What do you think?"

Silas smoked his pipe, considering Johnny's words before answering. "I used to think so, too, John. But I'm afraid you're right. A big problem lies in the fact that the two cultures are so different. One wants to *own* the land, setting down roots, calling it his own. The other has no such feelings. They've lived for generation after generation on the land, living off the bounty it provided. They've lived happily with all they had, *not* owning it, but giving thanks to the Great Spirit for providing it for them. No, son, I doubt there'll ever be a peaceful solution. Each believes their way is right, and will apparently fight to the death to uphold those beliefs." He took a pull on his pipe, and then exhaled slowly, the smell of tobacco filling the air. Then he continued, "Men have long been driven by greed, Johnny. It doesn't matter if it's a desire for whiskey, women, or money. It's greed driving them, pure and simple. Now it's gold and land that seems to be the main quest, and we both know the outcome of that." He took another long pull on his pipe, sitting before his fireplace, looking into the flames, thinking.

"I never felt caught between the two cultures before," Johnny said. "My folks always made sure I felt comfortable being part of both peoples. But now, well, it's not that easy. I got pulled from my horse recently, right in Hastings, by a group of men—white men—who were working themselves into a frenzy, filled with hatred toward the Indians. They slammed me around a bit, but thankfully, both Eli and Nancy's pa jumped in and helped me. I don't know why Old Man..." Johnny looked sheepish at calling the old man that, and looked quickly at Silas. "Sorry. I meant Mr. Pearly," he said, hoping to sound more respectful. "I don't know why he helped me."

"No offense taken," Silas said. "He never did much good, mostly drank and got mean-spirited after, far as I know. I'm glad he turned this other side. Did some good, you know. I'm sure the good Lord will see to it he gets credit for it, someday. Nancy will be glad to hear of his actions, when I tell her later," Silas said.

"I hope Doc can fix him up," Johnny replied. "He looked bad. He'll be stayin' at the hospital awhile, I guess. Miz Denton's got that old house that used to belong to Mr. Clark, the banker, turned into a fine hospital. A place where folks don't just go to get some medicine, or a bullet dug out, but where a fellow that's real sick can stay till he's all better."

"That's a fine idea," Silas replied. "Course out here in the woods there's everything we need growing wild at our doorstep. We don't need a fancy hospital. God provides for us here."

Johnny nodded, in understanding. "Well, I want to get an early start, so I'd better turn in. It's getting late."

Silas showed him to the room, where many years before, his mother had slept in the same small bed, the night she and his father stopped on their return journey to Standing Elk's village. "Night, John. I'm sorry about your pa. He was a fine man. Fine, indeed." Silas said, and he walked from the room, glad to have had the chance to talk with Moses' son.

Times were sure different, he thought. He'd never had any trouble with the Indians. Many a time, when the winter snows were deep as a man's chest, they'd stop by on the way back to their villages, and offer him some of the venison they'd shot, in exchange for a small bag of sugar, or an offering of coffee. They were a noble people, as far as he was concerned, except of course, for the Pawnee. He'd never heard any good words about them, and hoped he'd never have reason to deal with them.

Johnny rode into the village, surrounded by the many braves who'd seen him coming and rode out to greet him. Brave Foot had been among them, and had ridden quickly to his friend's side, crying out his joy at seeing him. Then side-by-side they entered the village. Small children ran here and there, anxious to see what it was that had caused excitement in the camp, happy smiles upon their faces. Brave Foot raised his arm, his bow clenched tightly within his hand, and pointed with it to a little girl who quickly disappeared into a nearby tepee. "My child, Black Hawk," he said, smiling proudly. Johnny was glad to see his friend's look of pride, but wondered where Laughing Water was. He had not seen her amongst the young women, as they'd entered the camp.

Stopping in front of Standing Elk's tepee, the old chief walked from it, just as Johnny slid from his horse. There was warmth to his voice, as he spoke in English, welcoming Johnny. "You are well, Black Hawk?" he asked.

"I am," Johnny answered, noticing the slight haze that covered the old man's eyes. "I am happy to be in the village of the great chief, Standing Elk. I have missed you, and the others."

"Come, we will smoke the pipe in thanks for your safe return. Then you must go to see your mother. Red Bird has missed you."

Johnny and the other braves entered the chief's tepee. He nodded toward the chief's wife who sat to one side, and she smiled at him, and then hurried away. She wanted to be the first to tell Sarah that her son had returned, knowing the joy it would bring her.

When Johnny left the chief's lodge, he was glad to see Brave Foot waiting for him. "Come to my lodge, later, Black Hawk. We will talk," he said, reaching out his hand to clasp the shoulder of his friend.

Johnny smiled, agreeing to come, but wondered if he could stand doing so. He still hadn't seen Laughing Water, and felt that Brave Foot would realize his love for her, if he saw them together. There was no way he could avoid going without hurting his friend's feelings, however, so he quickly agreed, then watched as Brave Foot turned to go. He watched him grab up the little girl, swinging her up into his arms, laughing at something she'd said, and Johnny's heart felt heavy. How could he sit in Brave Foot's tepee, he wondered, when his heart was filled with such love for his friend's wife? He hadn't planned to have such feelings. But one look, and he had known. And later, when he'd held her in his arms, whispering that he had to leave, he knew no words to describe the way he'd felt when her arms went around him. It was as if, in her arms, he was "home." He'd left soon after, knowing it was the honorable thing to do. The *only* thing to do. But she had stayed with him—in his heart—every day, no matter how far he traveled. He took a deep breath, certain that what he felt was a feeling that did not come often in a man's lifetime.

Sarah looked up, just in time to see Johnny approach. She hurried to him, the long-awaited embrace she had looked forward to, happening at last. He held her close, joy filling him. Their reunion, all he had imagined as he had journeyed far across the land. "Mother," he whispered, holding her gently within his strong arms.

"Oh, Johnny. I've missed you so," she said, not wanting to let him go. Then she drew back, looking at his face, having noticed the bruising of one cheek. "Are you well?" she asked, a look of concern upon her face.

"I am," he answered, starting to grin at her.

"What?" she asked, reaching up to touch her face, wondering why he was looking at her as he was.

"I see you now wear spectacles," he replied.

"Oh, those," she said. "Such bothers. I'll never get used to them, if I wear them a hundred years."

"I have much to tell you," he said, then. "Not the news you had hoped for, however, where my father is concerned." He looked long into her eyes, a sadness filling his, searching for the right words.

Sarah reached out, squeezing his hand, saying, "Come. It's cold out here. We can talk in my tepee, after you've had some food."

She didn't want to spoil the happy fact of his return by any sad talk. It had been so very long since the war had ended. It had been almost as long since she'd given up hope of Moses ever returning. She didn't want sadness to mar the joy of having her son back. There would be plenty of time for such talk, later.

They visited while they ate, bringing each other up-to-date on events in each of their lives. She asked about their home place, Eli and his folks, Lilly and Jonas, and what was new in Hastings, and he answered all her questions, as best he could. He asked how life was for her with Standing Elk's people, if she was still happy to be with them, and how their friends were, Howling Wolf, and the chief. He noticed she did not ask for news of his father. And she noticed he did not ask for any news of Laughing Water. It was as if the subjects closest to their hearts were too dear to be mentioned, and both knew it.

Finally, she gave him the moccasins she had made for him, lined in soft rabbit fur. And when he'd placed them on his feet, glad to be able to discard the boots that no longer fit, she handed him the buffalo coat she'd also made for him. It was heavier than he would have liked, but he knew how much hard work had gone into making it, and was grateful. The snow was now above his ankles in depth, and he knew both would come in handy before the winter was through. Sarah noticed he was taller, and his facial features were more like those of his father now, and it made her smile. She had looked at him, expecting to see only her boy, not expecting to see his father in him. It was a nice discovery, one that brought back many happy and heartwarming memories.

When they had talked long into the evening, he said he wanted to walk over to Brave Foot's tepee to visit with him awhile. Sarah had the strongest inclination to warn him to "be careful," but held her tongue, knowing he was now a man. It was up to him to decide the path he would walk in life. If she'd learned nothing else while with the Indians, it was that we each have our own paths to follow. Hard as it was, she held her tongue, telling him only to have a nice time.

He hesitated then, looking at her steadily, weighing his words. Finally he spoke, "I looked everywhere. Any mention of someone of father's description, I checked into. I'm sorry I failed you...and Pa."

Sarah laid her hand on his arm, her eyes now damp with tears at his words. "He'll always be with us, Johnny, in our hearts."

CHAPTER 54

The night was still, only the sound of coyotes howling in the distance, and the occasional barking of a dog was heard, as Johnny walked through the Indian village on his way to Brave Foot's tepee. He looked up at the cloudless sky, seeing the sprinkling of stars that filled it, and shivered as the night air breathed its cold breath around him. His thoughts were tearing at his heart. He was not a man that would choose to hurt someone. Especially not a close friend like Brave Foot. They had always been friends, since first they met. Even when they were young children, he had been careful of his friend's feelings when they played together. And later, when Brave Foot's face had been slashed deeply, leaving a terribly disfiguring scar, he had been careful to say nothing that might make him feel bad, or shame him. Now he walked across the camp, anxious to see his friend, wanting to deny, yet knowing, that he was more anxious to see his friend's wife. He longed to hold her, to kiss her, to touch her, to have her close. He shook his head, silently praying for the strength to keep his feelings from Brave Foot, and thus, not hurt him.

He heard laughter from a tepee as he passed, and saw children playing at their mother's knee, at another, and there was a longing inside of him that grew at the sight. Like a raging wildfire it spread all through him, taking his breath away. He longed for the home he had known when he was young, the home filled to bursting with the love of two parents, the home he had missed ever since his father went away to war and did not return. His mother had found the place she wanted to be, and he was happy for her. His father had paid the ultimate price of war, and would not be coming home. Where then, he wondered, did that leave him? Where did *he* belong? In his body there flowed the blood of two nations, two peoples: the whites and the Indians. Yet he found no sense of belonging in either world. He stopped walking to watch a falling star, wishing with all his heart that he had a home to go to where the cold winds of night could not reach him. A home where his wife lay beside him, their bodies entwined, and his children slept nearby, safe and warm. But he knew that the woman he longed to have share that home, belonged to someone else, and slept beside *him*, and watched *their* child sleep nearby. And he was filled with a feeling of immense loneliness.

Brave Foot was happy to see him, as he entered the tepee, his contentedness and satisfaction with his life, apparent. His little girl played with a stick doll on a bearskin to one side, and Laughing Water smiled shyly at him, quickly looking away. Johnny felt his heart begin to pound at sight of her, and was glad that she showed no signs of what had transpired between them before he had left the camp, years earlier. Perhaps she's changed her mind, he thought, glancing over at her, seeing the way she went on with her work, as if he wasn't even there. She looked even more beautiful now. The four years he'd been away had only enhanced her looks, making her far more desirable, as far as he was concerned. There was a soft glow to her skin, it seemed. And though she smiled politely when she offered him a bowl of food, he saw that her eyes never made contact with his. He wondered at that, but had all he could do to keep his mind on the things Brave Foot was saying. It was when the little girl fell asleep, and Laughing Water bent to cover her, that he noticed the fullness of her stomach beneath the buckskin dress she wore, and suddenly he knew. She was with child. He had all he could do, not to cry out. He wanted to grab her, to ask her why? To tell her how deeply she had hurt him. To hurt her back, so she, too, would feel the pain that he was feeling. He looked up, to discover that Brave Foot was looking at him, a questioning look upon his face. Johnny had no words, no voice. He looked at the fire that burned before him, too devastated to speak. "Do you want to hunt tomorrow, Black Hawk?" Brave Foot asked, a second time. But still Johnny did not answer. "Are you ill, my friend?" he asked, a look of concern upon his face. Laughing Water glanced at Johnny, knowing he knew.

"I'm not feeling good," Johnny said, laying a hand upon his stomach. "Tomorrow we will hunt. Yes," he answered, getting to his feet. And he turned and left, with no further word, his heart breaking inside him.

One look at her son's face told Sarah what he had discovered during his visit to Brave Foot's tepee. She, too, had guessed that Laughing Water was with child, the last time she'd seen her. There was a beauty about her, far beyond her normal beauty.

Laughing Water had confided in Sarah, only the week before Johnny rode in, that her suspicions were correct. Sobbing her heart out, she had told Sarah that she loved Johnny, and worried that he would not believe it, if he returned and found out. Sarah knew her son to be understanding and levelheaded, but she also knew how hurt he would be. She sat with the distraught younger woman, trying her best to comfort and assure her that everything would be all right. But she had to admit; even she did not believe it. Now the time had arrived, as Johnny walked into her tepee, his shoulders slumped, and sadness filling his eyes.

"Johnny..." she began. But he held up a hand, motioning her not to speak, and laid down upon a buffalo hide on the far side of the tepee, his back to her. All through the night, he lay there grief-stricken, chiding himself for having loved Laughing Water. There would be no home for them, with children and warmth and happiness. There would be nothing for them. *Nothing*. As soon as I can get away from her, and everything that reminds me of her, he thought, the better. He wanted no part of her, no part of Brave Foot, no part of this place where she lived, and obviously, loved. He groaned aloud, the pain inside him burgeoning into a raging torrent of anger. The tears from his eyes scalded his cheeks, and dried the love in his heart, until it withered and became like burned ash within him. Then he slept.

His prowess during the hunt the following day exceeded all the expectations of the braves who joined Johnny and Brave Foot.

He raced across the land, throwing all caution to the wind. Taking chances no one else dared, he urged his horse on, faster and faster, not caring if the animal ran itself to death, or broke its leg in a hole. When they came upon the den of a bear, he pulled his knife, and jumped from his horse, ready to draw it from its den and kill it, not caring that it was far larger, and capable of ripping him apart with one swipe of its large paw. Brave Foot and the other braves looked on, as he teased and taunted the bear, looking as if his reason was gone.

"A fine coat you'll be, Bear. A fine coat for my mother. Come! Come to me, Bear, and see what I'll do to you. Come!" he shouted, and the braves looked on, whispering amongst themselves, not understanding. When the bear charged out of his den, moving slowly, yet angered, Johnny laughed aloud at him, still challenging the great beast. And as he did, its nails caught him on one shoulder, ripping the flesh from it. Plunging his knife into the bear's hide, he felt its teeth sink deeply into his arm, and knew he no longer could win his battle against the beast. The bear shook him, growling its rage at having been disturbed, and Johnny stabbed and stabbed it, till he could wield his knife no more. That was the last thing he remembered, and then his pain ended.

Three days later, he woke. He was in a large lodge, many stitches—sewn with buffalo sinew—covering his body. His mother sat at his side, anxiously watching him. His body felt on fire, especially his shoulder and one arm. He tried to raise his head to look, but found he could not. Then he drifted off into a silent world of black, gladly welcoming it.

The next time he woke, faces danced above him; the face of Brave Foot, and some of the other braves, the face of the chief, and his father's friend, Howling Wolf. He closed his eyes, as a spasm of pain coursed through him, and when he opened them, the face of his mother looked down at him. Then he drifted back to the world of black, his only companion the sounds that rifled through his consciousness of someone singing a Lakota song, and someone praying.

He saw many things, the next time he entered the world of dreams. He fought the bear, once again, in his mind. But as they fought, he heard the bear speak to him, asking, "Why have you challenged me, Little Brother?" And in his delirium he felt ashamed of having done so. "Is it not better," the bear then asked him, "to seek answers to the things that trouble you?" Johnny saw a mountain before him then, its peak covered with snow, and on either side of the trail through the mountain, huge rock cliffs abounded, reaching to the sky. He felt his spirit float up, up, amongst those cliffs, higher and higher, soaring like an eagle, above them. Then he was standing at the very top of the highest mountain, looking beyond it. A blazing sun—brighter than any he had ever seen—filled the sky. It was startling in its brilliance, and the heat from it warmed his body, healing the pain within him. He stood facing the sun, taking in the beauty of the land that spread out before him in every direction, a land rich with possibilities. And as he stood there, his mighty adversary, the bear, came to stand beside him, though not as an enemy. As Johnny watched, it stood up on its two hind legs, and pointed toward the trail, and the trail became red (a good sign among the People) and the bear became an old man.

Johnny was amazed by the things that he saw, and spoke, saying, "I do not understand the things I see, Grandfather."

And the answer came, whispered upon the strong winds that suddenly blew, whipping his hair back from his face and buffeting his body, "You must go from here, Black Hawk, during the Moon of Falling Leaves" (November). And as soon as these words were spoken the bear disappeared, and Johnny was again aware of his surroundings. He opened his eyes, seeing both his mother and Laughing Water standing over him, worried looks upon their faces. He smiled at them, and then closed his eyes, welcoming the healing sleep that now came.

CHAPTER 55

Aunt Hilda was hurrying along the hallway in the hospital, a tray in her hands with bowls of porridge and glasses of milk upon it, when she happened to glance into the parlor as she passed, and was shocked to see the curled up form of a person laying on the floor before the fireplace. She nearly dropped the tray, her surprise was so great. Pausing, she heard the deep snoring of the man, and realized that he was asleep. She hurried on down the hall, delivering the bowls to her patients, then rushed back to the parlor.

"What are you doing here?" she asked, nudging the man with her foot, afraid to get too close. The man snored all the louder, his gloved hands clasped together, his dark coat wrapped tightly around him. Aunt Hilda shook her head in disgust, wondering at the impertinence of the fellow. Mumbling to herself about her discovery, she turned and hurried down the hall, intent on getting a broom and using it to chase the intruder from their door. She could not believe a man would be so bold as to enter the hospital after dark, much less curl up on the floor where just anyone could discover him. I might have fallen over him, she thought, shaking her head, angrily.

"What is it, sister? Your face is as red as fire," Auntie Belle asked, as her sister rushed into the kitchen.

"You don't want to know!" Aunt Hilda replied, looking here and there throughout the kitchen.

"Well, at least tell me what it is you're looking for," Auntie Belle said, wondering at her sister's tone of voice.

"Oh, for heaven's sake, Dorothea. Can't you see I'm in a hurry? Why do you always have to ask me so many questions when I'm busy?"

Auntie Belle pursed her lips, saying, "I only wanted to help."

"Well, if you want to help, tell me what you've done with the broom. *Every time* I need something, you've *hidden* it somewhere," Aunt Hilda stated, still hunting for the missing broom.

"I've never hidden *anything* from you, Annathea. That's an out-and-out, bold face lie!" Auntie Belle said, her voice rising in a manner so uncommon to her. "You always blame *me,* sister, for every little thing that doesn't go your way. I didn't hide the broom. And just why you need it so badly, when we have breakfast to get out to our patients, is beyond me. Have you spilled the bowls? I told you the tray was too full, but far be it for you to listen to me," Auntie Belle said, her temper getting the best of her.

"Ladies! Ladies. What's going on?" Ophelia asked, looking from one to the other of her usually docile aunts. She had been in one of the upstairs rooms, sweeping the floor, and entered the kitchen just in time to hear their angry exchange. In her hand, she carried the broom.

"There's your old broom," Auntie Belle said, pouting, her chin rising defensively in the direction of her sister.

"We have company," Aunt Hilda said, ignoring her words, and turning to look at Ophelia.

"What do you mean? Company at this hour?" Ophelia asked, a concerned look upon her face.

"A saloon patron, I suspect," Aunt Hilda replied, taking the broom from her. "He's sound asleep on the parlor floor in front of the fireplace. A little smack from my broom, and I assure you he'll be out the door and on his way."

"But, you don't mean he simply walked in, in the middle of the night, do you?" Ophelia asked, incredulously.

"He must have. I checked on all the patients before I went up to bed, late last night, and he certainly wasn't there then," Aunt Hilda said, shaking her head. "Come see for yourself. As I live and breathe, I just don't know what this world's coming to. If you want *my* advice, you'd be far better off opening your hospital in a little town. A quiet, peaceful place. It doesn't surprise me one bit, Ophelia, that he just wandered in off the street. That's what you get for wanting to live in such a wild town."

Ophelia took the broom from her aunt's hands, and started down the hall, saying over her shoulder, "Hastings is a nice town, Aunt Hilda. It's much less wild than some I've heard about. Come."

The women peeked around the doorway to the parlor, Ophelia holding fast to the broom with both hands. Aunt Hilda standing behind her, a stern expression upon her face, and both her fists doubled as if she meant to hit their intruder if he so much as moved. And to the rear, Auntie Belle, who kept raising up on her tiptoes, trying to see past the others. As she leaned to one side, trying to see around Aunt Hilda, she lost her balance and quickly reached out, grabbing her sister's waist to steady herself. Aunt Hilda was totally surprised by being grabbed, and let out a squeal that could have been heard all the way to the jail! Then all three of the women turned as one, and fled back to the kitchen, trying to gain both their courage and their composure.

"Well of all the idiotic things to do!" Aunt Hilda exclaimed, verbally lashing out at her sister.

Auntie Belle looked at her, answering, "Well, I wasn't the one who squealed loud enough to wake the whole town, sister."

"Well if you hadn't..." Aunt Hilda began, but Ophelia stamped her foot to get their attention, both hands on her hips.

The two aunts looked properly scolded then, and both looked down at the floor, Hilda snorting her disapproval of the whole situation, and Auntie Belle beginning to giggle softly.

"Oh, shut up, sister!" Aunt Hilda ordered, causing Auntie Belle to twitter all the louder. Ophelia couldn't help smiling. She knew her two aunts had never gotten along all that happily, but had never heard them actually squabble so. She thought it so funny, at their ages.

"Now come with me, ladies," she ordered, softly. "I dropped the broom in the hall. First we'll get it in our possession, and then we'll have a look-see at our intruder." In single file, they made their way cautiously down the hall to the parlor.

The old man laid where he'd been, his long white hair and beard spilling over his coat collar and masking his facial features, as the women crept closer, holding their breath. They noticed the holes in his tattered coat, and then still more holes in the soles of his shoes. Creeping closer, they couldn't help but see the partially unraveled red scarf that was wound around his neck, and the new gloves upon his hands. They saw, too, the crusted drainage in the corner of his eyes, and how his nose had drained down into his beard, and did so yet.

"Oh, how disgusting," Aunt Hilda stated, shaking her head.

"The poor dear," Auntie Belle said, folding her hands as if in prayer. "Why he must have gotten cold, and come inside to get warm."

Ophelia spoke then, her voice firm, yet soft, "Sir? Sir, can you hear me? You can't sleep here. Do you hear me? Are you sick? This is a hospital, Sir. You can't stay on the floor." When the old man did not stir, she pushed gently against his leg with the broom, surprised when he still did not respond. She glanced back at her aunts, questioningly, and then bent down, touching the old fellow on the shoulder. When there was still no response, she told Aunt Hilda to keep an eye on him, and *not* to hit him with the broom, if he happened to awaken, and she asked Auntie Belle to please heat up a cup of broth from the soup she had fixed the night before. Then she hurried down the hall to get her coat and boots, and rushed off down the street to get Doc Valentine.

Arriving back at the hospital, she was surprised to find both aunts sitting in the parlor, one looking disgustedly at the intruder, and one throwing a blanket over the old man and whispering softly to him.

"Here he is, Doc," Ophelia said, removing her coat and laying it in a chair. "I don't know when he came in. Sometime during the night, it seems. He must have come in to warm himself."

"Let me see him," Doc said, tossing his own coat onto another chair and kneeling down beside the old man. He placed his hand upon the old fellow's shoulder, talking softly to him. There was no response. He felt his forehead, shocked to feel how hot it was.

"This man's burning up," he said, glancing back at Ophelia. Then he checked the man's pulse and looked closely at his head for any sign of wounds. "We need to get him into a bed. Do you ladies think you can help me lift him? If not, I'll need one of you to go get help."

"I'll go," Ophelia offered, reaching for her coat. "Ladies, we'll put him in the large room in the front. The room where Mr. Dunnevey was. That's the cheeriest room. It doesn't look to me like he's had much cheeriness in his life in a long, long time." She paused, then added,

"And we'll need plenty of hot water to wash him...and his clothes. I suspect he hasn't had a bath in a long time, either."

"I'll heat some kettles of water so we can wash his clothes," Auntie Belle said, wringing her hands and hurrying toward the kitchen, while repeating over and over, "the poor soul, the poor, poor soul."

"Shouldn't we be findin' out who he is, first?" Aunt Hilda asked.

"There'll be plenty of time for that, ladies, when he regains consciousness," the doctor stated. "First things first. Right now he needs a warm bed, some diligent care, and as soon as possible, some good food. By the looks of him, he's had little to eat, and none of the comforts of home for a long, long time. A shame. Such a shame."

CHAPTER 56

Doc Valentine walked from the room of the old man, a worried look upon his face. "He's been here a week," he said aloud, though no one else was near. Doc was happy that the old fellow's fever had finally broken. But though he had regained his ability to speak, the only thing he ever said was "home." Doc had tried to get him to speak. He'd asked him questions over and over again, patting him gently on the arm, telling him to rest, that he was safe and warm, and that later, when he was well, he could go home. The old man had only looked at him, giving no indication whether he understood, or not. Doc had even tried the few words of Spanish he knew, but the old fellow didn't react. He shook his head. He wasn't sure what his new patient had been through, but one thing was clear, he'd walked for many a mile, and for some unknown reason, he *could* not, or *would* not speak. Maybe a little rest will help, Doc thought, rest and good food. He'd seen how the old fellow had grabbed the bowl of Belle's good venison stew, wolfing it down in great gulps. It was a wonder he hadn't choked. That was the first day he'd regained consciousness, Doc remembered. He'd grabbed the bowl from Auntie Belle before she had a chance to think, and swallowed down its contents. What didn't go into him, had simply dribbled down his face into his thick, white beard, causing the man no concern whatsoever. Auntie Belle had been startled when he grabbed the bowl, then realized he was probably half starved, and stood back, relishing the thought of him finally getting some good, hearty food inside him. Aunt Hilda would have grabbed the bowl right back, she was sure, so she was extremely glad it was she who'd brought the stew to the old fellow.

Doc finished seeing the other patients, glad to see that most were on the mend. Little Mary Wright was doing exceedingly well, and that really pleased him. He'd thought for a while that she wasn't going to make it, and knew how hard that would be on her older sister, Juliana. Juliana had never left her side throughout the whole ordeal, and many times he'd found her crying when he'd walked into the room. He'd tried to talk to the young woman, hoping to comfort her and give her hope, but she'd only sat there, staring at the floor, not answering. Only once had she spoken, and he realized by her words, the terrible extent the trauma of the Pawnee attack had inflicted upon her senses, as she asked—her voice a mere whisper—"the Indians won't get us *here*. Will they?" He felt so sorry for her, realizing that she would live with the viciousness of their attack, and the deaths of, not only her folks, but her brother, too. The relief he'd felt when her little sister took a turn for the better, was immeasurable. All these thoughts accompanied him, as he hurried down the hall to check on his last patient of the day.

"Hello, Miz Belle," he said, walking into the bright and cheery room of the old man whom they'd found in front of the fireplace. "I see our patient has come back to us," he said, walking over to the man. "I'm Doctor Valentine. How are you feeling today?"

The old man looked at him, setting an empty bowl on the bed beside him, and wiped one hand across his lips. As he did, pieces of food that had fallen into his beard were now further embedded in it. He looked over at Belle, and then back at the doctor, a confused look upon his face, before he asked, "Where am I?"

"You're in a hospital in Hastings. Do you know your name, sir?"

"Of course, I know my name," he replied, followed by a puzzled look upon his face. Both Doc and Auntie Belle watched as he shook his head then, clearly confused. "I...guess I don't," he replied at last, looking down at the floor. He noticed then how cut and scraped his hands were, and looked up at Doc. "I'm afraid I'm having a hard time remembering."

Both Doc and Auntie Belle shook their heads, sadly, and then Doc asked, "Do you remember anything, sir. Where you're from? Who you were with? Anything that might tell us how you ended up here?"

The old man ran a hand through his long white hair, closing his eyes, as he tried to summon some image, some recollection from his mind. "A watch...I remember a watch. It was gold...and had a..." he shook his head, disgustedly. "I can't remember," he replied.

"Well, try not to worry about it," Doc said. "That's a start, anyway. A good sign, in fact. I'm sure your memory will come back. You've obviously been through something traumatic, and that's why you can't remember," Doc continued, having reached over to gently pat the old man's shoulder. "I'm sure if you rest and continue to eat the good food this lovely lady has provided, it won't be long before you're up and about, *and* remembering."

"Thank you," the old man replied, smiling at the doctor and Auntie Belle. Then, suddenly, he blurted out, "Juliana! I remembered her name. That's my wife's name. Juliana...Juliana!"

And as he cried out the name of his wife, Juliana Wright heard, and began running down the hall toward his room, not believing her ears. She ran into the room, to the surprise of Doc and Auntie Belle, crying, "Grandfather! Oh, Grandfather!" and flew into the arms of the old man, who held her close, though still not remembering.

CHAPTER 57

Johnny lay still, his mind on the things he had seen in the vision he'd experienced after his tangle with the bear. Ashamed of his actions, he knew he'd lost stature in the eyes of some of the braves because of how foolish he'd acted. Of course they didn't know why he'd acted that way—his mind so filled with anger at the knowledge that Laughing Water was with child—that he'd thought only of lashing out and destroying whatever was within his reach. Some of the braves, he noticed, now shied away from him, but not his friend, Brave Foot. Every day Brave Foot had come to see how he was doing. This made it harder on Johnny, and often he'd look away when he came, or close his eyes. One day Brave Foot came to him, asking him what was wrong, and Johnny had glared at him, saying, "Leave me alone. Go!"

Brave Foot stood quietly, saying nothing for a moment, then spoke, his words surprising Johnny. "I know you are upset, Black Hawk. I do not know why. I, too, have felt such anger. You see, my friend, my wife loves another. I do not know his name. She will not tell me. But she has refused to lie with me for many moons because of this. When my anger grew, I took her." He paused, a sad look upon his face. "Now she carries my child, and I am happy because of that. But at night I hear her weeping as she lays beside me, and it makes my heart sad." He placed a hand on Johnny's shoulder, and then spoke. "I was angry, at first, and wanted to find the one who had stolen her heart. My heart felt black as the night from the anger. I wanted to hurt her, like she'd hurt me. I wanted to kill her. But I saw her tears and heard her cries, and the blackness flew from me. Now my heart feels pain because I still feel love for her, and I know she is hurting, too. I will take another wife soon, a younger woman, very pretty. But it is not as I wished."

Johnny had turned toward him as he spoke, surprised by his words. He hoped Brave Foot did not know that it was he that Laughing Water loved, but saw no sign of it in his friend's eyes. "I'm sorry," he said, looking up at Brave Foot. "I'm real sorry, my friend."

Brave Foot smiled slightly, "My brother has two wives. My uncle has four. Perhaps this second wife will take the pain from my heart." Then he turned and walked slowly from the tepee.

Johnny felt as ashamed, as he did happy. There was no denying how bad he felt for having caused Brave Foot such sadness, but at the same time, he felt his heart soar with joy! Laughing Water had not betrayed the love they felt for each other. It was against her will that she had ended up with child. He had to go to her and tell her that he understood. He had to tell her that he loved her. He got to his feet, moving his legs, first one and then the other, getting some strength back into them. His shoulder still pained him, but the many stitches had closed the great tears securely where the bear's claws had ripped into his shoulder, and the marks of its teeth on his arm no longer seeped. He moved his arm and shoulder slowly, still cautious of opening his wounds. Then pulled on his buckskin shirt that lay nearby, and hurried from the tepee to find Laughing Water.

To his surprise, she was nowhere in camp. He'd walked from one end to the other, not seeing her. He'd even gone to Brave Foot's tepee, but she'd not been there. He grew worried, as time flew by, and still there was no sign of her. Rushing to his mother's tepee, he hurried inside, intent on grabbing his buffalo coat and gun, and setting out from the camp in search of her. But as he entered, he was surprised to find Laughing Water sitting with his mother, her face wet with tears. He stopped, the tepee flap closing behind him, not knowing what to say. Sarah looked up at her son, happy to see him, but also aware of the feelings he felt for Laughing Water, and she, for him.

She stood, laying her hand upon his arm. "I'll go get water. I'm glad you're feeling better." Then she took the nearly empty buffalo paunch that held their water, and walked from the tepee.

Johnny reached out to Laughing Water, holding her close, his heart bursting with the love he felt for her. He spoke her name over and over, as he held her, and kissed her face and cheeks and neck, her tears wetting his cheeks as he did so. His body responded to her as he held her close, though he knew this was not the time for such feelings. His mother would be back soon, and there were many things he wished to say to Laughing Water, before she returned. He edged back from her, his heart pounding in his chest, as he struggled with all the feelings and emotions inside him.

"There's little time. We must talk. I love you, Laughing Water, and I know you're with child. It doesn't matter. I know it was not of your choice."

Laughing Water looked surprised as he said this. "How do you know this?" she asked.

"Brave Foot came to me. He told me. He told me of the anger he had felt when he realized you loved another. He told me he forced himself on you." Laughing Water began to cry, as Johnny told her this, and he wrapped his arms around her, to comfort her. Then he continued, "In spite of the hurt he feels, he's forgiven you. He's a proud man. A good man. At first, he was terribly angry, as you know. But it's his love for the child you carry that has eased some of his pain, and the love..." Johnny hesitated, "the love he feels for you, even yet, that has softened his heart toward you. He doesn't know it's me that you love."

"I'm so sorry, Johnny. I never meant to hurt him...or you. When the baby is born, I will leave him. He's told me he will take a second wife soon. I've given it much thought."

"What about your children?" Johnny asked. "Brave Foot has much love for his children. I'm not sure he'll let you take them."

Laughing Water looked up at him, tears glistening in her eyes as she answered. "I will not take them. I know how strong his feelings are for our daughter, and also for the child I carry, though he has not held it, or seen it, yet." She was quiet a few moments, wiping the tears from her eyes, as she continued, "The children will stay with him. The young woman he has chosen, as second wife, is a friend of mine. I have watched her with my daughter, seeing her great love and kindness toward her. It is decided."

It was then that Johnny remembered the vision he had experienced during the time of his healing. He looked at Laughing Water, pulling her close, their hearts beating as one as he held her. "When I was hurt, I had a vision. I must leave during the Moon of Falling Leaves. I don't know where I am to go. Only the grandfather who gave me the vision, knows. But I must do as he has shown me. And he told her of his vision. Then he asked, "When is the baby due?"

Laughing Water hesitated, figuring her time. "It should also be in the Moon of Falling Leaves. In a few days," she answered.

Johnny laid his chin against her head, the sweet scent of her filling his senses, as he thought of what she'd just said. He had never realized that the child was due so soon, and was surprised at learning this. "How will the baby survive, if it has no mother's milk?" he questioned, glancing down at her.

"Another will have milk," she answered, rubbing her hands across his back, knowing they had only a few more moments before his mother would return. "It is the way of my people, if a mother can not feed her baby."

"I...I can't let you do it," Johnny said, speaking softly. "I don't want you to suffer the pain that leaving them would cause you." He stepped away, his thoughts troubled.

"I *must* go with you," she said. "We will have other children. Many children. I do not want to live without you."

"I know," Johnny said. And as he said this, his mother walked into the tepee. Laughing Water looked at Sarah, the tears in her lovely dark eyes telling Sarah how sad she felt. Sarah hung the paunch filled with water in its place, then turned, hugging the woman who so obviously loved her son. "We'll talk later," Johnny said, and Laughing Water smiled at him, a smile filled with sadness, and hurried from the tepee.

Sarah saw the worried look upon his face, and in her heart she grieved for the two young people. She knew how deeply they loved each other, and knew it was not an easy position they now found themselves in. She, too, had been in a similar position, once, and the feelings she had felt then had nearly torn her apart. She sat still, her mind traveling back to the town where she had lived, first with her father, and then with Moses. Moses, she thought. Why did you have to go to war, my love? It broke my heart the day you left.

She thought then of the other day; the day she had first realized the feelings she had for Cal. It had all been so innocent. She'd heard him yell for help, and looked toward the creek where it was deepest, just as he fell in, striking his head on some rocks near the surface. She still remembered how terrified she'd been when she saw him go under, knowing in his blindness, he might have drowned if she hadn't heard him yell. She saw it all, again, as clearly as if it was happening once more, and her heart began to race at the memory. Plunging into the water, she'd not given a thought to her own safety. Nor had she cared about her clothing getting wet, or even how cold the water had been. Her only concern was for his safety, as she called his name, over and over, and reached out, getting a tight hold on his shirt. It had taken all her strength to pull him out of the water, and she feared the worst when she saw the blood that ran down his face from the cut on his head. She sighed deeply, remembering. When he regained consciousness, she'd helped him to his feet, her arm around his waist to give him support, and then as she looked up at him, asking if he could walk, or stand, or if he could make it to the cabin—she no longer remembered exactly what she'd asked—he'd bent his head and kissed her. It had happened so quickly, surprising both of them. And yet she'd known all along, since the very first moment they'd met, that someday they would share that kiss. It wasn't that she didn't love Moses; she did. She loved him with all her heart. But there was a...a feeling...like she had never experienced before when Cal was near. A feeling that she knew he, too, had shared. She couldn't call it love, exactly. She didn't want to marry him. It wasn't like that, at all. It was as if in meeting him, she had discovered a kindred spirit, one with whom she shared an affinity. "Oh, Red Bird, old woman, you did the right thing," she said, speaking aloud.

It had taken strength for her to leave Hastings. Almost as much strength as it had taken to leave Cal. But hard as it was, she no longer had regrets about doing so.

CHAPTER 58

The heaviest snow came three days before the end of November. And when it stopped, Brave Foot was the father of a baby son. A healthy child that gave every impression of growing into a brave who would count coup on many, showing no fear.

Johnny was happy for Brave Foot, but concerned for Laughing Water. When he saw her with her baby, he saw the look of love on her face as she held him, and his heart grew heavy. His mother would not have given him up, even for love. And to expect Laughing Water to do so seemed the worst thing he could put her through. He sat in his mother's tepee, his conscience tearing at him. How can I ask such a thing of her, he thought. It was too big a price to pay, to his way of thinking. As for Brave Foot, did he deserve the loss of both his wife and his son? Not to mention, his friend? He would hunt them down for such a betrayal, and rightly so, Johnny thought. And he knew that in his place, *he* would do the same. These thoughts tore at him, more and more, till he could see no satisfactory outcome for any of them. Walking out into the snow, he paced back and forth beside the stream, his thoughts eating away at him. If only I hadn't seen her, he thought. If only I hadn't...he paced more, knowing there was no use thinking "if only." I *did* see her, he thought, and I *do* love her. Right or wrong, I love her.

The image of his boyhood friend flashed across his mind: Brave Foot teaching him how to hold his first bow during one of his many trips to the Indian village. Brave Foot on his belly, crawling along in

front of him, showing him the way to sneak up on the buffalo. Brave
Foot when they were older, hanging off the side of his horse, as they
raced along, bows drawn—guiding him on his first hunt. All of his
memories were of the friendship he had shared with Brave Foot ever
since the first day they had met. He held his head in his hands, wondering how he could ever make things right again. Then he stopped
pacing, staring out into the thickly falling snow.

Suddenly he knew where he was going! He crossed the stream,
heading through the woods to the west, hoping he could find his way.
As he walked, he remembered stories of his grandfather, John Bruce,
and how he believed that a man was always where he was *supposed*
to be. That there were *no* accidents. That belief changed a whole lot
of things, if he was right. Life was a gift from God, Johnny thought,
but what about destiny? Where did it fit in? Is it my destiny to hurt my
friend? He shook his head as he walked through the snow, scanning
the countryside for the signs he was looking for. The woods ended and
rock bluffs rose ahead of him, the snow now so dense that he had trouble seeing through it. He trudged along, wishing he'd worn his hat.
Then he saw it: A rock outcropping that resembled an eagle's wing.
And behind some thick brush nearby, the hidden entrance to a cave.
He'd come here many times over the years with Brave Foot. It was a
special place, where they had talked and talked, discussing boyhood
thoughts and feelings. And often times, they spoke of the stories they
had heard the elders tell, of the many feats of the great warriors: Crazy
Horse, the most humble of all warriors, it was said, and the Hunkpapa
Lakota, Sitting Bull, the most fierce. There were others, many others.
Long days had been spent in the cave by Johnny and Brave Foot, and
he smiled as he entered, seeing the drawings they had made on the
wall, just inside the cave's entrance. He located the large pile of sticks
they had left there, long before, and quickly went to work getting a
fire started. Then he sat down beside it, his eyes closed, and hands outstretched, palms up, listening.

After a while, he spoke, his voice echoing throughout the cave,
sounding strange to him. "Grandfather, I seek your guidance. Tell
me what to do. I do not want to hurt my friend, Brave Foot. Nor do I
want to hurt Laughing Water. Tell me what I must do." He sat quietly
then, listening. His back straight and head held high, he waited for an

answer, his arms still outstretched. The wind blew in great gusts at the entrance to the cave, howling it's mournful lament, and an eagle flew across the sky calling to its mate, but inside the cave there was only silence. He stayed, as he was, until he could hold his arms outstretched no more, and then lowered them to his side. Taking a deep breath, he opened his eyes and saw the reflection of the flames on the wall beyond. And as he watched, he saw the great bear take shape before him, its massive bulk covering the wall. He stared at the image of the bear, his heart pounding, and soon saw it rise on its hind legs before him.

The wind swirled now inside the cave, as well as out, its fierce roar hard to distinguish from the roaring of the bear, as Johnny closed his eyes, listening...listening. And as he did, in his mind he heard these words, "Go, Black Hawk. It is time. Hear me, Little Brother. There is much for you to learn. When you return in the Moon of the Popping Trees (December) understanding will be yours." Then as suddenly as it had begun, the roaring stopped and wind grew still, and Johnny Black Hawk knew what he must do.

Walking back into the village, he went directly to his mother's tepee, telling her he needed to talk to Laughing Water, asking her to go tell her to come to him. Sarah looked deep into his eyes, knowing she did not have a choice. She had seen that look before in the eyes of her first husband, Gray Eagle—on several occasions—and knew that Johnny had made a decision. She left her tepee, praying beneath her breath that it was a good decision, one that would bring no sadness or danger to her son, or Brave Foot and his wife. Her heart skipped beats, as she walked along, her worries many.

In only a short while, Laughing Water entered the tepee, going into Johnny's arms immediately. It was a moment or two before she noticed the determined set to his face, and seeing it, her smile faded. "What is it?" she asked, sitting down. "I see you have made a decision, Black Hawk. It will not please me. Am I right?"

Johnny stood where he'd been when she'd entered the tepee, looking at her, knowing he had no choice. "You must stay with your children, Laughing Water, until I return. In the cave that is west of here, once more the great bear came to me. It spoke, telling me many things. Do you know where I mean?"

"Yes," she replied, her voice edged with sadness.

"The cave is a place that I visited all through my childhood. It's where Brave Foot and I hid from the other boys. It's a good place, safe from all intruders, and known only to the People. In the cave today, the great bear came to me again. He spoke, telling me of the journey I must make. He told me I will return in December; in the Moon of the Popping Trees." He waited for her to say something, but instead she stood and walked to him. Wrapping her arms around him, she held him, not wanting to let him go; yet knowing she must do as he asked.

"You will go soon?" she asked, tears welling up in her eyes.

"In two days time," he replied. "I love you, Laughing Water. Trust me. It is as it must be, though I do not understand the reason."

"I trust you, Johnny Black Hawk. I will wait for your return, and ask Wakantanka to guide you on your journey." Then she rose up, quickly, onto her toes, and kissed him long and hard. It seemed the kiss would never stop, as the two young people held each other, not knowing if they would ever see each other again. Then she pulled away and hurried from the tepee, never looking back.

Johnny ate a piece of pemmican as he waited for his mother to return. Now he would tell her of the visions he'd had, and explain that he must leave. It would be terribly hard for both, as he had been with her only a short while. He sat down before the fire, knowing in his heart that what he was doing was right. It was a good feeling. He also knew that wherever his journey took him, Laughing Water would be with him in his heart.

CHAPTER 59

The following day Johnny went to the tepee of his father's old friend, Howling Wolf. He had spoken to him only in passing since his return to the camp, and did not want to leave without spending some time with him. Johnny had told him there'd been no other word of his father, although he now had his medallion. That an old man had been wearing it who claimed he'd taken it from Moses' body where a great battle was fought, at a place called Gettysburg. Howling Wolf had nodded, saying that he was sorry to hear this. Other than that, they hadn't had a chance to talk.

Now, as he sat in Howling Wolf's tepee, passing the pipe, he told him of the visions he'd had, and Howling Wolf listened, shaking his head. They spoke, too, of the many things that had transpired in previous years. How the whites had come in great number, wagons cutting across the lands where the bison grazed. And of the killing of the buffalo. As many, it was said, as the stars in the sky. The two men grew silent as they thought about this. It was not as if the whites needed the meat. No. They killed for the hide, leaving the bodies to rot in the sun. Now there were few buffalo for the tribes to hunt. Few for meat, to feed the People, few hides for their shelter and clothing, or bones for their tools: buffalo shoulder-blades for hoes, or even small bones for use as needles, and awls for punching holes. Even the dung that they needed to heat their tepees had also become scarce.

Howling Wolf spoke of these things, and Johnny heard his concern for the People in his voice.

"I see no end to them coming," Johnny said, and he told his friend of the many wagons he had seen, not only near Hastings, but also on his journey to look for his father. "I've heard the soldiers are building more forts, as we speak."

"Yes, it is true. Long Hair (General Custer) went into the land of our people in the Black Hills with many soldiers, though it broke the white man's promise, to do so. He saw the yellow metal there. Then the Great Chief in Washington wanted our land, so men could come to dig the yellow metal that the whites call gold. We were told we had to sell our land, or many would come to take it from us. There has been much unrest since, many battles, and much talk of war. And not only among our people, but the Blackfoot, Cheyenne, and many others, too. Though the whites talk long, Black Hawk, their words are like the blowing wind," Howling Wolf said.

"I heard of the treaty at Fort Laramie in '68. I was thirteen at that time," Johnny said. "I think that was the year."

"Yes," Howling Wolf replied. "It said the land would be ours as long as the sun shall rise, as long as the rivers flow, and as long as the grass grows. But again, the words of the white man were like the wind. Some think the day will come when the Black Hills will not belong to our people," Howling Wolf said. "I do not understand how that could be. Can Mother Earth be sold?" He shook his head, a questioning look upon his face. "I do not see an end to the broken promises of the whites, Black Hawk, or to the pain of my people. The great herds of buffalo roam the land no more, and we too, will soon be like the buffalo, it is said."

Johnny looked at his father's friend, seeing the strong muscles of his arms, his hair now laced with gray. His many victories—both in battle and on hunts—were seen in the vividly colored drawings that covered the dew cloth on the inside of his tepee. Their meanings, not all clear to Johnny. Deerskins and buffalo robes were placed around the edges of the tepee, and a raised bed of woven branches covered with soft moss served as a mattress. The dew cloth was spread out around the lower half of the tepee, to keep drafts out, and along with the raised bed, it provided a warm and comfortable shelter. Johnny had learned of these things, when younger, as he watched his mother set up her tepee, and build her own raised bed. As he looked around, he thought then of Laughing Water and his friend, Brave Foot. Their tepee was much like Howling Wolf's, though the designs on their dew cloth told different stories. Johnny closed his eyes, attempting to rid his mind of these thoughts which brought him pain: thoughts of Laughing Water and Brave Foot. He looked back at Howling Wolf, noticing the bear-claw necklace he wore, and the intricately beaded design on his medicine bundle. Like Johnny, he wore buckskin pants, shirt, and warmly lined moccasins. A parfleche (bag) hung from one of the tepee poles, and Johnny knew it held extra clothing. From the other poles hung a rawhide shield, bow and arrows, a pipe bag to hold Howling Wolf's everyday pipe, and a finely decorated tobacco sack.

A sadness filled Johnny as he looked at these things. How he wished that the whites—especially those in Washington—could feel the tranquility of an Indian dwelling, and understand the ways of the People, as he did. But he was certain this was not to be, and felt great sadness. He felt even greater sadness as the feeling suddenly came to him that he would not see the things he'd seen today, nor ever share the warm company of his father's friend again. As he thought that, Howling Wolf's eyes met his, and *both* knew that this was goodbye.

Johnny walked back to his mother's tepee, troubled by his thoughts. He knew, beyond a doubt, that he would not see Howling Wolf again—though he couldn't explain just how he knew—and it caused him to wonder if he should be leaving. What of Laughing Water? he thought. And Mother? He had been amongst the Indians long enough, however, to know the importance of the vision he had received, and knew he would do as the Grandfather bid. He didn't understand why he had to leave, but it was clear he must. Setting aside these troubling thoughts, he decided to stop at the tepee of his friend, Brave Foot, to say goodbye.

Brave Foot welcomed him, telling him of his new son; of all the hopes he had for him, while Laughing Water sat nearby, her face pale.

She looked like she had been crying. Johnny smiled at her, a quick smile, while in his heart he longed to pull her to him, proclaim his love, and if necessary, fight to the death his lifelong friend, in hopes of taking her with him. Instead, he told Brave Foot it was a fine son he had, one who would surely count many coup in the years to come. Brave Foot smiled at his words, great pride showing on his face. Laughing Water left the tepee then, to Johnny's surprise, her tiny, black-haired baby boy asleep in his cradleboard, tied to a tepee pole high above the floor. Her little girl slept peacefully nearby.

Soon after, Johnny rose to leave. Brave Foot stood, reaching his hand out to him, looking at him in a way Johnny found odd. Still clasping his hand, Brave Foot looked into Johnny's eyes, a long time. Then he spoke, "Laughing Water...will miss you, Black Hawk. And I will miss the friend of my childhood. We have had many good times. I will remember them always."

Johnny looked at him, hearing the words he had *not* said. He looked down, momentarily, then back up at Brave Foot, replying, "I will miss *you...both...my* friend."

CHAPTER 60

Johnny knew the hardest goodbye of all was the one he had to say to his mother. Many thoughts entered his mind, sitting there in her te-pee, watching her sew with bone awl a fine shirt for him to take on his journey. He hadn't told her he was leaving, her mother's instinct had. That, and the tears she had seen on Laughing Water's face, he sup-posed. He cleared his throat, intending to speak, but sat watching her instead, knowing how much he would miss her. She was no longer the young mother he remembered who had taught him to read, spending long hours teaching him, always teaching him. He also remembered the lessons she had tirelessly tried to teach him, over and over again, about numbers. He smiled as he thought back to how frustrated she'd become when he inserted "twenty-seven" in between numbers, when counting, and hardly *ever* where it belonged. It had been a silly habit, that had only grown stronger, the harder she tried to correct him. And perhaps, he thought now, *because* she tried so hard to correct him. He hadn't always been the best at behaving, that was true. I tried never to disobey, he thought, but my mind would see something interesting, and I'd get caught-up in it, missing supper, or my chores. Sometimes, I wouldn't even answer her when I was sitting right beside her, if something had my attention. He watched as she sat there, a tender smile upon her face. A face that showed a few wrinkles and lines, now that she was older, but a face still so beautiful. I've seen her laugh and seen her cry, he thought, and all those times—good and bad—she always looked beautiful to me. In his mind, he saw her then—years back—standing before the fireplace at their home near Hastings, stirring a large pot of venison stew, wisps of hair curling around her face as she stood there. He saw her, too, sitting out by the barn on the old fallen log, the apron she wore full of peas that she was shucking, a smile on her face as she watched his father fixing the gate. Life can sure bring about some changes, he thought. Once, when he was little, and his pa was still with them, he'd seen them wrestling together down by the old apple tree. They were laughing and playing together like children, and she was squealing with delight, and jumped up and began to run. His pa had raced after her, tackling her, and he watched them then as they kissed. He had thought it so funny, seeing them like that. Except for the kiss, he'd thought that was awful. Being young then, I couldn't imagine anything as terrible, he thought, as kissing a girl—even Mother. He closed his eyes, resting them, as he tried to decide just what he would say to her. But to his surprise, his mother spoke first.

"When do you leave, son?"

He opened his eyes, studying her. It had always been this way between them, as long as he could remember. They seemed to know the other's thoughts, and unspoken words. He smiled, looking down at his hands, before answering. "You always know what's bothering me, don't you?"

"Sometimes," she answered, a slight smile on her lips.

"When I lay hurt, I heard the medicine man's prayers, but all of a sudden they were unclear to me. Louder than his words were the sounds around me. I saw the bear, and felt ashamed for having done what I did. It had come in a vision, Mother, and it spoke to me. I saw high mountains more beautiful than any in the books you taught me to read. And the sun, so bright, that it hurt my eyes to gaze at it. And the bear became a man and spoke to me, telling me I must make a journey in the Moon of the Falling Leaves to learn...something. I don't know what. He said I would find the answers I seek, and I saw a red road through the mountains. Yesterday I had another vision. In the cave that only a few of our people know about, the bear came again, and became a man. He told me I must go *now*, but that I would understand in the Moon of the Popping Trees (December). I've told Laughing Water that I will return then." He stopped talking, waiting for his mother to say something, but she was still.

"I studied every day, Mother, learning all I could when I was growing up. I studied all your books, and those belonging to Miss Denton. Learning was easy for me, as you know. I always thought that I'd take up teaching. Teaching or preaching. Though I guess they're one and the same. I liked the stories you and Grandpa Angus told me about my grandfather, John Bruce. How he came to this country and got the professorship at that college in the East. I thought I might like to try my hand at teaching, like he did. Never told you that, did I?" He paused, thoughts running through his mind. "But now I'm not so sure. Things are changing. Times are changing. And, I guess I'm changing, too. I see things differently now. Men aren't like I once thought them to be. Not many of them, that is. They seem so set on taking, no matter what it is: another man's money, or goods, or land. Sometimes...even his...wife." He grew quiet then.

"Life doesn't always flow along on an easy path, son. I think we all have good intentions," Sarah said, looking over at him. "But sometimes things just happen, you know. It's not that we plan it, or even want it. Sometimes, for reasons we can't even figure, there's a moment when our minds...or our hearts, take over. Love is a powerful force, Johnny, more powerful—sometimes—than a raging river. It can turn your life upside down, and change a whole lot of things. I can't help but think back to when your pa and I first met. Oh, John, he just made me so mad! Always teasing and flirting and embarrassing me. But later, when I saw the way he was—inside—you know. When I saw how he was the day Melinda Rose almost died having her baby, my heart just filled with all kinds of feelings for him. And later, when he told me of losing his first wife like he had, I felt so much love for him that I never minded his teasing after that. Not much, anyway." Sarah sat there, a contented smile on her face, as her thoughts carried her back in time. She went there more and more, it seemed, the older she got, and doing so always made her happy. "And the day that you were born...oh, Johnny, I wish you could have seen how proud your father was! I told him I wanted to name you after your grandfather, John Bruce. He'd been my best friend, and of course, we knew then that he was Moses' real father. Anyway, I said I wanted to name you, John Black Hawk Gentry. Black Hawk because that was Moses' Indian name, you know. And as soon as I said it, your pa said, "Johnny Black Hawk. I like that." And I don't think I *ever* saw him happier." She sniffled then, and Johnny knew it was the memory of his father that caused it.

"Will you be all right, Mother, when I leave?" he asked.

"Well, of course. Why wouldn't I be?" she answered, surprised by his asking. "I belong here, Johnny. I have, ever since your father..." she stopped talking, not finishing her sentence.

"We have to talk about him," Johnny said, and he reached into his medicine bag and pulled out the round bone medallion.

"Oh!" Sarah exclaimed; her eyes widening as she saw it.

"I came across a fellow...ah...an old fellow who'd found it at one of the battle sights. All those years of searching for some word, and I met up with him just outside of Hastings. I didn't mean to upset you. I'm sorry."

When Sarah spoke next, her voice was soft and filled with sadness, "I expected...it," she said. "I always knew if he was alive, he'd come back home to us. There never was a doubt in my mind about it. I'm sorry, too, son. Sorry you had to find out, though I guess "inside" we always did know, didn't we? It's been *so* long. With every passing day, I guess I became more certain he was gone. I wouldn't have come back here, so far from Hastings, if I'd thought there was even the tiniest hope...you know?"

"I guess I knew, too," Johnny said. "He would have walked through raging storms, and even fire, to get back to us. I always knew that, too, but I *had to go look*. Just had to." As he spoke, he reached out and handed her the medallion. Sarah took it, pressing it to her heart, a tear running down her cheek as she did so. They sat quietly then, each lost in their own thoughts of life, as it was, when life was so perfect in the good old days.

Sarah broke the silence, telling Johnny that there was something else they had to talk about. It had been put off much too long; what with him being young, first, and then being gone to look for his father. "We need to talk about the mine, Johnny, and all that money your Grandpa Angus put in our name. There was more money than you could shake a stick at," she said, smiling. "At first, it went to my head. I felt like running right to town and buying all the pretty dresses and fancy shoes and things. And maybe some hats, too, with all kinds of feathers going ever which way all over them. Hats like the really rich ladies wore in places like England, you know? And me not even liking hats!" She laughed aloud as she said this, and Johnny had to laugh, too. "Well, after about a week, I guess it was, the urge just sort of flew away. I guess you could say I got all my sense back. That's what Moses used to say. He'd be teasing me something fierce, telling me he was thinking of getting himself some of the pants like those English "dandies" wore. The kind of pants that hugged their behinds so tight that they could barely sit a horse. Oh, and a top hat! We'd get to laughing so hard at our "imagined finery." I think we had more fun talking about it, than we ever would have had, buying it." She sighed, softly, her eyes closed, remembering. Johnny sat quietly, enjoying her memories, and seeing her so happy. Soon she continued, "Anyway, enough of a silly old woman's memories. Your pa invested most of the money. He told me he bought up a large piece of land on the side of the big lake. You know, the lake where Cal Dunnevey owns some land. We would have ended up neighbors; if...things had turned out differently. Anyway, he also invested in the railroad. I don't quite understand how he went about it, but he said it would make us rich forever, if those big, ugly machines kept running down those tracks. I never was very good at figures. Better than you, though, with that number "twenty-seven" you stuck in everywhere when you were counting," she laughed, and Johnny laughed, too, as she continued. "I let your pa do all the investing and buying and such. Well, I didn't really "let" him, that's just a figure of speech. I kept my hand out of it, is what I meant. He said he'd made deals all over the country, can you believe it? Just to make sure those ugly tracks and trains kept running. I wonder what he'd think about them now, if he could see how much they've hurt the Indian people? I think he'd be sorely tempted to demand all his money right back. I've never seen the tracks, of course, but Silas has. He told me about them when he brought my spectacles. He said they stretch as far as the eye can see, all across the land. And worse yet, the trains belch awful black smoke and frighten horses, and even kill any animals or people who get on the tracks. Of course, the buffalo they hit usually get them off track. I guess you could say *I've* gotten off track, too. I was telling you about the money. All the papers are at the bank. Your pa said if anything happened to him, you could just go to Mister...well, whatever his name is. I imagine there's a new fellow there now, of course. You just go in there, son, and tell them your name. They can get the papers, and you'll see how good your pa did, investing. As far as the mine, I'm not even sure exactly where it is. That paper is buried near our old cabin. It's buried in an old bottle under the fence post closest to the barn, about four or five feet down, I think your pa said, maybe a little deeper. Michael won't mind you digging it up, I'm sure. Just tell him there's money there, and more under the posts nearest the outhouse, too. I do hope those posts are still standing. Your pa did a lot of good with all that money, Johnny. He helped a lot of folks get a start. You know, I sometimes think he and Angus had sort of a contest going, to see who could do the most good. They'd argue over how to help some of those poor folks, some of those Irish, you know. Would take them things they needed, when they saw that they were needful. It made me so proud, knowing that was the kind of man your pa was. A good man, Johnny—one of the best. And your Grandpa Angus, the same."

She stood then, as did Johnny, and she reached up, laying her hands on either side of his face. She looked at him a long time, memorizing every feature, so she would never forget a single detail. "I've finished the shirt. It'll keep you warm. And the buffalo robe coat will protect you from the winter winds. We've shared things this day, son, worth far more than money and gold."

"Yes, I know we have," Johnny replied, hugging her tenderly. Then he laid down on the far side of the tepee, and soon drifted off to sleep.

Early in the morning, while most of the camp still slept, they woke and shared a quick meal. Then Johnny got his things together, and readied his horse for the journey. It was cold that morning, but not as cold as it had been some other days. Snowflakes drifted down, and in spite of the cold, they gave a magical essence to the surroundings. It was the kind of morning Johnny especially liked, with its silent stillness and spiritual beauty.

Sarah watched, as he checked his gun and then holstered it, hoping he would have no reason to use it. She knew he was not one to use it unless he had to. He was a peaceable man, like his father had been, and she couldn't have been prouder of him. Hating to see him go, she knew that what he had spoken of the night before was resting heavy on his mind; the indecision, that is, of what he would do with the rest of his life. He had always been drawn toward helping folks. Probably got that from his father, she supposed. It was just his nature, it seemed, to want to help people. Being a teacher, *or* a man of God, either one would lend itself to that. She also knew that all the things he'd studied so diligently, ever since he was young, had been to that very purpose. And though she hated to see him go, she trusted the knowledge she had about visions, to believe he was right to do so.

At last, he was ready. Walking over to where she stood watching him, a terrible feeling of sadness filled him. "It's time," he said, smiling down at her.

"I know," she replied. Then she put out her hand, and in it he saw the round bone medallion. "This is yours now, Johnny. I want you to have it. It was a gift of love, son, from your father to me, just as you are." She slipped the medallion's rawhide strap over his head, her eye's brimming with tears.

Johnny wrapped his arms around her, whispering, "I love you, Mother."

Sarah held him close, answering, "And I love you, Johnny." And once again she stood watching as her son rode away.

CHAPTER 61

Johnny rode all that day, and the next, not hurrying but trusting God, Wakantanka, and the visions he'd had, to lead him where he was to go. The air was clear and no longer was the snow falling. His thoughts rode with him, bringing questions to mind: Why was it necessary for him to leave the village by the last day of November? And how far would he be traveling, if the Grandfather in his vision had told him he would be returning in December?

The second night he made camp in a sheltered cove, sitting by the fire he'd made, eating food his mother had prepared. He smiled as he thought of her. Other mothers would have wept and pleaded, he supposed, if their son was leaving. But she had not. She wasn't like any woman he'd ever known. She'd simply hugged him to her, telling him she loved him, then stepped back, her head held high and chin slightly raised, as was her habit. Her strength is what I admire most, he thought. She'd always seemed to have more than other women. That was made even more obvious by the choice she'd made to live with the Indians. Few, if any, women he knew would have chosen to do that. He made a thick bed of branches, wrapping his buffalo robe coat more tightly around him. And using his saddle as a pillow, he lay down, and was soon asleep.

That same night, on a hill a fair distance from Standing Elk's village, a cavalry officer stood surveying his troops as they made camp for the night. The moon was partially hidden behind the clouds, and he was glad. Except for a few murmurs, and the clinking of some gear, occasionally, a person would have a hard time discovering they were there. Of course, them Injuns seemed to have some kind of sixth sense, seemed able to almost see in the dark, he thought. He shook his head and ran a hand through his thick white hair. Be a cold day in hell, he thought, before they see me coming. He hated Indians. Had hated them for as long as he could remember. They were animals, cunning and sly as fox. Heathen devils. He cleared his throat, and then looked around cautiously, wondering if any were, at that very moment, creeping up on him. His collar rubbed against his throat, making his neck itch. But it was too cold to remove the uniform jacket. And besides, he wanted to look his best. He wanted to look impressive. He wished he had his flask with him. Could use a drink. Little did his troops realize that after tomorrow, he would be looked upon as a great officer. As great as that young up-start everyone was talking about...George Armstrong Custer. If there was anyone he hated more than the injuns, it was Custer! He cleared his throat again, and spit off to one side. His horse nickered softly, and he glanced around quickly, checking again for any sign of intruders. There was a stillness in the air that seemed somehow unnatural. A stillness and quiet unlike any he'd felt before. As if all creation was waiting, uneasily and expectantly, for the morning, and the task that lay ahead. As if even the earth was holding its breath.

Well, he thought, tomorrow would tell. Tomorrow would separate the men from the boys. He smiled into the darkness and scratched his neck, then ran his hand across his stomach, noticing the coarseness of his uniform jacket. How he wished he had a drink. A little whiskey would really hit the spot, he thought. Would ease the tension and maybe stop his hands from shaking. He licked his lips, unaware that he did so, savoring in his mind the last taste of whiskey he'd had. He'd gotten drunk that night, drunk as all git out. Had fallen on the ground, crying like a baby. Hadn't even remembered it, till one of his fellow officers teased him about it, the next day. He felt his cheeks burn with embarrassment at the memory. His retirement was not far away. This was his chance, he thought, to make a name for himself. His chance to gain the respect and admiration he'd so long deserved.

He hacked and spit, as these thoughts stirred up a mouthful of bile. Again he spit, wiping his mouth on his sleeve, wondering if it was going to snow.

All anyone ever spoke of nowadays, it seemed, was that arrogant young fool the Indians called "Long hair." Every time he turned around, there was some tall tale goin' around of his bravery and daring. Ha! I'd like to see him, all alone, face to face with a bunch of redskins, he thought. See just how brave he is then. He smiled, a smile filled with loathing. Yes, sir, he thought, I'd just love to see him up to his neck in a whole slew of them murderin' savages! He walked over to his horse, absently patting its neck a time or two. I've been out here in this injun country for near on how many years, and is there ever a pat on the back for all *I've* done? No, sir! Has there ever been *one—just one*—ounce of recognition for the work I've done, or the suffering I've gone through to make this land safe from those red devils? No, sir, he thought, his face getting redder, the madder he got. Well, tomorrow's gonna change all that. Tomorrow's *my* chance to get a little glory. He smiled again, a smile that was more a sneer; his eyes narrowing like a hawk sighting its prey. Custer ain't the only one who can make a name for himself by killing hostiles. It's *my* turn now. He scratched his stomach, wishing again that he had his flask with him. A drink would take the edge off. Would settle his stomach, he thought, and make the night air less chilling. He turned and walked on down the hill toward his tent, shivering slightly as the cold edged its way into his bones. Tomorrow, he'd show all those in command that he was the one who could be counted on to get the job done. He stopped, glancing around, seeing that his horse followed behind. Glad it was only his horse he'd heard, and not one of them heathen savages sneaking up on him. He clenched his hands into fists, wishing their shaking would stop. Then he turned, hurrying to his tent, knowing that tomorrow things would be different!

CHAPTER 62

The screech of a hawk woke Johnny the next morning, and he stood, brushing a light covering of snow from the buffalo robe coat that had kept him comfortably warm during the night. He walked back and forth, stretching his legs; glad for the fur-lined moccasins his mother had made him. He had a strange feeling, he began to notice, as he ate a piece of the pemmican she had provided. An uneasy feeling of some sort, that grew, till it became so intense that it seemed to shake him to his very bones. Placing a hand upon his heart, he stood still, not certain why he was feeling as he was. He closed his eyes, trying to determine the source of the feeling, and an image of his mother came to mind. And as it did, a great uneasiness filled him. "Mother," he said, aloud, and he couldn't shake the feeling that she needed him. Throwing handfuls of snow on his campfire to make sure it no longer burned, he saddled Buck, moving as quickly as he could. Then he mounted, and raced back toward Standing Elk's camp.

He remembered the stories his father had told him of how he, too, had gotten feelings such as those. Feelings that tore at him, years earlier, when his mother had lain desperately ill in a cave far from camp. And how she would have died, if his father hadn't trusted his feelings enough to race to her side, though he had no proof, whatsoever, that she was at the cave, until he arrived there and found her. Guess I've got your "sixth sense," too, Johnny thought as he urged his horse on faster, knowing he had two full days ride ahead of him before he'd reach the camp.

He had no way of knowing that at that very moment, his mother, Sarah Elizabeth Justus Gentry, was on her way to talk to her friend, Little Moon, on the other side of the encampment when she heard the sound of approaching horses. Thinking it was Chief Standing Elk and some of his braves returning from an early morning hunt, she turned to watch their arrival, a soft smile upon her lips. In mere seconds, however, her smile turned to a concerned frown, as she saw the blue uniforms of a cavalry troop as they cleared a rise, brandishing guns, some with swords drawn. There was no doubt in her mind: they were attacking!

She screamed out a warning, dropped the basket she had been carrying, and began to run. Though she was still fleet of foot for her age, she knew she could not outrun their horses. Besides, the snow was more than knee high in most places, and made running difficult.

She saw Little Moon hurry out of her dwelling, saw the look of astonishment upon her face quickly turn to fear. Sarah grabbed up a little girl, no more than two years of age, who had heard her yell and, toddled outside of her family's dwelling, knowing the child would be trampled if she remained where she was. The sound of the cavalry no longer far behind, their thundering reverberations matching the pounding of her heart! She could hear the soldiers' shouts, the crack of rifle fire, and the cries of the Indian women and children as they tried to escape the harrowing attack and find some safety in the woods beyond the creek, the snow hampering them in their attempt to escape. The little girl's mother rushed out of their lodge, a terrified look upon her face as she realized the nearness of their attackers, her little one still clutched within Sarah's arms as she ran.

"Run!" Sarah screamed, as she came abreast of the woman. She flung the terrified child into her mother's arms when she was close enough to do so, and saw the young mother turn and race as fast as she could toward the creek, and the safety of the forest beyond, to her left. A soldier close behind! Sarah veered to the right, knowing another soldier was closing in on her. She could hear the rapidly expelled breath of his mount as he came along side of her, and feel the spray of saliva as its head nearly touched her shoulder. Then suddenly, she was knocked to the ground, as its body slammed into her. She screamed as she fell, hitting the ground hard, in spite of the snow. Moving quickly, she had the presence of mind to roll away from the thundering beast, before she could be trampled. Suddenly, out of nowhere, Brave Foot appeared, running to her defense! She watched in horror as the soldier shot him, one bullet hitting him just below the eye, two more in the chest. He crumpled beside her, his young life snuffed out in his attempt to save her.

The soldier pulled up on his reins, causing his horse to rear and shy away from her. He wore the same insignia that her father had worn, and she knew he was a captain, just as her father had been.

"What in tarnation...?" she heard him say, as she looked up at him. His eyes were filled with a harshness devoid of warmth or even the slightest vestige of human kindness. "Well, what have we got here?" he said, sneering, his hatred for Indians burning deep into Sarah's heart. His horse pranced before her, its hooves barely missing her. She tried to inch back away and catch her breath, hearing the shouts, shots, and screams filling the air behind her, but the drifted snow prevented her from doing so. She knew without looking that only a few of the Indian people were still alive.

"You'll pay for this," she hissed between clenched teeth, as she lay upon her side, her feet drawn up out of the way of being stepped on by his excited mount.

For just a moment the soldier paused, glancing around as if he were checking to see if anyone was watching him. Then, seeing that his troops were far ahead, actively pursuing the few Indians still alive, he smiled at Sarah, a smile that left no doubt of the evil he was capable of. "We'll see about that, Injun lover," he threatened, his voice challenging. Then he raised his saber and slashed downward in one swift movement. The blade cut through the air, a brilliant flash from the sun reflecting upon it, blinding the eye, like an eagle's wing, turned silver. Having no weapon with which to defend herself, Sarah kicked up at him, hoping to frighten his horse, and somehow avoid the blow! The blade of his saber struck her just above the ankle of her left leg, slicing downward through her moccasin, severing a deep wedge of flesh at the ankle. She screamed as the pain tore through her. Pain worse than any she had ever known. Nearly losing consciousness from the pain, she fell back, her whole body shaking as she laid there, her hands drawn into fists, her teeth bared and eyes tightly clenched from the agony she was suffering. Tears coursed down her cheeks, and she moaned, unaware that she had bitten her lip until it, too, bled.

After awhile, she opened her eyes, realizing to her great surprise that the soldier had ridden off. He'd gone to join his returning troops, their shouts of victory filling the air, where they were assembling. Yelling out orders, the captain sounded pleased with himself, so certain was he that now his name would also be spoken of with pride by those in positions of authority. Certain that he, too, would be hailed as a hero, like Custer, who got praised for even his slightest foray.

Sarah raised up on one elbow, no longer reeling from the pain of the cut. Instead she felt only a calmness pervading the stillness all around her. She saw the rapidly spreading pool of blood coloring the snow beneath her leg. Saw, too, the severed piece of flesh that lay on the ground beside her. She started to reach out, wondering for just a moment, if she could stifle the flow of blood, but knew she could not. Already an imposing weakness was spreading throughout her body. She lay back, realizing she now felt only an all-encompassing calm. She knew she was dying. The thought did not frighten her. It was as if all sense of emotion had left her. She did not cry, or lament the fact; she simply felt a growing sense of acceptance. She had wondered what it would be like to die. Had even feared it, somewhat, over the years. Never dreamt that it would be like this...a simple...letting go.

Her thoughts turned to the time her mother surprised her with her very own dolly that she had sewn, just for her, from scraps of material. How she had loved that doll. And she thought of how happy her father had been the day he returned from town with news of his impending wedding to Rosie...dear, dear Rosie...with her lovely Irish brogue and joyful countenance. She remembered then, how her father had whirled Rosie around the dance floor the day of Nancy Pearly's wedding to Silas Haverty, the memory soon crossing her mind of how Moses had teased her mercilessly that day. Oh, how he had infuriated her! And how she had grown to love him in the years that followed. Wonderful years. Happy years. Oh, yes, how very dearly she had loved him. It had nearly killed her, when he didn't return from the war. He had nearly burst with happiness the day their son was born. He'd helped deliver him, and then rocked him, holding him close, telling her how happy she had made him, and how proud he was to be a father. John Black Hawk Gentry had given both Moses *and* her the healing they needed from the loss of their first children; Moses' child with his first wife, Sarah Mathews, and her, from the loss of Gray Eagle's child. Both had died before they could be born, but that never made their loss any less painful.

She stirred, realizing her eyes were closed. Slowly she opened them, aware that she was no longer wearing her spectacles. All was still. Above her the sky was a soft gray. It had been a most glorious morning, decidedly colder than the previous one. But the sun had soon come up, its rays glistening across the snow, its warmth a blessing. She turned her head, slightly, finding it most difficult to do so. She knew it would not be long before she would lack all strength, and wondered how long she had lain there. It was then that she noticed the others that lay nearby: young braves who had fought so valiantly, but never had a chance. She saw Little Moon, over by her lodge, a dark stain in the snow beneath her head, her lovely black hair—the texture of finest silk—now matted with her blood. Wind Runner, wife of Chief Standing Elk, lay beside her, a small boy—his eyes already glazed—cradled within her stiffening arms. Brave Foot, along with some of the old ones, lay nearby, and Sarah shuddered, feeling tremendous grief at the sight, and yet was strangely detached from it, somehow. She felt numb, as though her feelings and senses were no longer connected to her, but held at a protective distance. Turning her head slowly, to look to her other side where the creek was, she saw that the young mother she had told to run, lay face down in the snow at the water's edge, her pretty little, dark-haired, baby daughter sitting beside her, one of her small legs caught beneath the dead weight of her mother's body. The little girl looked unharmed, but was crying pitifully, and touching her young mother's face; a frightened look in her dark eyes.

Sarah turned away, once more looking up toward the sky. Carrion eaters flew above now; circling patiently, and she knew it would not be long before their stomachs would be full. The thought did not bother her. It simply was the truth, and she was detached from the horror of it.

She wondered then where Johnny was. Wondered where his journey had taken him. She smiled, thankful he was not there with her. Pride filled her as she thought of him. He would choose his path in life, not only because of his grandparents, Singing Raven and John Bruce, but because of the other good people in his life: Rosie, Angus, and of course, his father, Moses. She closed her eyes, her breathing shallow, her mind at peace, as a gentle warmth enveloped her.

It was then she sensed movement in front of her. A cloud surrounded her. Not threatening, but embracing. Figures appeared within it, the cloud-like haze separating as they slowly approached. She recognized her father, and beside him, her mother, and Angus; his beautiful white hair shining like an ethereal halo. He smiled at her, the smile she remembered so well. At his side, she saw her dear friend, John Bruce, and felt his love for her as he looked at her. She reveled in it, feeling profound happiness. Then they faded back into the haze, leaving only one figure in the mist. She watched him approach, her heart brimming with joy!

"Hello, darlin'," she heard Moses say, and reached out to him, as the most brilliant light appeared just beyond his shoulder. Stepping forward, she could feel herself being drawn into its radiance. And then Sarah Elizabeth Justus Gentry—affectionately known as Red Bird among the Indian people she loved so dearly—left her earthly cares behind, and went home to meet her Maker.

THE END.

EPILOGUE

And so it came to pass that early on a crisp and cold winter morning, while most were still asleep, all those within Standing Elk's camp, including Sarah Elizabeth Gentry, died. Massacred, because a cavalry officer sought glory and recognition. None of the Indians in camp that day lived to tell of the injustice done them. It was just one more act of savagery, committed in the name of peace. Committed not by the so-called savages, but by the whites who spoke of justice and goodwill, and signed treaty after treaty, breaking them as fast as they were signed.

The Indians had fought valiantly, as more and more of their lands were taken, in spite of the treaties and promises they were given. Finally, all the buffalo, land, and freedom to live as they had always lived, were gone. What the whites didn't destroy, the white man's diseases did. Few ever knew the extent of the suffering the Indians endured; fewer cared.

The cavalry captain led his troops back to the fort that day, heads held high, proud of their day's adventure. Behind them, thirty-three people lay dead in the snow. Most were women and children. Those that weren't dead, would be, by the time dark fell. Buzzards, wolves, and below freezing temperatures, would see to that. It was a good day. They had accomplished much. Only four soldiers had been wounded, and none had died. A good day, indeed.

"Let's see Custer get all the hurrahs today," the captain thought to himself, a sly smile spreading across his face, as he rode. He had no idea that he would soon be transferred to the place the Indians called Greasy Grass. The place the whites called Little Big Horn. And the following June, he would witness Custer and his entire 7th Cavalry troop die, due to Custer's own impulsiveness. That battle would go down in history as "Custer's Last Stand," and Custer would forevermore be proclaimed a hero. This would infuriate the captain, who, as it turned out, did not receive any recognition for his brutal attack on the Lakota village.

The only ones to survive that day were Laughing Water and her two small children. She had gone with them, earlier that morning, to explore the cave that Johnny had mentioned, a few days before.

OTHER BOOKS IN THE OUTCAST SERIES BY SUSAN ILEEN LEPPERT INCLUDE:

Courageous Outcast

Time of Remembering

Red Road Home